The
MOFFATT
NEW TESTAMENT COMMENTARY

Based on *The New Translation* by the
REV. PROFESSOR JAMES MOFFATT, D.D.
and under his Editorship

THE ACTS OF THE APOSTLES

The Moffatt
New Testament Commentary

MATTHEW
BY THEODORE H. ROBINSON, M.A., D.D.

MARK
BY B. HARVIE BRANSCOMB, M.A., PH.D.

LUKE
BY WILLIAM MANSON, D.D.

JOHN
BY G. H. C. MACGREGOR, D.D., D.LITT.

THE ACTS OF THE APOSTLES
BY F. J. FOAKES-JACKSON, D.D.

ROMANS
BY C. H. DODD, D.D., F.B.A.

I CORINTHIANS
BY JAMES MOFFATT, D.D., LL.D., D.LITT.

II CORINTHIANS
BY R. H. STRACHAN, D.D.

GALATIANS
BY GEORGE S. DUNCAN, D.D., LL.D.

COLOSSIANS, PHILEMON
AND EPHESIANS
BY E. F. SCOTT, D.D.

PHILIPPIANS
BY J. HUGH MICHAEL, D.D.

THESSALONIANS
BY WILLIAM NEIL, M.A., B.D., PH.D.

THE PASTORAL EPISTLES
BY E. F. SCOTT, D.D.

HEBREWS
BY THEODORE H. ROBINSON, M.A., D.D.

THE GENERAL EPISTLES
BY JAMES MOFFATT, D.D., LL.D., D.LITT.

THE JOHANNINE EPISTLES
BY C. H. DODD, D.D., F.B.A.

REVELATION
BY MARTIN KIDDLE, M.A.
ASSISTED BY M. K. ROSS.

THE
ACTS OF THE APOSTLES

BY

F. J. FOAKES-JACKSON

D.D.

Union Theological Seminary,
New York

Fellow of Jesus College,
Cambridge

HARPER AND BROTHERS PUBLISHERS
NEW YORK

EDITOR'S PREFACE

MOFFATT'S NEW TESTAMENT COMMENTARY

THE aim of this commentary is to bring out the religious
meaning and message of the New Testament writings. To
do this, it is needful to explain what they originally meant
for the communities to which they were addressed in the
first century, and this involves literary and historical criticism ; otherwise, our reading becomes unintelligent. But
the New Testament was the literature of the early church,
written out of faith and for faith, and no study of it is intelligent unless this aim is kept in mind. It is literature written
for a religious purpose. ' These are written that ye might
believe that Jesus is the Christ, the Son of God.' This is
the real object of the New Testament, that Christians might
believe it better, in the light of contemporary life with its
intellectual and moral problems. So with any commentary
upon it. Everything ought to be subordinated to the aim of
elucidating the religious content, of shewing how the faith
was held in such and such a way by the first Christians, and of
making clear what that faith was and is.

The idea of the commentary arose from a repeated demand
to have my New Testament translation explained ; which
accounts for the fact that this translation has been adopted
as a convenient basis for the commentary. But the contri-
butors have been left free to take their own way. If they
interpret the text differently, they have been at liberty to
say so. Only, as a translation is in itself a partial commentary, it has often saved space to print the commentary
and start from it.

As everyman has not Greek, the commentary has been
written, as far as possible, for the Greekless. But it is based

v

upon a first-hand study of the Greek original, and readers may rest assured that it represents a close reproduction of the original writers' meaning, or at anyrate of what we consider that to have been. Our common aim has been to enable everyman to-day to sit where these first Christians sat, to feel the impetus and inspiration of the Christian faith as it dawned upon the minds of the communities in the first century, and thereby to realize more vividly how new and lasting is the message which prompted these New Testament writings to take shape as they did. Sometimes people inside as well as outside the church make mistakes about the New Testament. They think it means this or that, whereas its words frequently mean something very different from what traditional associations suggest. The saving thing is to let the New Testament speak for itself. This is our desire and plan in the present commentary, to place each writing or group of writings in its original setting, and allow their words to come home thus to the imagination and conscience of everyman to-day.

The general form of the commentary is to provide a running comment on the text, instead of one broken up into separate verses. But within these limits, each contributor has been left free. Thus, to comment on a gospel requires a method which is not precisely the same as that necessitated by commenting on an epistle. Still, the variety of treatment ought not to interfere with the uniformity of aim and form. Our principle has been that nothing mattered, so long as the reader could understand what he was reading in the text of the New Testament.

JAMES MOFFATT.

PREFACE

THIS commentary is designed, not for specialists, but for those readers who require a plain statement of the contents of the Acts of the Apostles. It has been my object to give an independent view of the interpretation of this remarkable book, regarding it as a whole in its present form as a work of the greatest literary value and historical interest. With this end in view I have endeavoured to avoid the technicalities of modern criticism and to present my own impressions without attempting to produce an exhaustive exposition of what has been hitherto accomplished in the field of criticism. The only credit I can claim is that, here and there, I have seen difficulties which appear to have been generally ignored, and have made a few suggestions which I venture to hope are original.

The translation by Dr. James Moffatt is an invaluable exposition in itself, and if I have in any way differed from his conclusions, it is a testimony to his generosity that I have been permitted to do so.

F. J. FOAKES-JACKSON.

NEW YORK,
July, 1931.

INTRODUCTION

THE Acts of the Apostles is unique in the literature of the New Testament, and indeed in that of the primitive church. It is an historical work, written before about A.D. 90, the like to which nothing has survived. Apart from its religious importance, its value to the historian of human affairs is inestimable, since without it he could know nothing of how the religion now professed by a large part of the human race came into being. Without it, had we even the rest of the New Testament, the origin of the Christian church would be a subject for ingenious conjecture ; and when we lose its guidance we are frequently left entirely in the dark as to the course of events. The book has been the subject of many doubts and controversies ; but, even if its accuracy is questioned, it is the only source we have. Some at least of the epistles of St. Paul were written before it, but it is impossible to construct the story of the sequence of events out of a collection of letters which, weighty as they undoubtedly are, are very brief, and allusive rather than informative in regard to events. The gospels are not so much historical as biographical, and stop short with the career of the Great Figure with whom they are concerned. They tell us how Jesus lived, taught, and died, but are silent as to what happened when his career on earth was done.

The question is first, how did such books as Luke's Gospel and Acts come to be written ? and on this point the unnamed author has given us some satisfactory information. A person of the name of Theophilus, otherwise unknown, but evidently a man of importance, had heard by repute about Jesus Christ and his followers, and probably desired further information. He received two little books—we might almost call them pamphlets—one relating the life, death, and resurrection of Jesus ; the other a continuation, telling of what occurred immediately afterwards—how the followers of the Christ formed a society, how they received a divine commission, and how they proclaimed in Jerusalem and elsewhere that their crucified Master was the expected Messiah. Theophilus was informed of the adventures of a remarkable member of the group, named Saul or Paul, how he preached the gospel in the great cities of the Empire, and finally reached Rome under a criminal charge brought against him by his Jewish enemies. These two books are known respectively as the Gospel according to Luke and the Acts of the Apostles, and it is very generally agreed that the author or compiler of both was the same.

This writer tells us that he had made a careful selection of the sayings and doings of Jesus, and, in the Gospel, we have the opportunity of judging of the use he made of some of his materials. As regards Acts we are not so fortunate, but we can infer something from the author's employment of a narrative common to those of Matthew and Mark. The authorship of the Third Gospel and the Acts will ever be a subject for discussion, despite the fact that from the first it has always been attributed to St. Luke, the ' beloved physician ' mentioned by St. Paul in his Epistle to the Colossians, where his name appears among the Gentiles, as it does also in the little letter to Philemon. The reasons for disputing the unbroken tradition of the Christian church are invariably subjective. No other name has been suggested, and if Luke is the author, his qualifications to write the book are indisputable. The so-called ' We sections ' of Acts, where the first person plural is employed, point to one who was a constant and faithful associate of St. Paul during the last years of his ministry. He had been his companion for some time at Caesarea, and certainly travelled with him to Rome. Thus he was in a position not only to ascertain the facts of Paul's life, but also to become acquainted with the eye-witnesses of the ministry of Jesus, and of the early church in Jerusalem. Thus Luke fulfils the conditions necessary for a biographer of Paul, since at Jerusalem and at Caesarea he had opportunities for ascertaining facts regarding Jesus and the early story of the church. He was evidently comparatively so unim-

portant in the Christian community, that the ascription of
two books to him cannot be purely arbitrary.

On the other hand, there are indications that the writer of
Acts was not always intimately acquainted with the facts of
the life of Paul, and that he was not familiar with his epistles.
Moreover, the attribution of the two books to Luke is comparatively late, and cannot be, any more than the gospels of
Matthew and Mark, traced to apostolic times. Further, it is
contended that there are traces both in the Gospel and Acts
of borrowings from Josephus, who wrote in the last quarter of
the first century. But although the authorship of Acts can
never positively be proved, in this commentary the writer
will be called ' Luke.'

Whatever may be the date of Acts, and whether the ' We
sections ' are the work of the man who later brought the book
into its present shape, or of the writer of the whole, it is certain
that a definite plan is manifest from first to last. The author
begins from the birth of the Christian church, and traces its
growth till he leaves Paul preaching without hindrance in
Rome. It has been observed that the first part is divided into
different sections, each marking the progress of the Christian
community, at first as confined to Jerusalem, then spreading
its influence throughout Judaea and Samaria, and developing
along the coast of Palestine and Syria till it found its second
great centre at Antioch. For awhile the central body in
Jerusalem is very conservative and Jewish, but gradually the
Gentiles gain admission to the church, first under protest, but
soon obtaining equal rights with the Jewish members, though
as new converts they were free from the obligation to be
circumcised. Thus the first part of Acts has been steadily
leading up to the time when the Christian church ceased to be
Jewish, and became a world-embracing institution, open to
the whole race of man irrespective of birth or origin. Paul
now becomes the central figure. Having gained that for which
he had long contended, Paul's work in extending the gospel to
the world is the one object of interest to the writer of Acts,
who relates how the great cities of Macedonia and Hellas,
Philippi, Thessalonica, Athens, and Corinth, received his

message. Next he tells how Paul and his company crossed the Aegean and won Ephesus to the faith. Finally, we learn how Paul returned to Jerusalem, where his life as an itinerant missionary, as far as Acts is concerned, ended. The rest of the book is a history of the attempt of the Jews to embroil Paul with the Roman government, riots at Jerusalem, trials before the Sanhedrin, the procurators, and Agrippa II, followed by the dramatic story of the shipwreck and the arrival of the Apostle in Rome.

This seems to be a well-thought-out and skilfully constructed story, and the next subject for inquiry is how Luke obtained his material. He tells us, in the preface to the Gospel, that a beginning of Christian literature had been made, since many had already undertaken to write about Jesus, in accordance with the tradition of those who had actually witnessed and even taken part in what had happened. As for himself he was determined to set forth his statements in order and after proper investigation. From his preface we may gather two facts of importance for our purpose. First, that Luke stored up all the oral traditions he could collect ; and secondly, that he had written sources at his disposal.

Ever since the Old Testament began to be the subject of higher criticism, increasing attention has been paid to what are known as ' sources.' It must not, however, be forgotten that, except when a source is extant, or has been mentioned by an author, no results of higher criticism, even if generally accepted, can be final, but are at best the conjectures of able and acute scholars. As regards Acts source criticism must be devoted mainly to the first fifteen chapters, after which the writer was almost certainly in touch with St. Paul, whose adventures are the theme of the rest of the book. Till the ' We sections ' begin, relating how Paul crossed from Troas to Macedonia, Luke could have had no personal knowledge of what had happened in the Christian community, though he may have heard of the death of Stephen and of Saul's conversion from the Apostle himself. He must therefore have relied on what he had been told and on what he had read. That he had documents at his disposal is evident, but what the originals were we have no means of determining. All that can be done here is to mention four of the many theories in regard to them :

(1) The late Prof. A. von Harnack says that there are two accounts of the gift of the holy Spirit : the earlier is found in the fourth chapter, the later in the second. If this is so, there is little doubt that Luke used two separate stories of the same event. Nevertheless, Luke displays no little skill in handling two apparently contradictory sources ; for the narrative, as it now appears in Acts ii.–iv., is a continuous one, one event being made to lead on to the other. Admitting therefore the principle of a variety of documents or oral testimonies, it must be allowed that Luke dealt with his materials as a master of literary craftsmanship ; and this makes it no easy task to disintegrate his material.

(2) An attractive theory was advanced some years ago by Prof. Torrey of Yale in which he ascribes the whole of Acts i.–xv. to an original Aramaic source which Luke translated into Greek with such meticulous accuracy that he renders phrases into untranslatable Greek which are perfectly simple when put back into Aramaic. This view has probably not yet commended itself to the majority of expert scholars, and even those who are not such masters of the two languages as is Dr. Torrey may raise serious objections to his theory. Nevertheless, if Dr. Torrey has failed to prove his case, his method is so excellent and his knowledge so extensive that those who cannot accept his conclusions are sure to rise from the perusal of his statement gainers by having shared in his extensive knowledge and searching criticism.

(3) The same may be said of M. Loisy's opinion, that Acts is in its present form a redaction by a later hand of an original document, which gave a much plainer if less interesting account of what really happened. The whole subject of sources needs much fuller treatment than the limits of this work allow.

(4) There is one source which it is confidently asserted must have been used by Luke, namely, the writings of Josephus. Whether the author of the Third Gospel and Acts

employed them or not is, and must be, a continually open question. Luke undoubtedly differs from all other New Testament writers in the interest he shews in external events. He displays a peculiar knowledge of the family of the later Herods, he alone mentions the name of Roman emperors, or alludes to events in Jewish history. The accuracy with which he ascribes to the Roman officials their correct titles has frequently been noticed, and it is the same when he comes to speak of the cities visited by Paul. This and various linguistic and other considerations have made scholars suppose that Luke must have had some historical work to rely upon, and, as the only document of the kind known to us is the *Archeology*, better known as the *Antiquities* of Josephus, that Luke must have waited for its appearance before producing Acts. As Josephus did not complete his great work before A.D. 90, this theory affects the date of Luke's book.

Despite the multiplicity of instances produced by such scholars as Krenkel, and the ingenuity displayed by Prof. Burkitt and others, it is very difficult to accept as final the view that Luke depends on Josephus. Plausible as some of the arguments are, none seems really to clinch the matter, and therefore the number of suggested proofs adduced does not really decide the case. One feels inclined to recall the famous trial of Lord Strafford for high treason, when it was argued that though he could not be proved to have done one treasonable act, the mass of evidence was enough to convict him as a traitor, and the reply was, ' No amount of black rabbits can make a black horse.' The part of Josephus which relates to the times treated of by Luke is towards the close of the *Antiquities*. If the reader will examine books xviii.–xx. for himself, collecting all that can possibly bear on the story of the Gospel and Acts, he will be surprised to find how scanty is the material, since a large part of the narrative is occupied by such episodes as the career of Herod Agrippa (*Antiq.*, xxx.), the adventures of the Babylonian Jews Asinaeus and Anilaeus (*Antiq.*, xvii.), and the story of the life and conversion of Izates, king of Adiabene (*Antiq.*, xx.).

It will, then, seem strange that Luke should have bestowed

so much time on a book which gave him so little information, and inquired so minutely only to fall into such errors as the mention of Theudas and Judas of Galilee (Acts v. 36 f.) and of Lysanias, tetrarch of Abilene (Luke iii. 1). Most of the persons he mentions were of public notoriety, and so familiar to everybody that it was not necessary to read an historical work to discover them. Had Josephus informed us that Sergius Paulus was a proconsul, that Philippi possessed magistrates who liked to be called praetors, that Gallio was proconsul in Achaia, or that Ephesus had a ' scribe ' (γραμματεύς), there might be something tangible to prove that Luke depended on his *Antiquities*. As it is, Luke owes little or nothing of his knowledge of the world of his day to Josephus. Considerations of this kind forbid a hasty acceptance of the view that the works of Flavius Josephus are among the ' sources ' of Acts. Here and there, as in the account of the miracles wrought by Peter in the cities of Judaea, e.g. Lydda and Joppa (Acts ix. 32–34), there seem to be indications that there was a book, Marcan in character, which continued the story of the Gospel. But we should constantly remember that source-criticism in the New Testament is largely guess-work.

The speeches recorded in Acts are of deep interest as illustrative of the preaching of the gospel in the earliest days of the church. It was the practice of ancient historians, apart from Polybius, to tell part of their narrative by means of speeches put into the mouth of the chief actors, and it seems evident that they did not intend their readers to believe that these were other than their own compositions. Luke may have listened to what Paul actually said towards the end of Acts, and have given us summaries of the words of the Apostle on certain occasions. But he assuredly never heard Peter on the day of Pentecost, or when he addressed the Jewish rulers, or Cornelius, nor was he present when Stephen defended himself before the Sanhedrin, or when Paul preached at Pisidian Antioch or at Athens (cf. 1 Thess. iii. 1). Reports of such utterances may have been preserved and formed part of the sources of Acts, but the student of classical literature will find it difficult to believe that they are not compositions of the writer.   Whatever these speeches may be, it cannot be disputed that they are wonderfully varied as to their character, and as a rule admirably suited to the occasion on which they were delivered.   Luke seems to have been able to give us an extraordinarily accurate picture of the undeveloped theology of the earliest Christians, and to enable us to determine the character of the most primitive presentation of the gospel. However produced, the speeches in Acts are masterpieces, and deserve the most careful attention.

It is, however, a mistake to attempt to justify the theology of later days by an appeal to Acts as supporting modern ideas of church organization and discipline.   The view given of the nature and person of Christ does not appear to be that of a subsequent age, but is the more interesting because of its very crudity.   In the same way we are not justified in expecting to find in Acts evidences of a developed Christian ministry. For this reason I am disposed to question whether *episcopos* ought to be rendered by *bishop* or *presbuteroi* by *presbyters*, thereby implying that the government of the church was episcopal or presbyterian.   Nor does it appear to be legitimate to suppose that ' laying on of hands ' always signifies what we mean by ' ordination.'   We shall be nearer the truth if we try to picture to ourselves the church described in Acts as more fluid in its organization than some might wish it to be.

The purpose of the book of Acts has been the subject of much controversy.   Two views of this may here be mentioned as characteristic of modern conjectures on the subject.   Not satisfied with Luke's statement, that he wrote in order that Theophilus might have a certain knowledge of what he had been taught by word of mouth (Luke i. 3), efforts have been made to account more elaborately for the real purpose of the writer.   Was the intention of Acts (*a*) irenic, or (*b*) apologetic ? Was it designed to reconcile the two great parties of the church, or to be a defence of the Christian religion, whether addressed to a friendly pagan or to the Roman government ?

(*a*) In last century the famous school of Tübingen advanced a theory of early church history which long held the field. The clue to this was found in the so-called Clementine literature, in which the Jewish Christian party headed by Peter and James are represented as antagonistic to the Gentile section led by Paul, whose identity is thinly disguised under that of Simon Magus. In process of time the dispute was amicably adjusted, and the Catholic church was the result. This must have occurred in the second century, and Acts was written with the object of harmonizing the two rival conceptions of Christianity. Thus the author is scrupulous in assigning equal honour to Peter and Paul, the miracles wrought by them respectively being made to correspond in such a way as to shew that one Apostle was no less endowed with supernatural power than the other. This Tübingen hypothesis cannot be dismissed hastily, although it has declined in popularity. It has at least pointed to a possible solution of what happened in a very obscure period of church history, though it is open to certain objections, not the least of which is that the Clementine books represent a heresy which was probably confined within a small circle, and that the whole supposition is due to the subjectivity of a philosopher like Hegel, rather than to the experience of the practical historian.

(b) A second attempt to account for the appearance of Acts assumes that Theophilus was not a Christian inquirer but a Roman magistrate, and that Luke wrote in defence of the new faith or possibly of Paul himself. In fact, the whole of the book may be of the nature of a brief prepared for the trial of the Apostle.

Such a view would be based on the fact that the last few chapters of Acts, which form a considerable portion of the entire book, are occupied with legal matter. Thus chaps. xxii.–xxvi. are devoted to Paul's case, culminating in his appeal to Caesar. The biography of Paul from xvi. onward is really a catalogue of his acquittals. Even before he claims his Roman citizenship, the magistrates of Philippi order his release. The politarchs of Thessalonica refuse to listen to the absurd accusation of treason. At Corinth Gallio, one of the most eminent men in the Roman Empire, dismisses the charges against him with contempt. The Asiarchs of Ephesus, the richest and most influential men in their country, stood his friends at the time of the great riot, and the town clerk of the city in a public speech pronounces Paul and his friends innocent and peaceable men. Claudius Lysias at Jerusalem, except once when provoked by the clamour of the Jews, treats Paul with consideration ; Felix and Festus, the procurators, refuse to condemn him or to hand him over to his enemies. Finally, Agrippa II, himself a Jew, pronounces a solemn sentence of complete acquittal. ' This man might have been set at liberty if he had not appealed unto Caesar.' After his arrival at Rome no definite accusation seems to have been preferred ; and Paul remained there two years in his hired house, preaching the word without molestation.

This theory has much to recommend it, although it may be urged that the less ingenious any explanation of unknown circumstances may be, the more likely is it to be correct. Luke's own declaration that he wrote his books for the instruction and edification of a friend unknown to us, named Theophilus, may prove a sufficient explanation of his writing the Gospel and Acts.

If this be so, one cannot but admire the skill with which Luke performed his task. Had the Third Gospel alone of the ' four ' survived, it would rank, apart from the deep religious interest connected with it, among the literary masterpieces of the world. The theme of Acts lacks the sublime beauty of the Gospel, but this does not prevent its being a supreme literary achievement. Let us assume that Theophilus had been a heathen, perhaps converted to, but certainly interested in, the faith of Jesus. His friend would have to tell him how the movement originated, how it developed, and how finally, in the person of Paul, its greatest human exponent, it reached Rome. He was almost certainly limited as to space, as his book had to be written out by scribes. His two books had to be brief, and the material at his disposal was immense. With as little elaboration as possible he had to trace the course of some thirty years, the most eventful in religious history. He had to exercise no little judgment in what he selected or omitted. He had no room for disquisitions or explanations, and was debarred the use of footnotes, so con-

venient to the modern author. He had further to interest
Theophilus in the subject, and to consider what it was advisable for him to remember. The remarkable feat Luke as a
man of letters accomplished is that he has given a very condensed narrative written for an individual in two books which
can to-day be read with absorbing interest. Herein he shews
real literary genius. We are often blind to the excellences of
St. Luke and Acts, because, like the Aeneid and Odyssey, we
read them in short portions, and examine their every word,
forgetting that they are not school exercises or fields for expert
ingenuity, but literary masterpieces. To be understood such
a book as Acts must be admired, and it should be appreciated
before it is criticized. Too many commentators forget how
Alexander Pope annihilated Dr. Bentley, whose erudition was
justly regarded with admiration by the learned of his age, in a
single couplet :

> Great Aristarchus, whose unwearied pains
> Made Horace dull, and humbled Milton's strains.

And for many generations the erudite have done their best to
depreciate Luke's workmanship in the composition of Acts.
Some write as though they considered that they could have
done better themselves ; but could they produce anything
comparable to the brief account of the birth of the church and
the career of Paul as they appear in Acts ? Like other men
of genius Luke is at times careless, uneven, and open to criticism, but when he rises to great heights, as in relating the story
of the conversion of Cornelius, in his report of Paul's speech
to the elders of Miletus, or in his delineation of the Apostle's
greatness in the account of the shipwreck, Luke is simply
unsurpassable.

The textual criticism of Acts is of special importance, presenting problems which affect not only the New Testament but
all ancient literature. Elsewhere it is largely a question of
occasional words, phrases, grammatical forms, and in the
Gospels attempts to harmonize one evangelist with another.
But in Acts far graver issues are involved, as it is not a matter
of different texts but different editions. Codex D, presented

by Theodore Beza to the University of Cambridge in the sixteenth century, and some Syriac and Latin MSS., contain not merely small varieties of reading but deliberate alterations on one side or the other. Whether the text of the great MSS. or that of this small group, which will be described in this commentary as ' the western text,' is the original is still open to discussion. Here the differences, as shewn in J. H. Ropes' masterly edition of the text of Acts, will be noted, and the most important of them will be discussed.

It must be acknowledged that, apart from Acts, the Pauline letters, the Apocalypse, and a few notices by heathen writers, our ignorance of the first age of the church is well-nigh abysmal. The beginner in the study of the earliest church history finds that there is before him a vast amount of literature and of archaeological study, behind which are hardly any facts, but only interpretations of such as we have or inferences drawn from fragmentary inscriptions. There is no positive evidence even of what was the ultimate fate of Peter or Paul, and when some adventurous scholar presumes to doubt the current belief that they died as martyrs in Rome, he is met not by evidence but either by a not unreasonable rebuke for questioning the authority of the Catholic church, or by the crushing but less merited retort that some great authority has decided otherwise. Were it not for St. Luke we should know almost nothing, and if we reject his evidence, as some do, we are left to vague and contradictory hypotheses, and have to construct our history by our own philosophical conceptions of what ought to have happened, a process which possibly is interesting, but is assuredly unsatisfactory.

This commentary is critical in places, but it is frankly an appreciation of the work of Luke. At the bar of history the evangelist and historian is at least entitled to a fair hearing, with as little needless interruption as possible, and we may quote in regard to this from his own book the words of King Agrippa to Paul :

' Thou art permitted to speak for thyself.'

THE ACTS OF THE APOSTLES

i.

In my former volume, Theophilus, I treated all that Jesus began 1
    by doing and teaching down to the day when, after issuing 2
    his orders by the holy Spirit to the disciples whom he had
    chosen, he was taken up to heaven. After his sufferings 3
    he had shown them that he was alive by a number of
    proofs, revealing himself to them for forty days and dis-
    cussing the affairs of God's Realm. Also, as he ate with 4
    them, he charged them not to leave Jerusalem but to wait
    for what the Father promised—" for what you have heard
    me speak of," said he ; " for John baptized with water, but 5
    not many days after this you shall be baptized with the
    holy Spirit."

' Acts,' ' Acts of Apostles,' or ' Acts of the Apostles ' is not
the title given by the writer to this book. To him it is evidently the second volume of the Gospel. What we term ' the
gospel' did not in the mind of Luke end with the departure of
Jesus from the visible world. His sojourn on earth was only a
beginning of a work which was destined to continue. It may
even be that the Third Gospel is not, so to speak, rounded off
by the story of the Ascension, because to Luke the climax of
the work of Jesus has never been reached. To him there can
be no *finish* to the gospel in this world.

There is an ambiguity in the second verse, which can be
translated in two ways. Did Jesus teach, or did he choose
disciples by the holy Spirit ? If the Spirit was the vehicle by
which he taught, Jesus inspired them to receive his instructions. If, on the contrary, it was the Spirit who caused the
choice of the disciples, then the meaning of Luke may have
been that the Spirit whom the disciples of Jesus were about
to receive co-operated in their selection. Whichever view

I

we adopt, a theological difficulty is presented, i.e. as to how Jesus could be said to be inspired either to teach or to choose disciples, since he spoke with authority received directly from the Father ? The doctrine of the work of the Spirit in Acts develops as the narrative proceeds.

The subject of the discourse of the risen Lord with his disciples is here said to be the future of the **Realm** or kingdom of God, which is prominent in the preaching of Jesus. Whether Jesus intended to found a Church or not is keenly debated, but Luke has no doubt that this was his intention. Indeed, the whole purpose of Acts, as a sequel to the Gospel, is to relate the first steps in establishing a society or **Realm** in which God was to be acknowledged as king. Those who accepted Jesus as Lord were to be the nucleus of an empire which, as it is said later, was to spread to the uttermost parts of the earth.

In Acts alone is it said that the Lord was *forty days* with his disciples after he had risen. The reader scarcely needs to be reminded that in the Bible ' forty ' is a highly symbolical number. Moses was in the mount receiving the law for forty days (Ex. xxiv. 18), and the law of **God's Realm** was communicated during a similar period.

In ver. 4 there is a very difficult word, rendered in the text of the A.V. by ' being assembled ' and in the margin ' eating together with them.' The word is fairly common in classical Greek, and means ' to assemble.' But the Latin versions are in favour of ' eating together ' ; and it must not be forgotten that special stress is laid on the fact that the Risen Lord revealed himself to his disciples at a meal, which he often **ate with them** (Mark xvi. 14, Luke xxiv. 30, 41–42, John xxi. 9–12, Acts x. 41).

Luke's object in Acts is to shew that the Church was founded in Jerusalem, where the risen Lord appeared to the disciples, and where he ordered them to remain till they should receive the promise of the Father, **what you heard me speak of** (or, as W has it, ' which ye heard through my mouth '). There is a discrepancy here in the different accounts of the appearances. In Matthew the eleven disciples first see the Lord in

Galilee ; in Mark (xvi. 7) the women are to tell Peter and the
disciples that Jesus is going before them to Galilee ; in John
xxi. (the supplementary chapter) he is seen 'at the sea of
Tiberias.' But in Mark's secondary account (xvi. 14-18) Jesus
appears to the Eleven at a meal—the place not being specified ;
and in Luke, Acts, and John xx., the scene of the manifestations after the Resurrection is Jerusalem. In Matthew and
Mark the commission to preach is given by the risen Lord, who
in John xx. 22 bestows on his disciples the gift of the Spirit.
Luke, as we shall see later, is careful to mention the connexion
between the Baptist and Jesus, and to contrast the baptism of
John with that of the Spirit.

**Now when they met, they asked him, " Lord, is this the time 6
you are going to restore the Realm to Israel ? " But he 7
told them, " It is not for you to know the course and
periods of time that the Father has fixed by his own
authority. You will receive power when the holy Spirit 8
comes upon you, and you will be my witnesses at Jerusalem, throughout all Judaea and Samaria, and to the end
of the earth." On saying this he was lifted up while they 9
looked on, and a cloud took him out of sight. As he 10
went up, their eyes were fixed on heaven ; but just then
two men stood beside them dressed in white, who said, 11
" Men of Galilee, why do you stand looking up to heaven ?
This Jesus who has been taken from you into heaven will
come back, just as you have seen him depart to heaven."
Then they made their way back to Jerusalem from the 12
hill called ' The Olive-Orchard ' ; it is close to Jerusalem,
only a sabbath day's journey from it.**

Luke now indicates the scope and purpose of Acts. In
answer to the natural but somewhat simple question of the
disciples, the Lord explains that the kingdom was not of an
earthly domination, to be brought about immediately by a
catastrophic intervention by God, but must come into being
by the more peaceful process of the Apostles acting as witnesses to what they had themselves heard and seen. [After

Jesus had risen from the dead and manifested himself to his disciples, they had no doubt that he was the Messiah ; but they expected him at once to fulfil the Messianic office of making Israel supreme on earth. The Lord silences their curiosity as to the time of the restoration of Israel, and assures them that his **Realm** will embrace the world, though not in the way they had anticipated. Its growth will be sure, but it will be gradual ; and this corresponds with the plan of this book : the testimony that Jesus has risen from the dead, and is therefore the Messiah, must first be given in the Holy City, the scene of his sufferings (chaps. ii.–vii.). Those who were dispersed by the persecution about Stephen spread the news (viii. 1) in **Judaea and Samaria,** i.e. among those who worshipped the true God, whether regularly or schismatically. Then the Gentile servants of the God of Israel were approached in the person of Cornelius (Acts x.). Finally, Paul preached in Rome, the capital of the world ; and thus was attained the possibility of spreading the word to the ends of the earth.

With the promise that the gospel would be preached throughout the world and the kingdom become universal, the Lord vanished from sight. Luke is the only evangelist who describes the Ascension. In his Gospel it is said that the Lord was parted from the Eleven in the act of blessing them, though some MSS. omit **and was carried up to heaven** (Luke xxiv. 51). The story of the Ascension, of which Luke was not an eye-witness, is told with reserve, and not as a spectacular marvel like Elijah's ascent into heaven ' with horses and chariots of fire.' Jesus was parted from his disciples, and a cloud **took him out of sight** (' enveloped him, and he was lifted up,' W, omitting ' as he went up ' in 10). Fully to grasp Luke's meaning we must remember that whenever he describes an important spiritual event which he did not personally witness, he adopts a dramatic method of narration. We have only to turn to the stories of the descent of the Spirit in Acts ii., of the Conversion of Paul in Acts ix., and of the vision of Peter in Acts x., to see how the event is made vivid to his readers. Thus, in his account of the Ascension it is not the place to discuss the question of ' levitation ' nor of a localized heaven. All that Luke really relates is that Jesus was with his disciples for the last time on earth at Bethany on the Mount of Olives, and that there he mysteriously disappeared, and was seen no more. The important matter to determine is Luke's teaching as to the nature of the Resurrection. He is certainly anxious to insist upon the fact that Jesus had risen bodily from the grave. Yet the risen body of the Saviour was not subject to ordinary conditions ; for it could appear and vanish at will, and was only seen by a favoured few (Acts x. 41).

The story of the Ascension as Luke records it bears a striking resemblance to those of the empty tomb and the appearances to the disciples after the Resurrection. The **two men** in glistening garments at the tomb (Luke xxiv. 4) are analogous to the two **dressed in white** apparel, who here announce the return of the ascended Lord to the disciples. The disappearance of Jesus at Emmaus after Cleopas and his companion had recognized him in the breaking of the bread finds its parallel in the Gospel account of the appearance to the Eleven, when the Lord ate of the piece of broiled fish and the honeycomb, and explained that he must suffer, led them out as far as Bethany, blessed them, and was parted from them (Luke xxiv. 36–53). It must be borne in mind that Luke only records two manifestations of the risen Lord, and that the Ascension in Acts is the same story as that in the Gospel, somewhat amplified and dramatized. It is true that Luke hints that there were other appearances of the risen Lord (Luke xxiv. 34, Acts i. 2) ; but here he has seen fit to concentrate the record of the final charge and revelation that the risen Christ had left to his disciples into one unforgettable picture. ' The Mount called Olivet ' (A.V.) is rightly rendered *Olive-Orchard* ' (Lat. *olivetum*). It was fitting to emphasize the fact that the mount which had been the scene of the agony and humiliation of Jesus (Luke xxii. 39) should also witness his triumph, when he parted from his followers, assuring them of certain victory.

Before passing to the Acts of the Apostles proper, we must note that in these chapters Luke prefers to present, not a connected story but a series of descriptions of what he considers

5

to be the best illustrations of the first days of the Church. This he does without giving any notes of time, and often, it would seem, he tells what appears to be virtually the same story in different words. Nevertheless, it will be apparent that whatever may be the oral or written sources employed by him, he has arranged them in such a way as to give his readers an idea of the continuous progress of the work of the followers of Jesus in spreading his gospel from Jerusalem to the end of the earth.

13 On entering the city they went to the upper room where they were in the habit of meeting ; there were Peter, John, James, Andrew, Philip and Thomas, Bartholomew and Matthew, James (the son of Alphaeus) and Simon who
14   had been a Zealot, with Judas the son of James. All these men resorted with one mind to prayer, together with the women, with Mary the mother of Jesus and with his brothers.

The upper room was apparently known to Luke or his source as the meeting-place of the disciples of Jesus. It is, of course, an open question whether or not it can be identified with the scene of the Last Supper or with the house of Mary (Acts xii.). The Latin word for it is *cenaculum* (the dining-room), usually on the third storey, and approached from the outside by steps. The room was used as a place of **meeting.** In Acts xx. 8 the Christians at Troas met in an upper room to hear Paul's farewell address, and the lad Eutychus fell from the third storey (A.V. loft) and was taken up dead.

The original company of the followers of Jesus is given in vers. 13 and 14. It consisted of the Eleven, the women (W adds 'and children'), the mother of Jesus, and his brothers. The four lists of the Apostles (Mark iii. 16–19, Matt. x. 2, Luke vi. 13, and here) differ slightly from one another, but as regards the first eight only in order. Whether **Simon who had been a Zealot** had belonged to the fanatical sect who in the Jewish war assumed the name is open to question. The rest of those here enumerated are (1) **the women** who accompanied Jesus from Galilee (Luke xxiv. 10 ; see Mark xv. 40 and xvi. 1,

Matt. xxvii. 56-61, John xix. 25) ; (2) **the mother of Jesus,**
nowhere else mentioned in Acts, nor by the synoptists, but see
John xix. 25 ; (3) the **brothers** of Jesus, whose names are given
in Mark vi. 3 as James, Judas, Joseph, and Simon. Their
precise relationship to Jesus has been keenly debated since
the fourth century. Epiphanius, a native of Palestine and a
learned traditionalist, says they were the sons of Joseph by
a former wife. Jerome, a contemporary, maintains that they
were not brothers but cousins, and some at least were members
of the apostolic college. A Roman opponent of Jerome,
named Helvidius, who tried to counteract the exaggerated
position of celibacy as a Christian virtue, declared in favour of
taking the word **brothers** in a literal sense. Lightfoot, in his
commentary on **Galatians**, pronounces in favour of the view of
Epiphanius. In the first days of an Oriental religion, the
kindred of the founder are almost invariably held in high
honour. James, 'the Lord's brother' (Gal. i. 19 ; see
Acts xii. 17, xv. 13, xxi. 18), was later the chief man in the
church of Jerusalem. Paul speaks of brothers of the Lord
(1 Cor. ix. 5).

Now during these days Peter stood up among the brothers 15
    (there was a crowd of about a hundred and twenty persons
    all together). " My brothers," said he, " it had to be 16
    fulfilled, that scripture which the holy Spirit uttered
    beforehand by the lips of David with regard to Judas who
    acted as guide to those who arrested Jesus. Judas did 17
    enter our number, he did get his allotted share of this our
    ministry. With the money paid him for his crime he 18
    purchased an estate ; but swelling up he burst in two, and 19
    all his bowels poured out—a fact which became known to
    all the residents in Jerusalem, so that the estate got the
    name, in their language, of Akeldamach or The Ground of
    Blood. Now it is written in the book of psalms,   20

           Desolate be his residence,
             may no one dwell in it :
    also,
           let another man take over his charge.

According to the speech put into the mouth of Peter, Judas had been dead some time, and posterity had preserved a tradition that he had died miserably of a disease which was a horribly just retribution for his crime. Luke follows the historical method of his day, and puts what would now be a statement into the form of a speech. How Judas died is uncertain. Matthew relates that in his despair the traitor hanged himself. Papias, bishop of Herapolis (*c.* A.D. 120), according to Eusebius, had preserved a tradition that Judas swelled to an immense size, and was crushed in a narrow street by a wagon. That Mark tells nothing is an indication that the tradition of his miserable death was not part of the original story. The word *prênès*, rendered ' headlong ' (A.V.) or ' on his face,' is of doubtful meaning. Moffatt's translation assumes that it is formed from the Greek verb *pimprêmi*, and means ' swollen.' In the MSS. there is practically no variety, and the meaning of *prênès* in the versions is ' headlong.' The quotations from Pss. lxix. 25 and cix. 8 are not prophetic but imprecatory, and illustrate the method of using detached portions of Scripture to confirm statements, which till comparatively recent times was employed both by Jews and Christians. The word ' bishopric ' in the A.V., which Moffatt renders by **charge,** is perhaps an echo of the controversies as to church government in the sixteenth century, and is intended to emphasize the view that each Apostle had his own episcopate.

21 Well then, of the men who have been associated with us all the
22 time the Lord Jesus went in and out among us, from the baptism of John down to the day when he was taken up from us—of these men one must join us as a witness to his
23 resurrection." So they brought forward two men, Joseph
24 called Bar-Sabb'as (surnamed Justus) and Matthias; and they prayed, " O Lord, who readest the hearts of all, do thou single out from these two men him whom thou hast
25 chosen to fill the place in this apostolic ministry which
26 Judas left in order to go to his own place." Then they cast lots for them, and the lot fell upon Matthias, who was assigned his position with the eleven apostles.

Great importance was attached to twelve as the number of the Apostles who were to witness to the fact of the Resurrection, and to act as rulers of the Church. Thus Augustine, at the end of ver. 26, has, ' And he was reckoned along with the eleven apostles as the twelfth.' They must be twelve to correspond with the twelve tribes of Israel. Indeed, in some ancient lists of the Twelve, we have a tribe assigned to each Apostle. To be one of the Twelve, the *human* qualification was to have seen Jesus after his Resurrection, and the *divine* to have been specially chosen by him. Hence the selection of two undoubted witnesses, the prayer for guidance, and the choice by lot as when Saul was made king. Strange to say, Luke does not develop the subject any further. We hear no more of Matthias, nor, except for Peter and John (and his brother James who was killed by Herod), of any of the remaining Apostles. In fact, as the narrative proceeds, the Twelve entirely disappear. The selection of Matthias may be intended to shew that the infant Church possessed the power alike of organization and continuance. In the second chapter we shall see how the work of spreading abroad the gospel began.

The second chapter is an account of how the Spirit came upon the Church and prepared it for its task of converting the world. Luke does it dramatically (see above, p. 4), endeavouring to bring the scene before the reader's eyes. Yet, vivid as is the picture, we are left in doubt as to the details. Nothing is said as to where the disciples were assembled (in the Upper Room or in the Temple ?), where the crowd came together at the sound of the wind, how three thousand persons could have joined the community by being baptized at Jerusalem, and the like, but we observe the analogy between the gift of the Spirit on the day of Pentecost and his descent at the baptism of Jesus. On both occasions the heavens are opened (Mark uses the expressive words ' rent asunder '), a voice is heard, and the Spirit descends in visible form. It is as though the Lord gave his disciples the same experience as that through which he himself had passed, when he submitted to baptism at the hands of John, and was declared from the open heaven to be accepted as the Son of God.

ii.

1 During the course of the day of Pentecost they were all together,
2 when suddenly there came a sound from heaven like a violent blast of wind, which filled the whole house where
3 they were seated. They saw tongues like flames distributing
4 themselves, one resting on the head of each, and they were all filled with the holy Spirit—they began to speak in foreign tongues, as the Spirit enabled them to express
5 themselves. Now there were devout Jews from every
6 nation under heaven staying in Jerusalem. So when this sound was heard, the multitude gathered in bewilderment,
7 for each heard them speaking in his own language. All were amazed and astonished. "Are these not all Gali-
8 leans," they said, "who are speaking? Then how is it that
9 each of us hears them in his own native tongue? Parthi-ans, Medes, Elamites, residents in Mesopotamia, in Judaea
10 and Cappadocia, in Pontus and Asia, in Phrygia and Pamphylia, in Egypt and the districts of Libya round
11 Cyrene, visitors from Rome, Jews and proselytes, Cretans and Arabians, we hear these men talking of the triumphs
12 of God in our own languages!" They were all amazed and quite at a loss. "What can it mean?" they said
13 to one another. Some others sneered, "They are brim-full of new wine!"

We cannot fail to be reminded of the scene of the giving of the Law on Mount Sinai, when Israel became a strictly religious community, and there is reason to suppose that Pentecost was already the festival commemorating the giving of the Law. If Luke knew the Rabbinic tradition, the fact that the Spirit came to the Church at this season must have been impressive to him.

The opening words of the chapter are difficult to construe. Rendered literally, the Greek would represent, ' And in the day of the Pentecost's being fulfilled.' The verb of time only occurs once elsewhere in the New Testament (Luke ix. 51), and there it is rendered in the A.V. ' When the time was come that he should be received up'; in Moffatt's translation, *And the time for his assumption was now due.* The question here is whether Luke meant that the Spirit was bestowed on the actual day of Pentecost or during the Pentecostal season (the text of W is rendered by Dr. Ropes : ' And it came to pass in those days of the arrival of the day of Pentecost, while they were all together ').

More important is it for us to inquire into the meaning of the words, **they began to speak in foreign tongues.** It is clear that Luke wishes us to understand that those on whom the fiery tongues descended were enabled to make themselves understood in all languages, which, according to Rabbinic tradition, numbered seventy ; thus the miracle was symbolical of the coming universality of the gospel. But was the miracle as here recorded peculiar to this day or had the early preachers a continuous power of making themselves intelligible to all nations ? In other words, what was the so-called ' speaking with tongues ' mentioned elsewhere in the N.T. ? Was it, or was it not, a repetition of the Pentecostal gift ? The passages in which these ' tongues ' occur are Mark xvi. 17 (' they shall speak with new tongues '), Acts x. 46 (at the baptism of Cornelius), Acts xix. 6 (at the baptism by Paul at Ephesus). But the most important notices are to be found in 1 Cor. xii. and xiv., where to ' speak with tongues ' is acknowledged by St. Paul to be a spiritual gift, highly valued by the Corinthians. This, though possessed in a special degree by the Apostle himself, was liable to be exercised ostentatiously. As these ' tongues ' were not profitable unless someone was present who could interpret their meaning to the Christian assembly, they cannot be identified with the ' tongues ' on the day of Pentecost, in which foreigners recognized their native languages. Luke therefore cannot possibly mean that the sign of Pentecost, whereby everybody was edified by hearing the praises of God in his own language, was identical with the *glossolalia* or ' speaking with tongues,' the abuse of which was regulated by Paul in his Corinthian letter. Indeed, if the author of Acts were a companion of the Apostle, he must have known that the common phenomenon of ' speaking with tongues ' did not in any way resemble what is recorded to have taken place in Acts ii.

The list of nations enumerated as having been present at Jerusalem is scarcely what one would expect from a Western writer, and may conceivably have been derived from an Eastern source. It may be permissible to surmise that, as they were addressed by Galilaeans, the majority would at least have been able to understand them, since Aramaic in some form or other was generally understood by the inhabitants of the countries in which it was generally a *lingua franca* as the language of commerce. To the Jews from Parthia, Media, Elam, and *Mesopotamia*, Aramaic must have been familiar ; and, if by **Judaea** is meant not the province but all Palestine, the first five nations enumerated spoke, or at least understood, that language ; and, although the Alexandrian Jews probably spoke Greek, those of the rest of Egypt and Arabia may well have used Aramaic. A very early way of avoiding the difficulty of the mention of *Judaea* in this catalogue of nations, though unsupported by any MS. evidence, was by assuming that Armenia not *Judaea* was the original reading. In short, despite the fact that the Galilean language was considered to be corrupt in Jerusalem, Galilean believers could be widely understood, and the fact that every man heard them in his own tongue may be explained as allegorical of the future diffusion of the gospel to all nations.

That some **sneered** and derided those who had received the Spirit as drunken implies a certain confusion of mind in regard to the Pentecostal miracle, since it would have been unreasonable if the disciples had received, to quote the English Prayer Book, ' the gift of diverse languages.' On the other hand, if the tongues were like those alluded to in 1 Corinthians, it was a perfectly natural criticism. Luke, as has been suggested, may well have had practical experience of the ecstatic utterances described by Paul, which have repeatedly occurred in religious revivals, even in our own day. In 1 Cor. xiv. 23

Paul says that if in a Christian assembly a heathen came and
heard all exercising the gift, he would say they were raving.
Such being the case, it is not to be wondered at that those who
heard the believers at Pentecost speaking with tongues should
declare that they were brim-full of new wine.

But Peter stood up along with the eleven, and raising his voice 14
    he addressed them thus : " Men of Judaea and residents
    in Jerusalem, let every one of you understand this—
    attend to what I say: these men are not drunk, as you 15
    imagine.   Why, it is only nine in the morning!   No, this 16
    is what was predicted by the prophet Joel—
In the last days, saith God, *then will I pour out my* 17
       Spirit upon all flesh,
   your sons and daughters shall prophesy,
   your young men shall see visions,
   your old men shall dream dreams:
   on my very slaves and slave-girls in those days will I 18
       pour out my Spirit,
and they shall prophesy.
   And I will display wonders in heaven **above**   19
     and signs *on earth* **below,**
   blood and fire and vapour of smoke;
   the sun shall be changed into darkness   20
     and the moon into blood,
   ere the great, open Day of the Lord arrives.
   And everyone who invokes the name of the Lord shall be 21
    saved.

Men of Israel, listen to my words.   Jesus the Nazarene, a 22
man accredited to you by God through miracles, wonders,
and signs which God performed by him among you (as you
yourselves know), this Jesus, betrayed in the predestined 23
course of God's deliberate purpose, you got wicked men
to nail to the cross and murder, but God raised him by
checking the pangs of death.   Death could not hold him. 24
For David says of him,   25
   I saw the Lord before me evermore;
    lest I be shaken, he is at my right hand.

26   *My heart is glad,*
    my tongue exults,
    my very flesh will rest in hope,

27   *because thou wilt not forsake my soul in the grave,*
    nor let thy holy one suffer decay.

28   *Thou hast made known to me the paths of life,*
    thou wilt fill me with delight in thy presence.

29   Brothers, I can speak quite plainly to you about the patriarch David ; he died and was buried and his tomb

30   remains with us to this day. (He was a prophet ; he knew God *had sworn an oath to him that he would seat one of his*

31   *descendants on his throne ;* * so he spoke with a prevision of the resurrection of the Christ, when he said that *he was*

32   *not forsaken in the grave nor did* his *flesh suffer decay.* This

33   Jesus God raised, as we can all bear witness. Uplifted then by God's right hand and receiving from the Father the long-promised holy Spirit, he has poured on us what

34   you now see and hear.) For it was not David who ascended to heaven ; David says,
    The Lord said to my Lord,
     ' *Sit at my right hand,*

35   *till I make your enemies a footstool for your feet.*'

36   So let all the house of Israel understand beyond a doubt that God has made him both Lord and Christ, this very Jesus whom you have crucified."

   * Omitting [τὸ κατὰ σάρκα ἀναστήσειν τὸν Χριστὸν].

It is possible that some record of what Peter actually said on this occasion may have been preserved at Jerusalem in Aramaic. More probably, the writer of Acts put into the mouth of the Apostle what he might well have said to the astonished multitude. If, however, this and other speeches in the book are free compositions by Luke, they are valuable records, not only of the various appeals made by the believers in support of their Master's cause, but also of Luke's view of the development of the gospel message, and of the different methods of its presentation. In this speech we have an example of the most primitive preaching of the gospel to Jews.

However this address by Peter was composed, it exactly fits the situation. It should be observed that nothing is said of the miracle of the gift of tongues. All that is said of those who had received the Spirit is that they prophesied. This would not exclude the possibility of their having spoken with 'tongues,' because prophecy in the Old Testament means not only to foretell the future, but implies that he who exercises this gift is the mouthpiece of a spiritual being, or even a heathen god. Thus Saul was said to 'prophesy' in his madness because it was supposed that, not he but the Spirit which possessed him was speaking (1 Sam. xix. 24). Thus those who spoke with foreign tongues would appear to the bystanders as prophesying.

This Peter takes as the fulfilment of the prophecy of Joel that the prophetic spirit will be poured out **on all flesh.** As we shall have frequent occasion to point out that in the New Testament many passages in the Old are taken completely detached from their context, it is to be noted that the little prophecy of Joel must here be taken as a whole, because it not only explains the sign of the Spirit, but gives the keynotes of Peter's address. The land of Judah had been devastated by locusts, and the prophet called all to repent or rather to 'turn to God.' A solemn fast was proclaimed. 'Rend your hearts and not your garments, and turn unto the Lord your God.' Repentance would be followed by forgiveness, the rain would fall, corn and oil would again abound. Then God would 'pour out His Spirit upon all flesh (**blood and fire and vapour of smoke** is omitted in W) . . . before the coming of the great and terrible (Gr. *open* or manifest) day of the Lord.' Men would witness the restoration of Jerusalem, and once more would the Lord be the hope of his people. A more inspiring prophecy could not have been chosen when Peter announced to the people the triumph of the risen Master.

The fulfilment of the prophecy of Joel which the people had just witnessed was a sign of the beginning of the Messianic age, and Peter now directs the attention of his hearers to Jesus. There is some art displayed in the way Peter is made to address his audience. In his opening words he calls his hearers, **men of Judaea** (literally Jews) **and residents in Jerusalem ;** in ver. 22 he speaks to them as **men of Israel.** This is by no means accidental. A Jew or Judaean is a member of the nation or, as here, an inhabitant of Judaea. An Israelite, on the other hand, is the religious designation of the Chosen People, and, as such, Peter speaks of the deliverance Jesus had brought to his servants. Jesus is here called **the Nazarene.** As such he was known in Jerusalem, and his followers were known as Nazarenes (Acts xxiv. 5). The question is, what does the term mean ? Elsewhere the Jews called him Jesus of Nazareth from his home in Galilee. Some deny that there is any connexion between Nazarene and Nazareth. Upon the whole, however, the traditional view seems the less improbable. It is noteworthy that this is the only example of Jesus being thus styled by any believer, though the people of Jerusalem acclaimed him as ' Jesus, the prophet of Nazareth of Galilee ' (Matt. xxi. 11). Later, the Christians were called by their enemies Nazarenes or Galileans. That Peter should so style his Master in proclaiming to a Jewish crowd that he had risen, is singularly applicable to the situation.

The speech of Peter (vers. 14–36) is practically an exposition of three passages of Scripture, the first being the prophecy of Joel about the outpouring of the Spirit preceding the last days. This is (vers. 14–24) explained as the sequel of the life, death, and resurrection of Jesus. Jesus is presented as he had appeared to the Jews, a man **accredited by God,** as was shewn by the **miracles** he wrought. But he had been **betrayed** to the Gentiles, i.e. to men without the Law, and put to the most shameful death a Jew could conceive of ; for the Law had said that ' the curse of God is he that is hanged ' (Deut. xxi. 23), an ambiguous phrase used repeatedly by Jewish controversialists to prove that God had rejected Jesus. Despite this, God had decreed that Jesus should undergo this humiliation, because it was part of His eternal **deliberate purpose** (this finds an echo in 1 Pet. i. 20, a remarkable coincidence between this speech and the epistle). But God had rescued Jesus from this depth of shame by raising him from the dead, because it was not possible that death could conquer such a One as he.

Peter now begins to quote and expound a second prophecy, that of Ps. xvi, in which David, to whom all the psalms are attributed, had said that God would not allow the soul of His **holy** or favoured **one** (*chasîd*) to remain in the place of departed souls, nor his body to **suffer decay.** David could not have meant the words to apply to himself, for he had died, and his sepulchre was still in Jerusalem. He must have spoken of his descendant, the Messiah, whom God had actually raised from the dead. But not only did Jesus rise from the dead, he had ascended to the right hand of God as David had prophesied in Ps. cx., and had sent the sign of the Spirit, as all who heard Peter could witness. Consequently, the man who had been **crucified,** by his resurrection has been plainly proclaimed to be **Lord and Christ.**

This address to the people is possibly not meant to be taken as a speech, but as a prophetic utterance. The word **addressed** employed by the majority of the MSS. in ver. 14 is the same as is used in ver. 4, where those under the influence of the Spirit **express themselves.** The Bezan MS. saw the difficulty and changed it to ' said,' but according to the accepted reading Peter spoke to the people, like all the other recipients of the Spirit, prophetically.

When they heard this, it went straight to their hearts ; they 37 said to Peter and the rest of the apostles, " Brothers, what are we to do ? " " Repent," said Peter, " let each of you 38 be baptized in the name of Jesus Christ for the remission of your sins ; then you will receive the gift of the holy Spirit. For the promise is meant for you and for your children and 39 *for all who are far off, for anyone whom the Lord* **our God** *may call to himself."* **And with many another appeal he** 40 urged and entreated them. " Save yourselves," he cried, "from this crooked generation!" So those who accepted 41 what he said were baptized; about three thousand souls were brought in, that day.

These verses cannot be taken literally. The large number of **three thousand** is not as incredible as many are disposed to think ; so many Jews from all parts of the world may well have accepted Peter's message, and most of these would go home with the news that the Messiah had appeared in Jerusalem. But that so large a community was regularly formed in the city, as seems here to be implied, is wellnigh incredible. Probably Luke, as is his wont, desires to give a picture of the wonderful sequel to the Pentecostal miracle and Peter's speech. When the Apostles call on their hearers to **repent**, they re-echo the word with which John the Baptist and Jesus began their message (Matt. iii. 2 and iv. 17). The Greek means ' change your minds,' i.e. have a new object in view. The Latin rendering, which has rabbinical authority, is almost always ' do penance.' Probably it is the equivalent to the Hebrew ' turn ye ' to God, which is one of the keynotes of Joel's prophecy—' Turn ye with weeping, and with fasting and with mourning.' Yet the word ' turning ' to mean repentance is not biblical, though common in later Judaism.

The importance attached to Baptism by Peter in this address raises many questions : (1) Are we to suppose that on this occasion the Apostles insisted that instant submission to the rite must follow turning to God, as the first step towards acknowledging that Jesus had risen from the dead ? Or, granting that the acceptance of the sacrament was at a very early time a necessary prelude to becoming a member of the new community, may we assume that Peter is represented as at this time placing it in the forefront of his message because, when Luke wrote, it was acknowledged to be indispensable ? (2) How is it that water baptism, which is expressly contrasted with that of the Spirit, is assumed from the first to be the means by which the Spirit was bestowed ? (3) Is the baptism commanded by Peter essentially different from the baptism of John, to which probably many of his hearers had already submitted, or is it something else ? (4) What can be gathered from Acts as compared with the teaching of Paul as to the doctrine of the efficacy of baptism ? (5) Did Jesus insist on it as an absolute condition of discipleship, and institute the sacrament as such ? (6) Lastly, there is the formula of baptism and its significance. These important questions each need separate treatment, but they all assist us to determine the character of Peter's exhortation and the significance attached to it by Luke.

(1) That he meant these words to be taken literally is not easy to imagine. In the first place in the gospels, stress is laid upon the obvious fact that baptism on a large scale would only be administered where there was plenty of water (John iii. 23), and in the second place, in chap. iii., when Peter addresses the people after the healing of the lame man, he calls them to repentance without insisting upon baptism. According to some authorities, the narratives in Acts ii. and iii.–iv. are a doublet ; and certainly the omission of the exhortation to baptism seems more probable. (2) The contradictions in regard to baptism in the New Testament are perplexing. At a very early time in the history of the Church, certainly in Luke's time, it had become a sacramental rite, or a spiritual gift bestowed by an outward symbol. But the tradition of the Baptist's words persisted, or more probably the believers in Jesus practised the Johannine ceremony of baptism and gave it a fuller interpretation. (3) The author of Acts is disposed to emphasize the difference between the two baptisms, and thus he raises the whole question of the relation of the followers of Jesus to those of John. The importance of the Baptist in the gospel scheme cannot be overlooked and the constant insistence on the superiority of Jesus points to the fact that there was a hotly debated controversy on the subject. (4) It is evident that, whether the speech of Peter, as given in this chapter, is of a later date than the writings of Paul or not, it represents a far less spiritual and more primitive conception of baptism, namely, as a means for obtaining a miraculous gift of prophecy and tongues, rather than a cause of transformed character. (5) Whether Jesus instituted baptism himself turns on the saying recorded in Matt. xxviii. 19, and in a measure on the fact that in the Fourth Gospel the disciples of Jesus practised it, though Jesus himself did not (but see John iii. 26 and iv. 2). Peter's words on the day of Pentecost imply

that Jesus had ordered his followers to baptize their converts.
(6) It is clear evidence of the primitive character of Peter's
utterance that no formula of baptism is suggested. In the
N.T. (except in Matt. xxviii. 19) it is always in the Name of
Jesus. The whole question of the relation of the Spirit to
Baptism in Acts is of the greatest importance, and will be
dealt with as the narrative proceeds. Here it is sufficient to
enumerate the points raised in the introduction to the preaching of the gospel of the risen Lord.

The concluding words of Peter are that the promise of the
Spirit is intended for those who heard him, and for others who
were then far away, using the words of Isa. lvii. 19, and perhaps
hinting at the coming diffusion of the gospel to the whole
world. The Apostle also strikes an eschatological note exhorting all to whom he spoke to escape from a rebellious
generation about to be visited by the wrath of God.

42 They devoted themselves to the instruction given by the
apostles and to fellowship, breaking bread and praying
43 together. Awe fell on everyone, and many wonders and
signs were performed by the apostles [in Jerusalem].
44 The believers * all kept together ; they shared all they
45 had with one another, they would sell their possessions and goods and distribute the proceeds among
46 all, as anyone might be in need. Day after day they
resorted with one accord to the temple and broke bread
together in their own homes; they ate with a glad and
47 simple heart, praising God and looked on with favour by
all the people. Meantime the Lord added the saved daily
to their number.†

* Omitting [φόβος τε ἦν μέγας ἐπὶ πάντας, καί].

† Omitting [τῇ ἐκκλησίᾳ], although the omission makes it difficult to
get the above sense, or indeed any, out of the Greek.

This conclusion of the second chapter sums up the result
of the day of Pentecost, the birthday of the Church. The
believers are supposed instantly to have formed a society,
characterized by submission to apostolic authority, unanimity,
and devotion. The description of this society, henceforward

to be known as ' the Church ' (ἐκκλησία), is ideal rather than historical, and is in part duplicated later in iv. 32 ff. The word church occurs doubtfully in ver. 47 (A.V.), but Luke obviously implies its existence in the entire passage. Peter has warned the believers to flee the evil generation in which they lived, and they did so by forming an association. This was perfectly natural for a body of Jews to do. The Synagogue had enabled the Jews to combine with one another in all parts of the world ; and, despite the fact that at Jerusalem the Temple was the centre of worship, this did not prevent (see Acts vi.) the rise of synagogues in the holy city. Possibly, therefore, the rise of the Christian Church simply as a new synagogue, would cause no surprise, and if its members, like the Essenes, had religious customs of their own, this would be regarded as perfectly natural. Indeed, in Acts the writer insists that the new society was favourably regarded by the people. Its leading characteristics were : (1) attention to **the instruction given by the apostles** (W adds ' in Jerusalem ') ; (2) the sense of reverence owing to the apostolic miracles (some versions and MSS. add ' in Jerusalem' here) ; (3) the breaking of bread and prayers in common ; (4) the unity of the members and their charity to one another ; (5) their ' constant presence ' in the Temple ; (6) the rapid increase of the society, and its popularity owing to the simple and joyous character of its adherents.

(1) What is called the Apostle's **instruction** (Greek, *didachê*) proves the antiquity of the belief in the Christian Church that its doctrine must be traced back to the Twelve, who were the immediate companions of the Saviour. The idea first appears in the later epistles of St. Paul (cf. Eph. ii. 20, ' and are built on the foundation of the apostles and prophets,' etc.). It was assumed that the whole *corpus* of the teaching of the Church was derived from that of the Apostles during their sojourn at Jerusalem. Hence early Church law books were called ' The Teaching of the Apostles,' ' Apostolic Canons,' ' Apostolic Constitutions,' etc. This fact also explains the idea of Apostolic succession, and also of the Apostolic Creed, which a late legend explained as having been made by the Twelve

when they left Jerusalem to evangelize the world, each contributing in turn an article of belief.

(2) Acts lays stress on the fact that the Church was a supernatural society, in the sense that the Apostles at least were able to work wonders which amazed and awed men. Their miraculous powers of healing became widely known (cf. v. 12–16), and Paul says the same of spiritually gifted persons in the church of Corinth (1 Cor. xii. 10). In fact, miracles were regarded as the usual result of the foundation of an early Christian community, and these were not only beneficent, but as regards Ananias and Sapphira, also punitive (see 1 Cor. v. 5, and 1 Tim. i. 20).

(3) Whether by the **breaking bread** the sacrament of the Eucharist in commemoration of the Last Supper is here meant may be open to question. The expression ' to break bread ' is used of a Christian service in xx. 7 ; Jesus himself broke the bread when he fed the multitude (Matt. xiv. 19, Mark vi. 41, and Luke ix. 16), and he was known to Cleopas and his companion (who had not been present at the Last Supper) in the breaking of bread, or as Moffatt correctly renders it, *when he broke the loaf* (Luke xxiv. 35). The whole subject of the sacraments in Acts needs separate discussion. Here it is enough to say that, even apart from the Last Supper, the breaking of the loaf had a peculiar significance for the disciples of Jesus, and that a common meal, in which they believed themselves to be closely united to the Master, was partaken by the Christian community from the first.

(4) In the early chapters of Acts the condition of affairs is idealized with the object of shewing what the Church ought to be. Its unity should be unbroken, its charity unbounded. When we come to facts in chap. vi., we realize that even the loving care of **believers** for one another was a cause of dispute. It is generally assumed that Luke's object is to represent the original society at Jerusalem as purely communistic, in the sense that private property was not permitted. This would not be exceptional. Among the Jews, according to Philo, the Therapeutae resigned their personal possessions, and the small entourage of Jesus had a common fund entrusted to

Judas Iscariot. But according to this passage and Acts iv. 32 ff. there was no poverty in the community, because some-one was always to be found to **sell** his **goods** or lands to relieve it, and Barnabas, for parting with a farm to assist the Church, is mentioned as a conspicuous example of generosity. The sin of Ananias was not that he did not surrender all he had to the Apostles, but that he pretended to have done so, and Peter told him that the money he obtained from his land was his own to dispose of as he chose. The very fact that widows were specially relieved points to the fact that the majority of believers were not living on a common fund.

(5) It is remarkable that Luke, who was, according to tradition, the only Gentile among the New Testament writers, should dwell so much on the worship of the Temple (Luke i. 8 ff.). Here his object seems to be to impress the reader with the fact that the first believers were in every way exemplary as Jews, that they had no wish to break with the national worship and regarded the Temple with the utmost veneration. Yet both Jesus and his followers, though they resorted to it for worship and instructed the people in its courts, were accused of disrespect for the Temple. There may be an apologetic aim in this insistence that the earliest followers of Jesus so scrupulously **resorted to** the sanctuary.

(6) The concluding words of the chapter (rendered **to their number**) present an insoluble problem to the textual critic, as Moffatt points out. Prof. Torrey suggests that they are due to misunderstanding of an Aramaic original which really meant not ' together ' but ' exceedingly.' That the community increased rapidly and was in high favour need cause no surprise. The fact that a great prophet like Jesus had risen from the dead might easily be admitted by Jews, many of whom thought that John the Baptist might have been restored to life (Luke ix. 19) ; and, if Jesus had really been raised by God from the grave, why should he not be the Messiah and return to glory ? His followers were distinguished by the simple gladness of their lives—happiness was characteristic of early Christianity—and were irreproachable as regards their observance of the law. They claimed to be those

who were **saved** (i.e. ' the remnant ' of which the prophets had spoken, who would escape the judgment of the Lord), and people were naturally anxious to be of their number. Consequently, it could be said that ' the Lord was adding to the number of the saved exceedingly day by day.'

It is permissible to remark that, although the second chapter of Acts cannot be reckoned as an historical account of what actually happened, yet to the historian of Christian origins the author gives an invaluable description of primitive preaching and of his ideal of the Church at its inception.

The third and fourth chapters are sometimes considered to be taken from a source earlier than the second chapter, and to be another account of how the disciples received the gift of the holy Spirit (Acts ii. 4 and iv. 31–32, both repeating the words, ' And they were all filled with the holy Spirit '). But even if this is so, the author of Acts evidently intended these chapters to be a sequel to chap. ii. He has shewn how the Apostles had received the gift of the Spirit as a sign ; he now relates how the power bestowed upon them was confirmed by a miracle. Having related the favour the people shewed to the new society, he proceeds to describe the hostility of the Temple priesthood. The scene is now the Temple rather than the city, and the writer is able to describe the scene with a background less vague than in his story of the Pentecostal miracle.

iii.

1 Peter and John were on their way up to the temple for the hour
2 of prayer at three in the afternoon, when a man lame from birth was carried past, who used to be laid every day at what was called the ' Beautiful Gate ' of the temple, to
3 ask alms from those who entered the temple. When he noticed that Peter and John meant to go into the temple,
4 he asked them for alms. Peter looked at him steadily, as
5 did John, and said, " Look at us." The man attended,
6 expecting to get something from them. But Peter said, " I have no silver or gold, but I will give you what I do

have. In the name of Jesus Christ the Nazarene, [get up
and] walk!" And catching him by the right hand he 7
raised him. Instantly his feet and ankles grew strong, he 8
leapt to his feet, started to walk, and accompanied them
into the temple, walking, leaping, and praising God. When 9
all the people saw him walking and praising God, and 10
when they recognized this was the very man who used to
sit and beg at the Gate Beautiful, they were lost in awe
and amazement at what had happened to him.

The mention of **John** on two occasions as acting a silent
part in company with **Peter** is not easy to account for ; here,
and in chap. viii., the two appear as the official heads of the
community ; but in the gospels, James, the son of Zebedee,
ranks next to Peter. That a personage of such immense
importance in Christian history as John should be no more
than a spectator of what is done by Peter has caused some
scholars to hazard the opinion that by **John** is meant John
Mark, who was later regarded as the special attendant of
Peter ; but in Acts, whenever Paul and Barnabas, or Paul and
Silas act together, the first-named of the pair invariably
speaks and acts for the second, and the same rule may be
observed in the association of Peter and the Apostle John.

Ver. 2, as translated, gives the exact meaning of the Greek,
namely, that the cripple was being carried to the Temple as
Peter and John were going thither ; but it is difficult to
imagine why his hearers should not take the man to beg at the
gate in the morning instead of late in the afternoon. Probably
the meaning of the verse, even if somewhat awkwardly expressed, is that it was customary to carry the lame man to the
Temple and place him at the gate to attract the sympathy of
the worshippers. He was evidently a well-known character
in Jerusalem.

Peter and John are described as going **up** to the Temple.
If so, they must have resided in the Lower City, where the
Cenaculum, or traditional scene of the Last Supper, is situated.
The Temple, it should be remembered, was a vast building
consisting of a series of *courts* standing in an extensive oblong

space with porticoes or cloisters around the sides. This was
open to all, but only Jews were permitted to enter the Temple
itself. The entrance to the court from the city was on the
western side by gates and bridges, or steps from what was
known as the Valley of the Cheesemongers, or *Tyropoeon*. It
is not certain what the so-called **Beautiful Gate** was, whether
situated outside the large court, or at the entrance to the
Temple within the building itself. There is no gate of this
name in Josephus's description of the Temple, nor in the
rabbinic treatise called *Middoth*. The healing of a man known
to have been a cripple from his birth by virtue of the name
of Jesus Christ, the Nazarene, was sure to attract attention.
That this name could have such power was a sure proof that
he who bore it was, if not Divine, at least a Being in the highest
favour with God. In Acts xix. 14 those who tried to use the
name as a charm to exorcise demons brought shame and
danger upon themselves. Apparently, after the miracle,
Peter and John, accompanied by the lame man, entered the
Temple and performed their devotions, and on going into the
outer court the people, seeing one they knew well as a cripple,
surrounded him as he clung to the two Apostles.

11 **As he clung to Peter and John, all the people rushed awestruck
to them in what was called Solomon's portico. But when**
12 **Peter saw this, he said to the people, " Men of Israel, why
are you surprised at this ? Why do you stare at us, as if
we had made him walk by any power or piety of ours ?**
13 *The God of Abraham and the God of Isaac and the God
of Jacob, the God of our fathers has glorified* Jesus *his
servant,* whom you delivered up and repudiated before
14 Pilate. Pilate had decided to release him, but you
repudiated the Holy and Just One ; the boon you asked
15 was a murderer, and you killed the pioneer of Life. But
God raised him from the dead, as we can bear witness.
16 (He it is who has given strength to this man whom you see
and know, by faith in his name; it is the faith he inspires
which has made the man thus hale and whole before you
17 all.) **Now I know, brothers, that you acted in ignorance,**

26

like your rulers—though this was how God fulfilled what 18
he had announced beforehand by the lips of all the prophets, namely the sufferings of his Christ. Repent then, 19
and turn to have your sins blotted out, so that a breathing-
space may be vouchsafed you, and that the Lord may send 20
Jesus your long-decreed Christ, who must be kept in 21
heaven till the period of the great Restoration. Ages ago
God spoke of this by the lips of his holy prophets; for 22
Moses said,

*The Lord our God will raise up a prophet for you from
among your brotherhood, as he raised me :
you must listen to whatever he may tell you.*

Any soul that will not listen to this prophet shall be 23
exterminated from the People ;

and all the prophets who have spoken since Samuel and 24
his successors have also announced these days. Now you 25
are the sons of the prophets and of the covenant which
God made with your fathers when he said to Abraham, *all
families on earth shall be blessed in your offspring.* It was 26
for you first that God raised up his Servant, and sent him to
bless you by turning each of you from your wicked ways.''

According to Josephus, **Solomon's portico** was a magnificent
colonnade on the south side of the great court. It appears to
have been open to all religious teachers, and Jesus is said to
have ' walked ' there (John x. 23).

Peter's address on this occasion bears a resemblance to the
Pentecostal speech ; but this similarity must not make the
reader forget the difference of treatment. The object of the
address is to emphasize the power of the name of Jesus. The
miracle wrought by Peter and John is a conclusive proof that
he is still a living power, able to bring, not only a future
deliverance, but a present salvation into the world. The
scriptural proofs are different ; and, whereas in the second
chapter the call is to repent and be baptized, here it is to
repentance and obedience to the commands of Jesus, not so
much as the Christ, but as the prophet. As at Pentecost.
Peter says all that has happened is in accordance with the

eternal purpose of God. Jesus is here proclaimed as the παῖς of God, an ambiguous word which may be rendered ' child ' or **servant**. In accordance with the use of this term in the Old Testament, especially in Isaiah, the sense of servant seems preferable, as meaning the representative of God on earth. The implication throughout is practical rather than theological. God has sent in Jesus a second Moses, a Law-giver demanding from his generation the same implicit obedience as Moses required in the wilderness. The artistry of Acts as displayed in this speech is seen in its entire applicability to the occasion. As addressed to Jews, the argument is exactly of a kind to appeal to them.

The speech opens with the assurance that the people must not imagine that the miracle was wrought by **any power** inherent in the Apostles, but in the name of Jesus Christ. This is a proof that God has glorified his servant Jesus. Here we have a primitive Christology such as Jews could receive without any offence. What follows is eminently conciliatory. The gospel story of the Crucifixion is assumed to be well known ; the Jews had preferred the murderer, Barabbas, to a holy and innocent man, who, as the Apostle can testify, has risen from the dead. The cripple, because he believed in him, has been given perfect health, for here it is assumed that the miracle had been wrought upon a convert to Jesus. The people and their rulers had crucified Jesus, because they were ignorant, and also because God's purpose had to be fulfilled. Nevertheless, the people had only to repent and times of refreshment would come ; the Christ who had been foretold would return in the person of the triumphant Jesus. This seems to imply that the messiahship of Jesus was to be considered as belonging to a future, though not far distant. It is true that a speedy deliverance was often expected ; yet the very fact that God Himself was about to send His servant back to earth was at least calculated to prevent those disastrous outbursts which were directed to bring about a deliverance of Israel by physical violence. The risen Jesus is here presented as a law-giver and prophet now, and a Saviour and Messiah hereafter.

It is perhaps worth noticing that, wherever Peter speaks in Acts, his language appears to be unnatural in the mouth of the Peter of the gospel narrative. There are many words in this speech which it is hard to believe that a Galilean peasant could have used, and the same thing is to be observed in the address to Cornelius in Acts x. This is evident from the use of the word translated restitution or **Restoration,** a philosophical term expressing the theory of cycles. The Stoics taught that at the end of every ' period ' the world would revert again to what it had been at its creation, and that all that had happened in the former ' periods ' would recur. That Peter meant this is wellnigh incredible, though he may have assured the people that the world would be restored at the return of Jesus from heaven to its original purity, and that God would raise up a new Moses to be their prophet.

The quotation from Deuteronomy is a good illustration of the ancient method by which both Jews and Christians who followed them used the Old Testament. Taken with its context, the sense is plain enough : Moses, in Deut. xviii. 18, is exhorting the people to beware of false prophets, diviners, necromancers, and the like, but he assures them that they shall not lack Divine guidance, for God will raise up among them a prophet to instruct them in the right way. But the context mattered but little to the exegetes of the age, and of many generations to come. All Scripture was inspired, and detached words like those of an oracle might be of infinite importance. In their endeavour to prove that Jesus was the Messiah foretold in the Law, the Prophets and the Psalms, his followers collected a number of proof texts to shew that every act of his life corresponded to some inspired utterance. The most conspicuous example of this is the Gospel according to Matthew, in which a prophecy is adduced on every possible occasion. It is noticeable how skilfully this argument is introduced into the speeches in Acts. It only occurs in words addressed to Jews, notably in the two first speeches of Peter (in Acts ii. and iii.), in that of Stephen in Acts vii., and in the address of James in Acts xv. In ver. 26, one of the keynotes of the whole book is struck by the words, **For you first,** the author's object being to shew that although Christ had come to the world, his first message was to the Jews and through them to mankind.

The parallels in the speeches of chaps. ii. and iii. are very striking ; superficially the argument is the same, and some slight differences in language and treatment make it reasonable to suppose that Luke relied on two separate documents. Hence the idea that the two addresses to the people are really the same under a different form, or variously reported. Whether this is so or not, it appears that even in giving two versions of Peter's speech the author of Acts means to mark the progress of the first revelation of Jesus as the Christ to the people of Israel. The first speech is introduced by a sign from God ; the Spirit is sent with manifestations of storm and fire, which announce the divine presence. The second speech is prefaced by the story of a miracle in order to illustrate the fact that the Apostles of Jesus had been endued with special power to carry on their work. God has witnessed to their mission by enabling them to work miracles ' in the Name of Jesus Christ the Nazarene.' In chap. ii. the object is to shew that the outpouring of the Spirit proves that in Jesus the days of the Messiah have come, and Peter, in calling to baptism, indicates by what means this messianic Spirit may be obtained. The call to repent ' or turn ' is the same in both, but in Acts ii. Jesus is in heaven and God's Spirit on earth ; in Acts iii. it is otherwise. The Spirit has been manifested by words ; prophecy and ' tongues ' are the signs of his presence. The power of the Name of Jesus, on the other hand, is manifested in active work. Thus the first address of Peter lays emphasis on the new spirit, and the second is a proclamation of Jesus by two Apostles, Peter and John, who are able to prove by an astounding miracle that they act by his authority. Thus Jesus, as has been indicated, is the new Moses, the guide of his disciples on earth. In this way a fresh note is struck. The importance of these two speeches as introductions to the gospel as it was to be proclaimed can hardly be overestimated.

The theology, as might be expected, may be called rudimentary, but it is a proof of the artistic skill of the author that it is so. Throughout the book he is working his way to a more complete explanation of the meaning of the ministry and death of Jesus, and he employs different proclamations of the gospel to this end. Thus in a certain sense the speeches, whether taken from early sources or, as was not unusual in ancient literature, composed by the author, are selected with great skill, and are at least as important for our understanding of primitive Christianity as the strictly historical portion of the Acts.

iv.

While they were speaking to the people, they were surprised by   1
    the priests, the commander of the temple, and the Sad-
    ducees, who were annoyed at them teaching the people and   2
    proclaiming Jesus as an instance of resurrection from the
    dead. They laid hands on them and, as it was now even-   3
    ing, put them in custody till next morning. (A number of   4
    those who heard them speak believed, bringing up their
    numbers to [about] five thousand.)

The arrest of Peter and John is in conformity with what might be expected. If the descent of the Spirit at Pentecost and the preaching of Peter took place outside the Temple, it was natural that the followers of Jesus should not be molested. True, Peter had declared that the fire and tongues were a further sign of God's approval of Jesus, whom He had raised from the dead, but the Apostles had wrought no miracles by their Master's authority, and simply exhorted the people to be baptized in his name. But with the healing of the lame man all was changed. In the first place, the miracle was wrought within the precincts of the Temple, and in the second, Jesus had been openly declared to be not only the Christ risen and about to return, but an ever-present leader, the new Moses.

In the Temple, the high-priest occupied a position not wholly different from that of the Pope in the Vatican after 1870. He was in a sense a sovereign pontiff with considerable power. A disturbance in the city was an affair of the Roman procurator ; but the high-priest was in charge of the Temple. Seeing an excited crowd surrounding Peter and John, he had full authority to interfere, and accordingly he placed the two Apostles under arrest. The subject of their preaching was a matter for his cognizance, since they were proclaiming a doctrine, in his opinion, highly dangerous, both to peace and orthodoxy. To him and his associates **Resurrection** was not to be taken in our sense of the word. To the modern Christian it means that there is a future life, in which men will be held responsible for their actions on this earth. To the Jews at this time it meant imminent world-catastrophe, in which the powers on earth would be destroyed and a new order miracu-lously set up. To the priesthood a future life might be a matter of opinion, for on this point Judaism was not usually fanatical ; but the Resurrection implied political disturbance, of which they were most apprehensive, especially if it was to come very soon, and this was assured by the triumph of Jesus over death. Moreover, to the Temple authorities Moses meant the *status quo*, and Jesus, a new prophet like unto Moses, meant a revolu-tion. No wonder the priests instantly stopped the preaching of this new gospel.

The authorities enumerated are **the priests, the commander of the Temple,** and **the Sadducees.** The commander (στρατηγός) is absent in the western text, possibly because the scribe or editor did not know of such an official. But there was cer-tainly an armed guard of Jews whose duty it was to patrol the Temple precincts, and its commander was called in the rab-binic writings ' the man of the Mountain of the House.' Our Lord was arrested by armed servants of the high-priest (Matt. xxvi. 47, Mark xiv. 43, and John xviii. 3, but not Luke). In 2 Macc. iii. 4 Simon the Benjamite is said to have been ' governor of the Temple.' Although we hear but little of the differences between the Pharisees and Sadducees on the subject of a resurrection and a life to come, it is constantly stressed in the New Testament, notably in our Lord's answer to their question about the woman and the seven brethren. In Acts the resurrection is emphasized as the crucial point of difference between the two great sects. Paul wins the support

of the Pharisees on the ground that he shares with them ' the
hope of the resurrection of the dead ' (Acts xxiii. 6 ff.).   That
the Pharisees should be favourable to the followers of Christ
who kept the Law, and the Sadducees should be hostile to
them, is in strict keeping with Josephus's statement, when he
says (*Antiq.*, xiii. 10. 6) that the Sadducees were highly regarded by the rich and influential, and the Pharisees beloved
by the people.   The priests were the aristocracy of Jerusalem,
and as such, being wealthy and in an assured position, were
suspicious of any new movement, especially if it were messianic
in character.

Next morning a meeting was held in Jerusalem of their rulers, 5
    elders and scribes, which was attended by the high priest 6
    Annas, by Caiaphas, John, Alexander, and all the members
    of the high priest's family.   They made the men stand 7
    before them and inquired, " By what authority, in whose
    name, have you * done this ? "

* With a touch of superciliousness (' men like you ! '), which is perhaps better expressed in reading aloud than by any verbal periphrasis.

The account of this meeting should be compared with the
assembly of priests and elders after the arrest of Jesus.   It is
represented as having been held only a few weeks after the
crucifixion, when Pilate was still procurator, although at this
time he was almost certainly at Caesarea, the seat of the
Roman administration, and not in Jerusalem.   It is significant, however, that the Romans now were not asked to interfere, and that the priests dealt with the matter.   **Annas**, or
Ananias as he is called by Josephus, takes the lead, and
Caiaphas, who had long enjoyed the office of high-priest, takes
a secondary place, as, in a sense, he does in the Fourth Gospel,
where he is called ' high priest for that year ' (John xi. 49).
The popular notion used to be that Annas was the legitimate
high-priest, and Caiaphas only recognized as such because of
the Romans, but this seems to be due to misconception as
to the character of the office.   According to the priest's code,
Aaron was high-priest for life, and his dignity was to pass from

father to son as in a monarchy. Each successive high-priest was formally anointed and set apart for his office by being invested in the sacred garments. Thus Aaron was succeeded by his son Eleazar, and likewise Eleazar by Phinehas. After this we look in vain for any regular succession of these semi-royal priests till after the captivity, when the ceremony of anointing seems to have ceased ; and it is permissible, even if we admit that Aaron, Eleazar, and Phinehas were historical figures, to doubt whether the office of high-priesthood was not conferred upon them by the imagination of a much later age. As a matter of fact, in New Testament times there was no one who was strictly high-priest. Even in the Law he had no special function except on the day of Atonement, and the man who could perform them need only be an Aaronic priest in possession of the holy garments, of which the secular powers, whether Roman or Herodian, took charge, allowing them only to be worn on special occasions. The word ἀρχιερεύς (high-priest) in the New Testament is applied to all priests belonging to the ruling class, several families of which are spoken of in the Talmud. Since about 28 B.C. few men retained the priestly vestments for more than a year or two. Herod the Great conferred them on different persons, so did the *legatus* of Syria and the procurator of Judaea ; even when the right of appointment was given to a devout Jew like Herod Agrippa I (41–44), it was bestowed and taken away as repeatedly as by the Romans. His brother, Herod of Chalcis, and his son made and removed high-priests as suited their convenience.

Annas is a standing example of this ; he had been appointed by Valerius Gratus, who had constantly transferred the office to different incumbents, the last of them being Annas. Pilate deposed him and put in Joseph Caiaphas, the son-in-law of his predecessor. The procurator and Caiaphas seem to have got on excellently, both being opportunists, whose actions were determined by consideration of expediency rather than justice or morality. At anyrate they worked together and kept Judaea in comparative peace for ten years. Annas seems to have acquiesced in this arrangement, and reaped his reward in exercising great authority as a recognized leader of the priestly rulers. Josephus says he was the most fortunate of men, because his son-in-law and five of his sons were given the high-priesthood in his lifetime. Here he is placed at the head of the list of the great officials of the Temple and called **the high-priest,** but Luke's meaning may be that he was the recognized head of the priestly order by reason of his seniority to Caiaphas, who was *de facto* high-priest at the time.

We are too much obsessed with the idea that the high-priesthood as conceived in the Law was ever a practical reality. We are disposed to believe the office was in some way analogous to the Papacy, namely, that it was the prerogative of a single individual whose tenure terminated only with his life. But since the days of Nehemiah, the high-priesthood had not passed from father to son ; and whenever we meet with a notice of a high-priest in Josephus, he generally had a brother who was desirous of supplanting him. Practically, the high-priest was the head of the principal priests in the Temple of Jerusalem, who happened for the time to be recognized as such by the government, whether Roman or Herodian, and in this capacity he was allowed to wear the garments appertaining to the office. The author of Acts must here have had a source independent of Josephus, who says nothing of the priestly leaders **John** and **Alexander.**

Then Peter, filled with the holy Spirit, said to them : "Rulers 8
of the people and elders of Israel, if we are being cross- 9
**examined to-day upon a benefit rendered to a cripple, upon
how this man got better, you and the people of Israel must** 10
**all understand that he stands before you strong and well,
thanks to the name of Jesus Christ the Nazarene whom you
crucified and whom God raised from the dead. He is** 11
the stone despised by **you** *builders,*
which has become head of the corner.
There is no salvation by anyone else, nor even a second 12
**Name under heaven appointed for us men and our
salvation."**

The words of Peter are intended to be regarded as inspired. Luke has in mind the words of Jesus recorded in the Gospel

(Luke xxi. 14 ff.). This was the first time the Apostles were brought before synagogues and imprisoned, as Jesus had foretold (Luke xxi. 12), and the writer of Acts evidently has his words constantly in mind in recording the events of chap. iv. Peter's answer is a proclamation of the power of the **name of Jesus Christ the Nazarene** to work miracles. We are not told that the priests regarded this teaching as heretical, or that they objected to the magical employment of the name of Jesus. They seem to have been mainly interested in the maintenance of order in the Temple courts, and to have feared that the movement the Apostles were inaugurating might produce confusion. Their action is certainly not represented as due to any dogmatic apprehension, as the sequel will shew.

The quotation from Ps. cxviii. 22 about the corner-stone is attached, according to all the Synoptists, to the parable of the wicked husbandmen. Outside the gospels it is only found here and in 1 Pet. ii. 7, in connexion with Isa. xxviii. 16, which is also quoted in Eph. ii. 20. Evidently these passages in Psalms and Isaiah were considered proofs of the acceptance by God of Jesus ; and it is certainly striking that Peter, here and in the epistle, attached special importance to Ps. cxviii.

13 They were astonished to notice how outspoken Peter and John were, and to discover that they were uncultured persons and mere outsiders ; they recognized them as
14 having been companions of Jesus, but as they saw the man who had been healed standing beside them, they
15 could say nothing. Ordering them to withdraw from the
16 Sanhedrin, they proceeded to hold a consultation. "What are we to do with these men ? " they said. " It is plain to all the inhabitants of Jerusalem that a miracle has admittedly been worked by them. That we cannot deny.
17 However, to keep things from going any further with the people, we had better threaten them that they are not to
18 tell anyone in future about this Name." So they called the men in and ordered them not to speak or teach a single
19 sentence about the Name of Jesus. But Peter and John

replied, "Decide for yourselves whether it is right before God to obey you rather than God. Certainly we cannot 20 give up speaking of what we have seen and heard." Then 21 they threatened them still further and let them go ; on account of the people they found themselves unable to find any means of punishing them, for everybody was glorifying God over what had happened (the man on 22 whom this miracle of healing had been performed, being more than forty years old).

It would seem that most of the translations have missed the point of the fact that the Jewish rulers considered Peter and John to be unlearned men. Peter (ver. 8) had spoken **filled with the holy Spirit,** that is to say, God had put into his mouth the words he uttered. The priests had probably been informed that the Apostles were ignorant men, and were so amazed at the way in which Peter had addressed them that they had no answer to make to Peter's eloquent words, which are certainly given here in the briefest possible form.

It is evident that Luke is anxious to shew that by this time, very soon after the crucifixion, the priesthood had realized that in putting Jesus to death they had committed a fatal blunder : note their almost despairing words in v. 28. So far from destroying the work of Jesus, he had become a great power among the people, who were more than ever alienated from his judges ; and do or say what they might, they were powerless to stop the progress of the new teaching. When Peter and John defied them by declaring that they must obey God, they could do no more than utter empty threats. The conduct of the rulers may be compared with what is told us regarding the two miracles of healing by Jesus in Jerusalem, that of the cure of the lame man at the pool of Bethsaida (see John v. ff. as arranged by Moffatt), and the healing of the blind man later (John ix., x., also rearranged by Moffatt).

On being released they went to their friends and related what 23 the high priests and elders had said ; and on hearing this 24 the entire company raised their cry to God, " O Sovereign

25   Lord, thou art he* who made *heaven, earth, and sea, and all that in them is*, who said to our fathers † by the holy Spirit through the lips of thy servant David,

> *Why did the Gentiles rage,*
> *and the peoples vainly conspire?*

26   > *The kings of the earth stood ready,*
> *the rulers mustered together against the Lord and his Christ.*

27   In this very city they actually mustered against thy holy Servant Jesus, whom thou didst consecrate—Herod and Pontius Pilate, together with the Gentiles and the people

28 of Israel, mustering to carry out what thy hand had

29 traced, thy purpose had decreed. So now, O Lord, consider the threats of these men, and grant thy servants may

30 be perfectly fearless in speaking thy word, when thy hand is stretched out to heal and to perform miracles and

31 wonders by the name of thy holy Servant Jesus." At their prayer the place of meeting was shaken, and they were all filled with the holy Spirit, speaking God's word fearlessly;

33 the apostles gave their testimony to the resurrection of the Lord Jesus with great power, and great grace was upon them all.‡

* Omitting [ὁ θεὸς].

† Accepting Hort's suggestion that τοῦ πατρός is a corruption of τοῖς πατράσιν, though the text even then seems to include a gloss somewhere.

‡ Transposing ver. 33 to its original position after ver. 31.

The dismissal of the Apostles from the council of the priests of the Temple is followed by a meeting of the believers. The tale may be derived from some double narrative of the Pentecostal bestowal of the Spirit, in this instance following an earthquake, and not a storm (ver. 31). It has been thought that this represents an earlier tradition. But it seems evident that, if Luke used such a source, he inserted it in such a way as to mark the progress of his narrative. Peter's speech in Acts ii. is intended to shew how the coming of the Spirit was first presented to a Jewish audience. In chap. iii. we have a further declaration of the power of the name of Jesus. This is followed by a fearless proclamation of the

Saviour to the priests; and now we have a prayer which shews how what has happened affected the company of his followers. (After hearing this, in ver. 24, W adds, ' And recognizing the energy of God.')

The short petition (vers. 24-30) is one of those prayerful utterances found throughout the New Testament (cf. Luke xviii. 11). The Greek word *Despota* or **Sovereign Lord** is found in the Greek Liturgies. In the New Testament it is used, once, in the *Nunc Dimittis* of Simeon, ' Lord (*Despota*), now lettest thou thy servant depart in peace ' (Luke ii. 29), once in the Apocalypse (Rev. vi. 10), and also in 2 Pet. ii. 1, as in the similar passage in Jude 4. Although the second epistle of Peter is one of the latest compositions in the New Testament, it is interesting to note the use of the word in a letter traditionally ascribed to that Apostle. In the application of Ps. ii. it is to be observed that Herod, whom both Luke and Josephus are careful to distinguish as ' the tetrarch,' is implied to be king, as he is in Mark vi. Possibly here he is so called to indicate that the prophecy was fulfilled in Pilate as a ruler and Herod as a king.

We now pass to a passage involving several serious problems. The author abandons his recital of the course of events which he has sketched, if briefly yet in masterly fashion, in order to relate at some length an episode in the history of the church of Jerusalem ; this extends from iv. 32 to v. 11, after which he resumes the thread of his narrative. His object in doing this is clearly to contrast the liberality of Barnabas, who here appears for the first time, and the perfidy of Ananias and his wife Sapphira.

Now there was but one heart and soul among the multitude of 32 the believers ; not one of them considered anything his personal property, they shared all they had with one another. There was not a needy person among them, for 34 those who owned land or houses would sell them and bring the proceeds of the sale, laying the money before the feet 35 of the apostles; it was then distributed according to each individual's need. Thus Joseph, who was surnamed 36

37 Barnabas or (as it may be translated) ' Son of Encouragement ' by the apostles, a Levite of Cypriote birth, sold a
farm belonging to him and brought the money, which he
placed before the feet of the apostles.

The first two verses are a repetition of ii. 44–45 in order
to explain what follows. In one respect, however, there is a
difference. In chap. ii. it is implied that the organization of
the infant church was communistic ; here (after **believers** in
ver. 32, W adds, ' And there was no difference among them ')
it was only in so far that no member of it was allowed to be in
want, and whenever money was needed the wealthier brethren
sold their property to procure the requisite sum. The rise
of the imperfect tense in ver. 34 (**would sell**) is to be observed ;
the owners of land were accustomed to sell their property
and the Apostles to distribute the proceeds among the poor.

The liberality of Barnabas in this respect was considered
deserving of especial mention. That it was not necessary to part
with all one's property is shewn by Peter's words in v. 4. Care
for the poor has always been an honourable characteristic of
Judaism, and was naturally practised by those who had accepted
Jesus. The Gospel of Luke lays especial stress on this duty.

The introduction of Barnabas is significant ; we have now,
as it were, passed out of the circle of the immediate followers
of Jesus and met with a man destined to play an important
part in the development of the movement. Joseph the
Cypriot, of the tribe of Levi, was an Hellenistic Jew, living at
Jerusalem with property in or near the city. His relative,
Mary (Col. iv. 10), owned a house there, which was used by
the Apostles (xii. 12). He was evidently not only wealthy
but spiritually gifted, and was, as the name Barnabas implies,
regarded as a prophet by the Twelve. As will be seen there-
after, he formed a valuable link between the church of Jerusalem and the world outside.

v.

1 But a man called Ananias, who with his wife Sapphira had
2 sold some property, appropriated some of the purchase-
money with the connivance of his wife ; he only brought

part of it to lay before the feet of the apostles. "Ananias," 3
said Peter, "why has Satan filled your heart and made
you cheat the holy Spirit by appropriating some of the
money paid for the land? When it remained unsold, did 4
it not remain your own? And even after the sale, was
the money not yours to do as you pleased about it? How
could you think of doing a thing like this? You have
not defrauded men but God." When Ananias heard this, 5
he fell down and expired. (Great awe came over all who
heard of it.) And the younger men rose, wrapped the 6
body up and carried it away to be buried. After an inter- 7
val of about three hours his wife happened to come in,
quite unconscious of what had occurred. "Tell me," said 8
Peter, "did you only sell the land for such and such a
sum?" "Yes," she said, "that was all we sold it for."
Peter said to her, "How could you arrange to put the 9
Lord's Spirit to the proof? Listen, there are the footsteps
of the men who have buried your husband! They are at
the door, and they will carry you out as well." Instantly 10
she fell down at their feet and expired. The younger men
came in to find her dead; they carried her out and buried
her beside her husband. Great awe came over the whole 11
church and over all who heard about this.

Now they all without exception met in the portico of Solomon. 12
Though the people extolled them, not a soul from the out- 13
side dared to join them. On the other hand, crowds of 14
men and women who believed in the Lord were brought
in. Many miracles and wonders were performed among 12
the people by the apostles.* In fact, invalids were actually 15
carried into the streets and laid on beds and mattresses,
so that, when Peter passed, his shadow at anyrate might
fall on one or other of them. Crowds gathered even from 16
the towns round Jerusalem, bringing invalids and people
troubled with unclean spirits, all of whom were healed.

* Transposing the first clause of ver. 12 to the beginning of ver. 15.

There is a tendency for some commentators to shew that the
deaths of Ananias and Sapphira (vers. 1-11) are credible from

the standpoint of modern psychology. That is, the stern rebuke of Peter may reasonably be believed to have been the cause of the death of the unfortunate couple. Among primitive peoples the violation, real or supposed, of a taboo has been known to cause instant death; there is a well-known story of Edward I of England's terrible look of displeasure resulting in the sudden death of a bishop who had offended him. There is nothing therefore impossible in the account of Ananias and Sapphira, and it may well have been not a legendary event, but an actual occurrence. But the difficulty is not so much miraculous as moral. The whole behaviour of Peter is absolutely different from what one might expect of a disciple of his Master. It is not in keeping with the conduct even of Paul, who believed that he or the Church had the power of causing sickness in punishment for serious offences among believers. The delivery to Satan of the Corinthian guilty of an incestuous union is remedial, the object being to save the spirit by bodily punishment (1 Cor. v. 3–5; see also 1 Tim. i. 10). But there is no hint of any merciful purpose in Peter's dealing with this guilty couple. The brief narrative is frankly repulsive. Ananias and Sapphira are cross-examined, and the lie they tell is instantly punished by death! The duty of the commentator, however, is not so much to apologize for the story as to account for its presence in Acts.

(1) In the first place the object of the first two sections of v. 1–11 and 12–16 is to lay stress on the supernatural character of the apostolic Church. The Spirit which dwells in it renders all attempts to deceive the Apostles futile. The Twelve occupy a position of dignified separation from the other believers. It is not the name of Jesus, nor the faith of the patient, which cure the sick; the very shadow of Peter passing by was believed to be efficacious (ver. 15). In these sixteen verses we are transported into a strange and unnatural condition of things, entirely foreign to the more sober narration of the rest of Acts, and into an atmosphere of sternness and isolation on the part of the Apostles of Jesus, which finds no counterpart in the gospel narrative.

(2) The moral purpose of the section is to emphasize the

necessity for complete surrender in those who claim to become disciples of Jesus. It is useless to pretend to the holy Spirit that all has been given up, while something has been reserved owing to guilty or prudential considerations. Terrible indeed is the punishment as shewn by this story of those who attempt to deceive God.

(3) Parallels have been discovered with much ingenuity between Acts and the Book of Joshua (see below on xvi. 7). The sin of Ananias and his wife has its counterpart in Josh. vii. 1, and the same word (ἐνοσφίσατο) is used in Acts (**appropriating**) and in the LXX. As Achan, after the miracle of the walls of Jericho, had brought disaster upon Israel by his greed, so Ananias had disgraced the new Israel after the bestowal of the Spirit at Pentecost.

Even with Moffatt's skilful transposition of vers. 12 and 13 the meaning is by no means clear. It would seem from ver. 13 (**not a soul from the outside dared to join them**) that the multiplication of converts from without had ceased, though this is contradicted by ver. 14. The word κολλᾶσθαι (join) appears to mean what has been previously stated, and to connote intimate association (see 1 Cor. vi. 16, 17).

This filled the high priest Annas * and his allies, the Sadducean 17 party, with bitter jealousy; they laid hands on the apostles 18 and put them into the public prison, but an angel of the 19 Lord opened the prison-doors during the night and brought them out, saying, " Go and stand in the temple, telling the 20 people all about this Life." With these orders they went 21 into the temple about dawn and proceeded to teach. Meantime the high priest and his allies met, called the Sanhedrin together and the council of seniors belonging to the sons of Israel, and then sent to prison for the men. But as the attendants did not find them when they got to the 22 prison, they came back to report, " We found the prison 23 safely locked up, with the sentries posted at the doors, but on opening the doors we found no one inside! " On hear- 24 ing this the commander of the temple and the high priests

* See Note on next page.

25   were quite at a loss to know what to make of it. However, someone came and reported to them, " Here are the very men you put in prison, standing in the temple and teaching
26   the people! " At this the commander went off with the attendants and fetched them—but without using violence, for fear that the people would pelt them with stones.
27   They conducted them before the Sanhedrin, and the high
28   priest asked them, "We strictly forbade you to teach about this Name, did we not ? And here you have filled Jerusalem with your doctrine! You want to make us responsible
29   for this man's death! " Peter and the apostles answered,
30   " One must obey God rather than men. The God of our fathers raised Jesus whom you murdered by *hanging him*
31   *on a gibbet.* God lifted him up to his right hand as our pioneer and saviour, in order to grant repentance and
32   remission of sins to Israel. To these facts we bear witness, with the holy Spirit which God has given to those who obey
33   him." When they heard this, they were so furious that they determined to make away with the apostles.

* Blass's brilliant conjecture for the ἀναστάς of the ordinary text. It is not entirely without manuscript evidence.

Again it is possible that the arrest of the Apostles and their defence may repeat what is told us in chap. iv. Yet there are obvious signs of progress in this narrative. In the previous chapter the priests are powerless to inflict any punishment on the adherents of Jesus. But here it is otherwise : it is implied that the Temple authorities have the power to put the preachers of the gospel to death. This suggests that some time had elapsed between what is recorded in chaps. iv. and v. Supposing the first arrest to have occurred a few weeks or even months after the Crucifixion, say, in A.D. 32, Judaea would have been under the government of Pilate. It was then, as we are told, impossible for the ruling priesthood to inflict the death penalty, nor would the procurator be likely to encourage a persecution of the followers of a Jesus whom he had crucified only under pressure. But as Tiberius was drawing near his end, Pilate was evidently out of favour with

Vitellius, the *legatus* of Syria, and may well have had little power in Jerusalem. As, even before the death of Tiberius, Pilate was sent to Rome to answer for his violent attack on the Samaritans, there may have been no procurator in Judaea for some time ; consequently, the Apostles may have been in danger of their lives. The death of Stephen was probably possible under similar circumstances ; for directly the Jews had a king of their own, James, the brother of John, was executed by Herod Agrippa, as also was James, the Lord's brother, at a later time, when there was no procurator. Under any circumstances, the object of Luke is to shew that between chaps. iv. and v., the faith in Jesus had grown so powerful that the priesthood were resolved to suppress it at any cost ; the disciples were, therefore, in actual peril.

If the conjecture of Blass, accepted by Moffatt, be correct, this is the third time Annas is mentioned by Luke as taking the first place in the priestly hierarchy. Neither his name nor that of Caiaphas occurs in the trial of Jesus as recorded by Mark and Luke. From the fact that, according to the Fourth Gospel, our Lord was arrested and taken first to Annas, one may perhaps infer that when the priests acted on their own initiative, Annas took the lead ; and, when the Romans were appealed to, Caiaphas, the high-priest recognized by the Romans, was put forward. The Sadducean priests and the commander or captain of the Temple guards are mentioned in the similar narrative of chap. iv., and in both instances the supposed offence of the Apostles is disturbing the people in the Temple by preaching in Solomon's portico. The release from prison by an angel has its parallel in chap xii., where Peter is delivered by the same agency. It may not be superfluous to remind the reader that the word **Sanhedrin** is Greek transliterated into Hebrew letters, and may signify no more than an assembly. In the trial of Jesus, the court is associated with the high-priests and elders (Matt. xxvi. 57 and 59, Mark xiv. 55). In Mark xv. 1, συνέδριον means no more than a consultation (so both Moffatt and the A.V.) ; the Vulgate has *concilium facientes*. The word is, in fact, the common one for a council, and the use of the word Sanhedrin without qualification might lead to the idea that it was the Hebrew court, described in Rabbinic writers as part of the constitution of Judaism.

34 But a Pharisee in the Sanhedrin called Gamaliel, a doctor of the Law who was highly respected by all the people, got up and ordered the apostles to be removed for a few
35 moments. Then he said, "Men of Israel, take care what
36 you do about these men. In days gone by Theudas started up, claiming to be a person of importance ; a number of men, about four hundred of them, rallied to him, but he was slain, and all his followers were dispersed
37 and wiped out. After him Judas the Galilean started up at the time of the census, and got people to desert to him; but he perished too, and all his followers were scattered.
38 So I advise you to-day to leave these men to themselves. Let them alone. If this project or enterprise springs from
39 men, it will collapse ; whereas, if it really springs from God, you will be unable to put them down. You may even
40 find yourselves fighting God ! " They gave in to him, and after summoning the apostles and giving them a flogging, they released them with instructions that they were not
41 to speak about the name of Jesus. The apostles left the Sanhedrin, rejoicing that they had been considered worthy of suffering dishonour for the sake of the Name; not for a
42 single day did they cease to teach and preach the gospel of Jesus the Christ in the temple and at home.

The author of Acts consistently represents the Pharisees as upon the whole well-disposed to the believers, and in this he agrees with Josephus, who declares that they were mild in their judgments, and on the side of the people as opposed to the aristocracy. We must always remember that, according to Acts, the followers of Jesus were, at first, decidedly popular in Jerusalem ; and that the priests who controlled the Temple were greatly disliked. In this chapter a very wise and states-manlike speech is put into the mouth of Gamaliel, whom Paul in Acts xxii. 3 claims as his teacher.

As, however, the speech of **Gamaliel** raises an historical difficulty which no one yet has solved, it may be well to inquire what is known of him. He was the grandson of Hillel, one of the last ' Pair ' by whom the tradition of the Law was handed down. Hillel's rival was Shammai, and the two schools represent respectively mercy and justice. Consequently, Hillel and his grandson Gamaliel stand for the Pharisaic, and Shammai for the unbending Sadducean tradition. This Gamaliel is selected by Luke as the advocate of the Apostles. His admirers called him ' the Glory of the Law,' and he was one of the seven rabbis honoured by the pre-eminent title of Rabban. Very little, however, has been preserved of the doings or sayings of this highly respected teacher, who is often confused with his grandson, Gamaliel II. He is never so much as mentioned by Josephus ; that Luke should introduce his name is a proof that he had in his mind an independent tradition, ignored or unknown to the Jewish historian.

It is of course possible that Gamaliel spoke on this occasion and gave the advice attributed to him in Acts. It was eminently judicious and to the point : to put the Apostles to death would certainly cause great offence to the Roman authorities, nor did the circumstances warrant such a drastic proceeding. If this preaching of a Messiah were false, it would in due course inevitably prove itself to be so, and probably be brought to an end by the power of Rome. The wise thing to do was to leave the Apostles alone and to trust to God either to further or destroy the movement. Were this all, we might accept the speech as worthy of Gamaliel ; but unfortunately the author of Acts has inserted a statement which cannot possibly have been made on this occasion. He makes Gamaliel prove his point by pointing to an abortive uprising of a fanatic named Theudas, who is mentioned by Josephus (*Antiq.*, xx. 5) as having rebelled some years after the speech, although Gamaliel places him earlier than Judas of Galilee who (according to Luke) headed a movement against the enrolment ordered by Augustus at the time of our Lord's birth. The attempts to save the historical accuracy of Acts in this matter are more interesting than convincing.

The five chapters of Acts hitherto considered contain very

little positive information, and give us no indication of how long a period they cover. The author does not shew much knowledge of what actually occurred ; and if he was in contact with eye-witnesses of the events, they do not appear to have had much to impart to him, nor can the sources he may have employed have given him much first-hand information. When we consider the skill displayed in using the written sources which we may suppose Luke to have had before him, it is impossible to deny that he proves himself to be a consummate literary artist. In the remaining part of Acts his power of narration is equally undeniable. But these merits appear to be absent in the story of the primitive church in Jerusalem, the only actor portrayed being Peter ; and it cannot be denied that even his character appears here as formal and unnatural. The progress of the community of believers is indicated in bold outlines, but our interest in it is not quickened by any lifelike touches. Even though the narrative of the Gospel is resumed in the first chapter of Acts, it is not continued in the same spirit ; and we have only to compare the description of the walk to Emmaus with the final injunctions of our Lord to the Twelve to realize the difference between the Third Gospel and the Acts.

In justice to the Evangelist, however, the following facts must be borne in mind :

(1) Not only did the writer suffer from a possible lack of information : he was restricted as to space. Everyone engaged in literary work knows what this means, as he is often asked to deal with a subject in a strictly limited number of words. This applied with tenfold force to an ancient author, every copy of whose work had to be made by a separate hand. Luke had to compress an immense amount of material into Acts, which after all is a very small book, not much more than one or two chapters of a modern work ; and one can hardly blame him for at times being disappointingly brief.

(2) Again, Acts is not an historical treatise designed for the information of posterity, but was written for the benefit of an individual. The author had consequently to consider what it was important for Theophilus to know, and what would be

of most interest to him. Therefore he not unnaturally hastens over the first beginnings of the Church with which he himself was doubtless imperfectly acquainted, and gives more space to subjects on which he could speak with fuller knowledge and authority. What Theophilus almost certainly wanted to know was how the gospel spread throughout the Roman world, and what were the rights of those who had declared themselves to be the disciples of Jesus. The work of Paul was of especial interest to him, and Acts is mainly devoted to an account of the labours of this Apostle.

But when all has been said, these five chapters are of the highest importance ; and if the record is to us in some respects incomplete, it is nevertheless invaluable. Analyse it as we may, it is the only one we possess of the first days of the Church, and, as it stands, it throws a flood of light on the character of the Christian religion in its most primitive form. If we consider the words put into the mouth of Peter as inconsistent with him as he is represented to have been in the four gospels, we must not forget that the author intended to represent him as delivering not his own sentiments but inspired utterances, speaking in the name of God through the Spirit which he has received. The author, in fact, desires to depict the change which had come over the somewhat wayward Peter, now that he had become the spokesman of the redeemed Church. At the same time we may recognize in the utterances of Peter not the developed gospel of a later age but that which was preached at the time when the disciples realized that the risen Saviour was the Messiah and deliverer of a new Israel. The somewhat crude Christology and use of Scriptural proofs were in themselves an indication that the faith was capable of being more perfectly expounded as time went on and the experience of believers ripened ; and the reader of Acts is prepared for what is to follow when the record emerges into the fuller light of history.

As has been suggested, a clue to the order of events recorded in the early chapters of Acts is to be found if we regard each as marking the progress of the narrative by a series of separate

49

pictures, the background of each being varied as the tale proceeds. Or we may conceive of the opening of the book in the light of a drama with a succession of acts, not always closely connected. In the first five chapters the **dramatis personae** are the Twelve. The spokesmen are Peter and John, who are opposed by the high-priest and the Jewish rulers. The believers act as a silent chorus of saintly folks living in common, in perfect harmony, and obedience to the Apostles. The *ecclesia* or church which they have joined, greatly respected by the people of Jerusalem, increases day by day, and is unmolested in the city. But in the Temple it is otherwise : because the Twelve insist upon teaching in Solomon's porch and boldly proclaim their Master to be the Christ, they are subject to arrest and persecution by the dominant hierarchy. We have no means of knowing how long this state of things continued, or whether the record in Acts i.–v. embraces a few days or some years.[1] Perhaps the author of Acts was himself too desirous to describe the Church of the first days as the norm of what every church should be to pay strict attention to the exact sequence of events in point of time, although, as we have seen, he has in mind an orderly scheme as to the progress of the infant community.

vi.

1 During these days, when the disciples were increasing in number, the Hellenists began to complain against the Hebrews, on the ground that their widows were being
2 overlooked in the daily * distribution of food. So the twelve summoned the main body of the disciples and said : " It is not desirable that we should drop preaching the
3 word of God and attend to meals. Brothers, look out seven of your own number, men of good reputation who are full of the Spirit and of wisdom. We will appoint

* See Note on next page.

1 It is the same with the narrative of the four gospels, from which it seems impossible to determine how long the ministry of Jesus actually lasted.

them to this duty, but we will continue to devote our- 4
selves to prayer and the ministry of the word." This 5
plan commended itself to the whole body, and they chose
Stephen a man full of faith and the holy Spirit, Philip,
Prochorus, Nikanor, Timon, Parmenas and Nikolaos a
proselyte from Antioch ; these men they presented to the 6
apostles, who, after prayer, laid their hands upon them.

And the word of God spread ; the number of the 7
disciples in Jerusalem greatly increased, and a host of
priests became obedient to the faith.

* The western text of ver. 1 omits ' daily,' and adds at the end of the
verse, ' of the Hebrews.'

This portion of Acts is introduced by a formula (**during
these days**) found in Mark viii. 1, to introduce as a new episode
the miracle of the feeding of the four thousand, without
specifying the exact time.   Here no notion is given of what
may have occurred in the interval between chaps. v. and vi. ;
the Hellenist Christians, as distinct from the Hebrews, are
presented without any explanation.   It is evident that already there were two classes of believers in Jerusalem—the
original followers of Jesus, perhaps Galilaeans or natives of
the city who spoke Hebrew (i.e. Aramaic), and Greek-speaking
foreigners settled or temporarily residing in proximity to the
Temple.   Undoubtedly these **Hellenists** were present on the
day of Pentecost, but the majority had gone to their own
homes, probably leaving only few of their numbers who
believed in Jerusalem.   Evidently the acceptance of the
messiahship of Jesus had subsequently made great progress
among the Greek-speaking settlers in Jerusalem, who began to
feel that they did not receive proper consideration from their
Hebrew brethren.   How long it took for such a state of
things to be possible we have no means of judging.   The fact
that there seem to have been **widows** on the charitable roll of
the Church seems to imply that there was considerable interval
between chaps. v. and vi.   If one may hazard such a suggestion,
it may be possible that Luke, in his desire to make what
happened intelligible to his readers, is describing the diffi-

culties in regard to these ' widows ' in language which would be understood by people of a later time.

Solicitude for the welfare of the poor has always honourably characterized Judaism. The law insists on providing for the fatherless and the widow, and Christians cheerfully acknowledged their obligation to help the unfortunate. From the first widows are spoken of as though they were an order in the Church. Thus, when Peter at Joppa raised Tabitha, or Dorcas, it is said that ' all the widows ' stood beside him (Acts ix. 39), and that he called ' all the saints [i.e. believers] and the widows, and presented her to them alive.' At a later period the question of providing for the widows in a Christian community occupied the attention of the Church, as is seen from the fact that in the Pastoral Epistles a chapter (1 Tim. v.) is mainly devoted to the subject. Still, however, the difficulty remains how it came to pass that the widows had from the very first become a special charge on the Church.

The significance of what is meant by **the daily distribution of food** furnishes another problem. The Greek word is διακονία, and in ver. 2 the verb in connexion with tables is rendered **attend to meals.** Although the word διάκονος is neither here nor elsewhere applied to the Seven chosen by the Church, it is possible that Luke had the office of the deacon as he understood it in mind when he wrote Acts vi. But the words **daily distribution of food** and **attend to meals** are capable of two interpretations.

They may be taken literally : if so the widows may have been given doles daily, as was done in Rome, where meals were distributed by the wealthy to their dependents in baskets (*sportulae*). Josephus informs us that in the days of a great famine Queen Helena of Adiabene purchased a store of provisions in Egypt which she distributed to those who were in need (*Antiq.*, xx. 2. 5), so that a similar custom was not unknown in Jerusalem. Or it is possible that the believers, as is suggested in Acts ii. 46, met at a common meal which may have been already called ' the Lord's Supper.' In 1 Cor. xi. 21 ff. St. Paul's converts meet to eat a supper of the Lord, in which as each took his own meal, the poor were neglected, and scenes of disorder occurred. At a comparatively early date officers called deacons were charged with seeing that order was maintained and with directing the distribution of the eucharistic meal. It is possible that the author of Acts had this in mind when he described the appointment of the Seven in such a way as to make himself intelligible to his fellow Christians who belonged to the second or third generation of believers. Thus far Luke's object is evidently to shew that there are two spheres of activity in the Christian ministry, one of teaching and the other of administration (1 Cor. xii. 28, Eph. iv. 11-12).

But if, in describing the dispute between Hellenists and Hebrews in these early days, the writer has in mind the diaconate of a later date, he does not seem to connect the Seven, after their appointment, with administrative as contrasted with evangelistic work. On the contrary, no sooner are they chosen and admitted by the laying on of hands, than they, and notably **Stephen** and **Philip,** become the leaders of fresh missionary enterprise. From henceforward Stephen seems to stand to the Hellenists much as Peter did to the Hebrews, and Philip is represented as the pioneer Christian missionary outside Jerusalem. The Seven all bear Greek names, but this does not prove much, and it is remarkable how so large a proportion of them has survived, at anyrate in Christian legend. Only three, **Nicanor, Timon, and Parmenas,** have left no trace behind them.

Prominent as the name of Stephen is in Acts, it is strange that it is never mentioned in the Pauline epistles or in the rest of the New Testament, and the Apostolic Fathers. He was commemorated in the Church as early as the end of the fourth century ; and early in the fifth his body was said to have been discovered by a vision of St. Paul's teacher Gamaliel to Lucian a priest of Caphar Gamala, a village near Jerusalem. His feast in the western church is on December 26, the day after Christmas. In the East he is commemorated the following day, the 26th being in honour of Joseph and the Blessed Virgin. Philip was evidently a prominent personage in the Church. In Acts xxi. 8 he is called ' the evangelist, one of the Seven.'

As the first missionary to the cities of the maritime plain, it was but natural that he and his four daughters, who were prophetesses, should be residents at Caesarea. According to the Fourth Gospel, the Apostle Philip of Bethsaida was applied to by the ' Greeks ' who wanted to see Jesus (John xii. 20). The connexion of the name of this Apostle with the Greeks is remarkable, because in Christian tradition the Deacon and the Apostle are frequently confused with one another. All the ancient writers, quoted by Eusebius, i.e. Clement of Alexandria, Polycrates of Ephesus, and Polycarp of Smyrna, place Philip at Hierapolis, and call him an ' Apostle.' Nevertheless, all speak of him as having daughters as in Acts xxi. 9. In the apocryphal *Acts of Abdias* Philip lives at Hierapolis, and has many extraordinary adventures in company with the Apostle Bartholomew (see M. R. James, *The Apocryphal New Testament*, Oxford, 1924).

Of the Seven, two others, **Prochorus** and **Nikolaos,** the proselyte of Antioch, have their place in later history, or at least in the legendary lore of the Church. Prochorus is the name given to the writer of an apocryphal *History of the Apostle John*, a late work. There is a mediaeval tradition that St. John dictated his gospel to Prochorus. Like the rest of the Seven, he is included in the list of the seventy disciples chosen by our Lord.

In the Apocalypse the Church of Smyrna is said to be troubled by the teaching of the Nicolaitans (Rev. ii. 6 and 15). Tradition has naturally traced this heresy to **Nikolaos, a proselyte from Antioch;** but there is no positive evidence for this, and Irenaeus, the first writer on heresies, does not attribute this error to the Nikolaos of Acts vi.

The Seven were chosen by the brethren, and the Apostles **laid their hands upon them** after they had prayed. In like manner Barnabas and Saul were dismissed to their mission from Antioch by the laying on of hands, by fasting, and prayer (Acts xiii. 3). The purpose of the imposition of hands in both instances seems to have been rather a commission to discharge a particular task than a permanent ordination, such as may be implied by the ' laying on of the hands ' of the presbytery (1 Tim. iv. 14). In the Law *laying on of hands* is employed : (1) for the devotion of a sacrificial victim to which sin is transferred (Lev. iv. 4, 15, 29, xvi. 21—the scapegoat) and of a blasphemer about to be stoned (Lev. xxiv. 14) ; (2) for the transmission of authority (Moses laid his hands on Joshua, Numb. xxvii. 18–23). In the New Testament the rite is employed : (1) to heal the sick (Matt. ix. 18, etc.) ; (2) to confer the Spirit after baptism (Acts viii. 17–18, xix. 6). In **a host of priests became obedient to the faith** we have one of those notes of the early progress of the Church characteristic of the early narrative in Acts (cf. ii. 41, iv. 4). The priests in Jerusalem were very numerous ; nevertheless, there is no mention in the gospel of a priest as a personal follower of Jesus (but see John xii. 42).

Now Stephen, who was full of grace and power, performed 8 great wonders and miracles among the people. Some of 9 those who belonged to the so-called synagogue of the Libyans,* the Cyrenians, and the Alexandrians, as well as to that of the Cilicians and Asiatics, started a dispute with Stephen, but they could not meet the wisdom and the 10 Spirit with which he spoke. They then instigated people 11 to say, " We have heard him talking blasphemy against Moses and God."

* Reading Λιβυστίνων instead of the Λιβερτίνων of the text. This, as Blass points out, gives " the African Jews in the geographical order of their original dwelling-places."

In this passage Stephen is represented not as a server at tables but as a preacher and wonder-worker (W adds to ver. 8, ' By the name of the Lord Jesus ') comparable to the Apostles (cf. Acts v. 12). Whether it is implied that more than one synagogue was meant is uncertain ; each of the peoples mentioned (W omits, ' and Asiatics ') may have had its separate synagogue, as according to Jewish tradition there were as many as 480 in the city. The official worship of Israel in Jerusalem was naturally carried on in the Temple, and the synagogues were used for prayer, preaching, but above all in New Testament days for the discussion of the Law.

Thus we find Paul constantly disputing in synagogues and schools (Acts xvii. 17, xviii. 4, xix. 8–9). Of the people here mentioned those in our translation who are designated **Libyans** have been a fruitful cause of perplexity since Beza in 1556 suggested that for *Libertinôn, Libustinôn* should be read. ' Libertine ' is a Latin word, and would mean freedmen ; it has been usually explained to mean Roman Jews who had obtained their liberty and had formed a synagogue in the imperial city. If, however, the conjectural emendation be correct, the synagogue would consist of a group of natives of Africa, Lybia, Cyrene, and Alexandria. To these are added natives of the Roman provinces of Cilicia and Asia ; and it must not be forgotten that, as a citizen of Tarsus, Saul, the leader of the persecution, was a Cilician Jew. The phrase **talking blasphemy against Moses and God** is significant. Josephus tells us that the Essenes, whom he admires more than any other Jews, will endure any torture rather than blaspheme their ' lawgiver.' In the same way Christians, according to Pliny, were called upon to ' curse Christ.'

12 In this way they excited the people, the elders, and the scribes, who rushed on him, dragged him away, and took him
13 before the Sanhedrin. They also brought forward false witnesses to say, " This fellow is never done talking against
14 this holy Place and the Law ! Why, we have heard him say that Jesus the Nazarene will destroy this Place and change the customs handed down to us by Moses ! "

In one respect there is a marked difference between the trial of Stephen and that of Jesus or his disciples. Both the Master till his arrest and his followers from the first were favoured by the people. It was the party of the Temple priesthood who considered that the new teaching might prove dangerous, and resolved to anticipate it by dealing promptly with the preachers. With Stephen it was otherwise : the accusers are not the priests but the people. It is the same with Paul, when he visited Jerusalem for the last time, and the Jews of Asia raised a tumult against him for bringing Greeks into the Temple (Acts xxi. 27, xxiv. 18–19). It would

seem as though the native believers at Jerusalem were allowed
to exist in comparative security, except during the short reign
of Herod Agrippa I (Acts. xii. 1 f.). The people respected
them for their attendance at the Temple and for their con-
forming to the Law. With the Greek-speaking Jews it was
otherwise. These regarded the Christians as dangerous inno-
vators. Probably those who resided in the holy city were
more fanatical than the Hebrew-speaking natives, especially
as they had left their homes in order to dwell in pious proximity
to the Temple.

Another difference between the trial of Stephen and that of
Jesus is that there is no mention of any Roman official. It
has been suggested that, after the deprivation of Pilate, there
was no procurator in Jerusalem for a time, and consequently
that the Sanhedrin could try and condemn an offender in the
matter of religion. It is striking that there is nothing said
as to Stephen being a disturber of the peace, or guilty of any
offence cognisable by Roman law. The charge against him is
simply one of blasphemy from a Jewish standpoint, to which
no Roman authority would listen. It is assumed that the
high-priest and his Council was the only tribunal competent
to try the case. No similar charge of heresy is hinted at
as having been advanced in the first five chapters of Acts.
According to the strict interpretation of the law, confirmed
by the treatise *Sanhedrin*, stoning was the penalty, not of
presumptuous language about God but of blaspheming the
NAME, i.e. the sacred and unpronounceable word designated
by the consonants JHVH. The account of the martyrdom,
Acts vi. and vii., simply bristles with difficulties.

Then all who were seated in the Sanhedrin fixed their eyes on 15
    him, and saw that his face shone like the face of an angel. vii.
    He, full of the holy Spirit, gazed up at heaven and saw the 55
    glory of God and Jesus standing at God's right hand.
    "Look," he said, "I see heaven open and the Son of man 56
    standing at God's right hand!" With a loud shriek they 57
    shut their ears and rushed at him like one man. Putting 58
    him outside the city, they proceeded to stone him (the

59
60
witnesses laid their clothes at the feet of a youth called Saul). So they stoned Stephen, who called on the Lord, saying, " Lord Jesus, receive my spirit ! " Then he knelt down and cried aloud, " Lord, let not this sin stand against them ! " With these words he slept the sleep of death.

By thus leaving out for the present the speech in chap. vii. we have here a very beautiful and well-connected description of the death of the first Christian martyr,[1] and we realize that the omission of the defence brings out the intentional parallel-ism between the trial of Jesus and of his protomartyr. Nor can we fail to notice how closely the two narratives correspond. The accusation of the false witnesses regarding the Temple is identical. Stephen saw **the Son of man standing at God's right hand :** Jesus declared that his judges will see the son of man sitting at the right hand of power (Mark xiv. 62, Matt. xxvi. 64, Luke xxii. 69). Stephen prays, **Lord Jesus, receive my spirit :** Jesus commends his soul to the Father (Luke xxiii. 46). Both pray for their murderers (Luke xxiii. 34, Acts vii. 60). The insertion of the speech certainly detracts from the impressive character of the description of the death of Stephen, if only because Stephen's words contrast unfavourably with the dignified silence of the Christ before the high-priest.

Before, however, one can arrive at any definite theory in regard to the speech, it is necessary to discuss the argument which it was presumably intended to advance. Stephen opens by giving a sketch of the patriarchal history till the appearance of Moses.

vii.

¹⁄₂ Said the high priest, " Is this true ? "   " Listen, brothers and fathers," said Stephen. " The *God of glory* appeared to our father Abraham * when he was still in Mesopotamia,

---

* See Note on next page.

[1] In vers. 55–56 Stephen sees Jesus standing at the right hand of God, and calls him the Son of man. This is the only example of this title being bestowed on our Lord in the New Testament. This, and nothing said in the speech, convicted the martyr of blasphemy in the eyes of the Sanhedrin.

before ever he stayed in Haran, *and said to him, ' Leave* 3
your land and your countrymen and come to whatever land
I show you.' Then he left the land of the Chaldeans and 4
stayed in Haran. From Haran God shifted him, after his
father's death, to this land which you now inhabit. But 5
he did not give him any inheritance in it, not *even a foot of*
the land. All he did was to promise that he would *give it*
as a possession *to him and to his offspring after him* (he at
the time being childless). What God said was this : ' *His* 6
offspring will sojourn in a foreign land, where they will be
enslaved, and oppressed for four hundred years. But,' said 7
God, ' *I* † *will pass sentence on the nation that has made*
them slaves, and then they will get away to worship me in this
Place.' God also gave him *the covenant of circumcision.* 8
So Abraham became the father of Isaac, *whom he*
circumcised on the eighth day, Isaac was the father of
Jacob, and Jacob of the twelve patriarchs. *Out of jealousy* 9
the patriarchs sold *Joseph into Egypt ;* but *God was with* 10
him, rescuing him from all his troubles and *allowing him*
to find favour for his wisdom *with Pharaoh king of Egypt,*
who appointed him viceroy over Egypt and over all his own
household. Now a famine came over the whole of Egypt 11
and Canaan, attended with great misery, so that our
ancestors could not find provender. *But, hearing there* 12
was food in Egypt, Jacob sent our ancestors on their first
visit to that country ; at their second visit *Joseph made* 13
himself known to his brothers, and Pharaoh was informed
of Joseph's lineage. Then Joseph sent for his father 14
Jacob and all his kinsfolk, *amounting to seventy-five souls ;*
and Jacob *went south to Egypt. When he* and our ances- 15
tors *died, they were carried across to Shechem* and laid *in* 16
the tomb which Abraham had bought for a sum of money
from the sons of Hamor in Shechem.

* In Josh. xxiv. 2 it is interesting to note that Terah, the father of
Abraham, and his family ' served other gods,' thus supporting the
Mohammedan'tradition about Terah as a maker of idols in Mesopotamia.

† The ' I ' is emphatic. When the New Testament is read aloud, as
it was originally meant to be, such stresses can be brought out. They
often interpret the inner meaning of the text.

The recapitulation of the story of the patriarchs of Israel is a feature of later Jewish literature ; and it is remarkable that whereas the life of Abraham is a constant theme, and his example is continually held up for imitation, so little is said of him in the prophetical books of the Old Testament. Here the story is told with some slight deviation from the narrative of Genesis. **The God of glory** is unique in the New Testament : it occurs in Ps. xxix. 3. The glory of God is that by which he manifests himself, and the glory of Jehovah is almost a synonym for the Eternal. Perhaps the opening words may be paraphrased ' God revealed His glory to Abraham.'

God's command to Abraham, according to Gen. xi. 31-xii. 1, was given not in Ur of the Chaldees but in Haran. Nevertheless, throughout the Bible the migration of Terah, the father of Abraham, from Ur is implied to be due to a divine impulse (Gen. xv. 7, Neh. ix. 7). The figures given in vers. 4–14 are not identical with those in our Bible. Abraham did not leave Haran after his father's death, but sixty years before. The period of affliction was four hundred and thirty not **four hundred years** (see Ex. xii. 40) ; and only seventy not **seventy-five** persons came down to Egypt. There is a more serious discrepancy still. It is said that Jacob was buried in **Shechem in the tomb which Abraham bought from the sons of Hamor.** But Abraham bought the cave of Machpelah, near Hebron, from Ephron the Hittite (Gen. xxiii. 1 ff.), where Jacob was really buried (Gen. l. 13). Nothing is said of the burial of the twelve patriarchs in Canaan in Genesis, but only that at the time of the Exodus the body of Joseph was carried away by the Israelites and ultimately buried in Shechem (Gen. l. 25, Ex. xiii. 19, Josh. xxiv. 32), in the field which Jacob had purchased from the sons of Hamor (Gen. xxiii. 19). Various explanations have been given of these variations from the scriptural narrative ; but similar ones are to be found in both Philo and Josephus. Again, there is a curious addition to the promise made to Abraham which may possibly affect the argument of Stephen that God can be served elsewhere than in the Temple of Jerusalem. The words **they will . . . worship me in this Place** are taken from Ex. iii. 12 :

' When thou hast brought forth the people out of Egypt, ye shall serve God upon this mountain.'

As the time approached for the promise God had made to 17 Abraham, the people *grew and multiplied* in Egypt, till 18 *another king arose to rule Egypt who knew nothing of Joseph.* He took a cunning method with our race ; he 19 *oppressed* our ancestors by forcing them to expose their infants, to prevent them *from surviving.* It was at this 20 period that Moses was born, a divinely *beautiful* child. *For three months* he was brought up in his father's house; then he was exposed, but *Pharaoh's daughter adopted* him 21 and brought him up *as her own son.* So Moses was 22 educated in all the culture of the Egyptians ; he was a strong man in speech and action. When he had com- 23 pleted his fortieth year, it occurred to him to visit *his brothers, the sons of Israel.* He saw one of them being 24 badly treated, so he defended him, *struck down the Egyptian,* and thus avenged the man who had been wronged. (He thought his brothers would understand God was going 25 to bring them deliverance by means of him ; but they did not understand.) Next day he came upon two of them 26 fighting and tried to pacify them. ' You are brothers! ' he said, ' why injure one another ? ' But *the man who* 27 *was injuring his neighbour* pushed him aside. ' *Who made you ruler and umpire over us ?* ' he asked. ' *Do you* 28 *want to kill me, as you killed the Egyptian yesterday ?* '

The patriarchal history in the speech contains little applicable to the accusations brought against Stephen. In this section, however, we have what may be taken in the light of a parallel between the Lawgiver and the Christ ; and although the speech does not make this clear it may conceivably have been so understood by the Jewish council. Moses appears in Egypt to the oppressed Israelites as a messenger of peace, and tries to bring about harmony among his own people. But he is at once rejected and compelled to take refuge in the desert. Nothing is said in Exodus of the beauty, wisdom, and might of Moses in Egypt, although these things are prominent in Hebrew legend, and are dwelt on by Philo and Josephus.

29 *At that Moses fled ; he became a sojourner in the land of Midian,*
30 where he had two sons born to him. At the close of forty years *an angel (of the Lord) appeared to him in the flames*
31 *of a burning thornbush, in the desert of mount* Sinai. When Moses saw this, he marvelled at the sight ; and as he went
32 up to look at it, the voice of the Lord said, ' *I am the God of your fathers, the God of Abraham and Isaac and Jacob.*' Moses was so terrified that he did not dare to look at the
33 bush. *But the Lord said to him, ' Take the sandals off your feet, for the place where you are standing is sacred ground.*
34 *I have indeed seen the oppression of my people in Egypt, I have heard their groans, and I have come down to rescue*
35 *them. Come now, I will send you back to Egypt.'* The Moses they refused, when they said, ' *Who made you ruler and umpire ? '*—that was the very man whom God sent to rule and to redeem them, by aid of the angel who had
36 appeared to him in the bush. He it was who led them forth, performing *wonders and signs in the land of Egypt,*
37 at the Red Sea, and *in the desert during forty years.* (This was the Moses who told the sons of Israel, ' *God will raise up a prophet for you from among your brotherhood, as he*
38 *raised me.'*) This was the man who at the assembly in the desert intervened between the angel who spoke to him on mount Sinai and our fathers ; he received living Words to be given to us.

The commission to Moses, when God's glory was revealed by the angel in the bush which was aflame but not consumed— note the Alexandrian touch that not Jehovah but the angel appeared—is followed by a real burst of eloquence (vers. 36–38), where the Moses whom Israel had rejected appears as the great deliverer of the nation. Here we have a parallel between Moses and Christ, heightened by the reminder that Moses had foretold the prophet which God would raise up, ' like unto me.' This verse in Deuteronomy was used by Peter in Acts iii. 22–23, and was evidently taken in a messianic sense by the Jews of this age. It is here not directly applied to Jesus, though this may be implied. The rejection of Moses is linked to the rejection of the laws and customs which Stephen had been accused of trying to subvert. There is an applicability in the word **living** applied to the oracular message God had delivered to Moses. The Law, as Jesus had said, must live and be fulfilled.

But our fathers would not submit to him ; they pushed him 39 **aside and** *hankered* **secretly** *after Egypt.* **They told** 40 **Aaron,** ' *Make gods that will march in front of us! As for this Moses who led us out of Egypt, we don't know what has happened to him!* ' **They actually** *made a calf* 41 **in those days,** *offered sacrifice* **to this idol, and grew festive over what their own hands had manufactured. So God** 42 **turned from them, abandoning them to the worship of** *the starry Host*—**as it is written in the book of the prophets,** *Did you offer me victims and sacrifices during the forty years in the desert, O house of Israel ? No, it was the tent* 43 *of Moloch and the star-symbol of Rephan your god that you carried, figures that you manufactured* **for worship.** *So now I will transport you beyond Babylon!*

No sooner had the people received the living oracles uttered by God Himself on Mount Sinai than they turned to Aaron and requested him to make gods to lead them in the wilderness, so Jehovah gave them up to worship the host of heaven. The quotation which follows is from the book of the prophets, i.e. of the twelve so-called Minor Prophets (Amos v. 25). The difficulties in this quotation are : (1) that the prophet seems to deny that sacrifices were offered in the days of the wanderings, though the same idea is implied by Jeremiah when he says, ' I spake not to your fathers . . . concerning burnt offerings ' (Jer. vii. 22) ; (2) that there is no mention of the worship of the heavenly bodies in the Law (except in Deut. iv. 19, xvii. 3), this being a later form of idolatry, although Stephen would certainly have regarded the book of Deuteronomy as reproducing the exact words of Moses ; (3) that the

Hebrew version is entirely different from the Greek, both being equally unintelligible ; (4) that Amos has Damascus and Stephen **Babylon,** the prophet alluding to the captivity of Israel and the martyr to Judah's.

44 In the desert our fathers had the tent of witness as arranged by Him who told Moses to *make it after the pattern he had*

45 *seen.* It was passed on and borne in by our fathers as with Joshua they *took possession of* the territory of the nations whom God drove out before our fathers. So it

46 remained down to the days of David. He found favour with God and asked permission *to devise a dwelling for the*

47 *God of Jacob.* It was *Solomon,* however, who *built him*

48 *a house.* And yet the most High does not dwell in houses made by hands. As the prophet says:

49   *Heaven is my throne,*
      the earth is a footstool for my feet!
    What house would you build me ? saith the Lord.
    On what spot could I settle ?

50   *Did not my hand make all this ?*

Here the object of the speech is evidently to shew that no temple made by man is capable of containing God, a fact, by the way, which none of Stephen's opponents could deny. The noteworthy point is that the language of Stephen here bears a close resemblance to that of the epistle to the Hebrews, where the Tabernacle, built by divine revelation, is more important than the Temple, because it is the type of the true house of God revealed to Moses on the Mount (Heb. viii. 1–5).

51 *Stiff-necked, uncircumcised in heart and ear,* you are always *resisting the holy Spirit!* As with your fathers, so with

52 you! Which of the prophets did your fathers fail to persecute ? They killed those who announced beforehand the coming of the Just One. And here you have betrayed

53 him, murdered him!—you who got the Law that angels transmitted, and have not obeyed it! ''

54 When they heard this, they were furious and gnashed their teeth at him.

Here Stephen breaks off the narrative of Scripture for a furious invective against the Jews. It is supposed that he had provoked an outburst on the part of his judges ; but so far the speech as represented here had done nothing to call this forth. Only the concluding words have anything to do with what had hitherto been said, namely, that the Jews have received a divine law and have not kept it.

It is noteworthy that there is no hint in this that the Law is not obligatory. It had not been kept by those who received it, but that did not make it the less divine. According to Paul the Law is good, but cannot effect the salvation of man. So far from the Jews not keeping it, they are eager to observe it, but their zeal is not according to knowledge. Stephen, on the other hand, maintains that the Law is perfect, and that the Jews disregard it. Paul and Stephen agree that the Law came through angels, but to Paul the fact proves that it is inferior to what is actually divine (Gal. iii. 19), whereas Stephen maintains the opposite. The epistle to the Hebrews draws a distinction between the danger of disobedience to the word spoken by angels and to the commands of God Himself (Heb. iii. 2).

That the speech of Stephen contains the foundation of an argument in favour of the primitive Christian position has been demonstrated, but it is not so easy to shew that it was as applicable to the occasion on which it is said to have been delivered as are the rest of the alleged speeches in Acts. It must be borne in mind that Stephen was on his trial, and that the charge against him was that of blasphemy, because he had declared that Jesus would destroy the Temple and change the ancestral customs of the Jews. If the speech in Acts vii. was his defence, it is strange that he makes no mention of the accusations, but gives a recapitulation of the facts of the ancient history of Israel, concerning which all his hearers were perfectly familiar as well as being in agreement. Moreover, though the offence of Stephen was preaching in the name of Jesus, he never makes any allusion to him in the entire speech, except that the ancestors of his judges had murdered the prophets who had foretold the coming of the Just One (see James v. 6). The relation of the facts concerning the choice and deliverance of Israel is repeatedly given in addresses to the nation by patriot, prophet, and psalmist. It is found in the farewell address of Joshua to the people (Josh. xxiv. 2 ff.) ; in Samuel's speech, when Saul was acknowledged as king (1 Sam. xii. 6 ff.) ; in the long prayer of the Levites (Neh. ix. 6 ff.) ; in Pss. lxxviii., cv., and cvi.

In the Apocrypha the story of Israel is retold in the praises of famous men (Eccles. xliv.–xlix.), and in the speech of Mattathias to his sons (1 Macc. ii. 14 ff.). And the lesson frequently insisted upon in these is that the Israelites proved unworthy of all the benefits God had bestowed upon them; nor was it necessary to remind the Sanhedrin of the fact. There is nothing, even in the violent denunciation of Israel at the end of the speech, which would convict Stephen of blasphemy. It is an echo of the language of the ancient prophets who constantly expose the sins of the nation in equally scathing terms. Nor can we account for Stephen's outburst of indignation by supposing that what he had said before had provoked his hearers, who can hardly have seen the underlying argument, assumed to exist by those who see in the discourse a ' masterly defence.'

When we consider whether, if St. Paul heard the apology of Stephen, the words uttered could have affected the conversion or the subsequent opinions of the Apostle, we may, without laying stress on the speech as an influence upon Pauline doctrine, well believe that the behaviour of the protomartyr made a profound impression. It must be borne in mind that we know little or nothing of the teaching of St. Paul till some seventeen years after his conversion. His earliest epistles are either those to the Thessalonians or that to the Galatians ; and if we do not take into account the so-called ' Pastoral Epistles ' (1 and 2 Timothy and Titus), the period of his literary activity extends over little more than ten years. Yet in this period, though the Apostle cannot be charged with being inconsistent, he modified his opinions on such an important point as the immediate coming of Jesus. It is no disparagement of St. Paul to say that he was, to the end of his life, a learner alike by contemplation and experience, and to infer that, if his opinions deepened in the last years of his active life, he may well have modified his views in the interval between his conversion and his earliest epistles. The first utterance of Paul which can by any possibility be attributed to him is the sermon delivered in the synagogue of Pisidian Antioch. In this we have the usual sketch of the history of God's people. In no other respect does it resemble the apology of Stephen. Paul touches lightly on historical events and goes straight to David, then immediately to Jesus as the Christ. He attributes the Crucifixion to ignorance rather than malice, and dwells on the Resurrection, shewing that all that has happened is to fulfil the purpose of God as declared by the prophets. The message of the Christ is a reconciliation to God which the Law could not bring about. The concluding words are not denunciatory but admonitory, to beware of neglecting the proffered salvation. The sermon bears a closer resemblance to the words of Peter at Pentecost than to the fierce diatribe of Stephen.

The magnificent description of faith in Heb. xi. resembles Stephen's summary of Israel's story ; but is on a far higher plane. In it we are carried from Abel to the Maccabean martyrs in a rushing torrent of eloquence. With the refrain " By faith " ever sounding in our ears, we are led onwards to Jesus as consummation of all that the heroes of old had wrought. The defence of Stephen, on the contrary, is in the tone of an apology, the argument of which it requires no little ingenuity to discover.

Not that the speech in Acts vii. need for this reason be considered as unimportant. Like others put into the mouths of prominent persons by Luke, it is primitive in tone if not in date of composition. One peculiar merit of Luke as an historian is that, although he must have known the system of Paul, he does not allow his orators to present a purely Pauline Christology, either because he had access to early sources, or because he possessed the rare historical instinct of understanding what people thought before he himself came in contact with the teaching of the gospel. In fact, if the speech had been addressed to the Hellenistic enemies of Stephen it would have been appropriate, and have accounted for their bringing him to trial before the authorities at Jerusalem. The difficulty lies in accepting Stephen's words as a defence before the Sanhedrin.

Another explanation may perhaps be hazarded. In the infancy narratives at the opening of his Gospel Luke uses Hebraic poems, possibly of an earlier age, and puts them into the mouth of the persons he introduces. Such, for example, is the *Benedictus* (' Blessed be the Lord God of Israel '), which he attributes to Zacharias, the father of the Baptist (Luke i. 68–79), and also the *Magnificat* (' My soul doth magnify the Lord,' Luke i. 46–53), a poem obviously based on the Song of Hannah (1 Sam. ii. 1–10), put into the mouth of the Blessed Virgin, or perhaps of Elizabeth. Is it not therefore possible that the speech of Stephen is an earlier prophetic diatribe, popular among the earliest Christians, which Luke considered as a speech well suited to the first martyr when he stood before his judge ?

We have a later example of a similar literary device. The apology of Aristides was recovered by Rendel Harris in a Syriac translation, and shortly afterwards Dr. Armitage Robinson found that the original Greek had been inserted as the speech of the soothsayer Barlaam in the comparatively well-known ' Acts of Barlaam and Josaphat.'

What followed the dispersion of the believers from the city of Jerusalem is hard to explain, unless this chapter is regarded as consisting of a series of detached pictures. It would then fall into five separate and not closely connected scenes :

    I. The persecution by Saul and the burial of Stephen.
    II. Philip's preaching in Samaria.
   III. The conversion of Simon the magician.
   IV. The visit of Peter and John and the discomfiture of Simon.
    V. The conversion of the Eunuch.

The object of the writer is evidently to trace the progress of the gospel outside Jerusalem, but he has not carried out his design in a continuous story. The intervention of Peter and John, in a short section otherwise devoted to the missionary labours of Philip, one of the Seven, is by no means easy to understand, though Luke's intention seems to have been to remind his readers that the work of the Hellenistic preachers was carefully supervised by the Twelve, who remained at their post at Jerusalem. It is only by keeping each episode apart that we can appreciate the problem involved in this single chapter.

viii.

(Saul quite approved of his murder.)   1
That day a severe persecution broke out against the church in Jerusalem, and everyone, with the exception of the apostles,* was scattered over Judaea and Samaria. 2 Devout men buried Stephen and made loud lamentation over him, but Saul made havoc of the church by entering 3 one house after another, dragging off men and women, and consigning them to prison.

* W adds, ' Who remained in Jerusalem.'

I. This brief description of the persecution of the church in Jerusalem abounds in contradictory statements. If Stephen had been legally executed as a blasphemer (the words of ver. 1, ' Saul quite approved of his murder,' follow vii. 60), how could devout persons, probably Jews as well as believers, bury him with public expressions of grief ? On the other hand, if the martyrdom was the result of tumultuary violence, how could it have been followed by a regular inquisition on the part of Saul and the arrest of suspected persons ? If again the persecutions were as systematic as is implied, how could the Twelve have been allowed to remain in the city even in concealment, much less to act as directors of the movement ? When he stood before Agrippa II St. Paul declares that in Jerusalem he shut up ' many of the saints in prison, having

received authority from the chief priests, and when they were
being put to death I gave my vote for it, and punishing them
in all the synagogues, I forced them to blaspheme, and being
excessively mad against them I was pursuing them into the
cities outside ' (xxvi. 10–11). It would appear that there
was a *severe persecution in Jerusalem*, and that others besides
Stephen lost their lives ; but no definite record of it has survived. Thus the problems raised by what little we learn
from Acts are practically insoluble.

4 **Now those who were scattered went through the land preaching**
5   **the gospel. Philip travelled down to a town in Samaria,**
6   **where he preached Christ to the people. And the crowds**
       attended like one man to what was said by Philip, listening
7   **to him and watching the miracles he performed. For**
       unclean spirits came screaming and shrieking out of many
       who had been possessed, and many paralytics and lame
8   **people were healed. So there was great rejoicing in that**
       town.

II. The words **those who were scattered** are repeated in
xi. 19 in allusion to the Hellenists who had been driven out
of Jerusalem. In the next verse the adventures of Philip are
related, and the resemblance to what is said of Stephen (vii. 8)
cannot be disregarded. Like the Apostles these two prominent representatives of the Seven were workers of miracles
as well as preachers. Philip's ' signs ' attracted the crowds
as well as his words. This progress throughout was marked
by his power over rival spirits, and in restoring the paralysed
and the lame. There is some doubt as to the description of
the town visited by Philip. If the article is prefixed, it was
' the city of Samaria,' or Sebaste as it was called, since it had
been refounded by Herod the Great, and named in honour of
Augustus (Gk. *Sebastos*). This town was probably inhabited
by a mixed population with a large pagan element. If the
article is omitted any town in Samaria might be meant.
From what little we know of the Samaritans we may be sure
that the announcement that the Messiah had come would be
eagerly received, and Philip's proclamation, confirmed as it

was by miracles, caused, as Luke says, **great rejoicing in that
town.**

Now for some time previous a man called Simon had been 9
practising magic arts in the town, to the utter astonishment of the Samaritan nation ; he made himself out to
be a great person, and all sorts and conditions of people 10
attached themselves to him, declaring he was that Power
of God which is known as "the Great Power." They 11
attached themselves to him because he had dazzled them
with his skill in magic for a considerable time. But when 12
they believed Philip, who preached the gospel of the Reign
of God, and the name of Jesus, they had themselves
baptized, both men and women ; indeed Simon himself 13
believed, and after his baptism kept close to Philip,
utterly astonished to see the signs and striking miracles
which were taking place.

III. In order to understand the appearance of Simon in
this and the following section, it is advisable to confine ourselves to what is actually told us about him in Acts, and to
dismiss from our minds, at anyrate for the present, all that
Church writers have related concerning Simon, the Gnostic
heretic.

Rival miracles often mark the contest between a new and
an old religion. Nor must it be forgotten that preachers of
truth and disciples of error are both wont to claim to be gifted
with supernatural powers. Thus, when Moses confronts the
magicians of Egypt, both sides are able to work wonders;
and Jesus himself warned his disciples that their enemies
would show signs and wonders to deceive, if possible, the
elect. In the controversies between the Jewish rabbis and
the Christian preachers, the same rivalry in miraculous gifts
is displayed, and in later times St. Patrick and St. Columba
are opposed by the magic of the Druids, which is proved
to be inferior to the supernatural power displayed by the
missionaries of the Cross.

Philip as a wonder-worker is thus confronted by Simon,
the leader of the Samaritans, who declares that he must be

the so-called **great Power of God.** Simon, however, at once recognizes that he is in the presence of one far more gifted than himself, and submits to Philip, openly becoming his follower, and accepting baptism. Thus ends the first evangelistic mission of Philip, the deacon, who converts a Samaritan town and persuades its wonder-working religious leader to submit to his guidance.

14 When the apostles at Jerusalem heard that Samaria had accepted the word of God, they despatched Peter and
15 John, who came down and prayed that the Samaritans
16 might receive the holy Spirit. (As yet it had not fallen upon any of them ; they had simply been baptized in the
17 name of the Lord Jesus.) Then they laid their hands on
18 them, and they received the holy Spirit. Now Simon noticed that the holy Spirit was conferred by the laying on
19 of the apostles' hands; so he brought them money, saying, " Let me share this power too, so that anyone on whom
20 I lay my hands may receive the holy Spirit." Peter said to him, " Death to you and your money, for dreaming you
21 could buy the gift of God! You come in for no share or lot in this religion. *Your heart is all wrong in the sight*
22 *of God.* So repent of this wickedness of yours, and ask God whether you cannot be forgiven for your heart's
23 purpose. For I see you are *a bitter poison* and *a pack of*
24 *evil.*" Simon replied, " Beseech the Lord for me! Pray that nothing you have said may befall me! " ＇
25 After bearing their testimony to the word of the Lord and preaching it, the apostles went back to Jerusalem, preaching the gospel to a number of the Samaritan villages ;

IV. A new scene opens. Philip disappears, and the Apostles at Jerusalem send **Peter and John** (his silent but inseparable colleague, Acts iii. and iv. *passim*) to complete the good work. **The Samaritans,** it is true, have **been baptized,** but the supreme gift of the Spirit is not yet bestowed on the converts. Thus baptism, even **in the name of the Lord Jesus** (but see Acts ii. 38), is not enough ; the Spirit must be given by the apostolic laying on of hands. This would seem to be a later conception of the sacrament, though the story has every appearance of being very primitive. The gift is manifested openly, possibly (though this is not stated) by *glossolalia*. This so impresses Simon, though he has witnessed all the miracles done by Philip, that he offers money to purchase this apostolic privilege. For doing so he is sternly rebuked by Peter, and told to ask to be forgiven for being guilty of such a thought. Whereupon Simon manifests sorrow for what he has done, and begs Peter and John to pray for him to avert the calamity his folly has brought upon himself. There is no suggestion whatever that his prayer was not granted. But, although the two narratives of Simon-and-Philip and Simon-and-Peter-and-John may seem to us to be inconsistent with one another, their object is similar. Philip works true wonders in the presence of a famous magician, named Simon, who, admitting that his miracles cannot compare with Philip's, becomes his disciple, and is baptized. But when Peter and John arrive and give the Spirit to the newly baptized, Simon is prepared to buy the right of bestowing this great gift, presumably for a large sum. When Peter rebukes his wickedness, Simon is instantly convinced and professes penitence. The western text says that he ' wept much and would not leave the apostles '—a parallel to his adherence to Philip in ver. 13.

This explanation of the story of Simon would be sufficiently obvious but for the fact that in the second century a Simon made his appearance who greatly impressed the Christians of that age. About A.D. 150 Justin Martyr, himself a native of Samaria, speaks of an heretical teacher from the same country who had promulgated his views far and wide and received divine honours when he visited Rome. There he seems to have founded a sect of ' Simonians.' Justin says that people of many nations worshipped Simon as the ' first god,' and that he used to be accompanied by a woman named Helena, whom he declared to be the first conception of himself as the deity. At the end of the second century Irenaeus, the famous bishop of Lyons in Gaul, appears to have used Justin's lost work on heresies, and gives a description of Simon's views,

THE ACTS OF THE APOSTLES

which appear to have been those of the Gnostic systems prevalent at that time. A generation later, about A.D. 220, Hippolytus of Rome quotes from a book called the *Apophasis*, and hereafter the Church fathers generally regarded Simon as the man whom Peter had denounced in Acts and the founder of all heresy. All agree that he was a magician.

At the same time Simon became, as the great enemy of truth, the constant opponent of Simon Peter. At a much later date Simon, the founder of heresy and the foe of the prince of the Apostles, gave his name to the besetting sin of the western church, the purchase of offices or benefices which was known as Simony.

But in the book of Acts no hint is given that the Simon of the Samaritan city was destined to trouble the Church, or that Peter regarded him as a possible enemy. He is here little more than a worker of wonders, who, honoured as he was by the people, acknowledged Philip, or Peter, or both, to be invested with powers far superior to his own.

26   but an angel of the Lord said to Philip, " Get up and go south, along the road from Jerusalem to Gaza " (the
27   desert-route). So he got up and went on his way. Now there was an Ethiopian eunuch, a high official of Candace the queen of the Ethiopians (he was her chief treasurer),
28   who had come to Jerusalem for worship and was on his way home. He was sitting in his chariot, reading the
29   prophet Isaiah. The Spirit said to Philip, " Go up and
30   join that chariot." When Philip ran up, he heard him reading the prophet Isaiah. " Do you really understand *
31   what you are reading ? " he asked. " Why, how can I possibly understand it," said the eunuch, " unless some one puts me on the right track ? " And he begged Philip
32   to get up and sit beside him. Now the passage of scripture which he was reading was as follows :

> *he was led like a sheep to be slaughtered*
> *and as a lamb is dumb before the shearer,*
> *so he opens not his lips.*

* See Note on next page.

> *By humbling himself he had his doom removed.*   33
> *Who can tell his family?*
> *For his life is cut off from the earth.*

So the eunuch said to Philip, "Pray, who is the prophet 34
speaking about? Is it himself or someone else?" Then
Philip opened his lips, and starting from this scripture 35
preached the gospel of Jesus to him. As they travelled 36
on, they came to some water, and the eunuch said, "Here
is water! What is to prevent me being baptized?" So 38
he ordered the chariot to stop. Both of them stepped into
the water, and Philip baptized the eunuch. When they 39
came up from the water, the Spirit of the Lord caught
Philip away, and the eunuch lost sight of him. He went
on his way rejoicing, while Philip found himself at Azotus, 40
where he passed on, preaching the gospel in every town,
till he reached Caesarea.

---

* The Vulgate preserves the play on words in the Greek. *Intellegis
quae legis* brings out, as English cannot, the force of γινώσκεις ἃ
ἀναγινώσκεις.

V. In Acts xxi. 8 St. Paul is said to have gone to the house
of Philip the Evangelist, one of the Seven who had four
daughters, virgins, who prophesied. This was at Caesarea,
where we leave Philip at the end of this chapter, in which he
appears in the capacity of a prophet and evangelist. His
actions, like those of Elijah, are prompted by the Spirit, who
transports him from place to place and directs his every action.
It is to be noted that, as in chap. x., the angel of the Lord and
the Spirit appear to be interchangeable (viii. 26 and 29, x. 3
and 19). The conversion and baptism of Queen Candace's
treasurer is an incident separated from the rest of the narrative
and completely isolated from the rest of the history; it does
not seem probable that Luke had any design in relating it of
marking the progress of the story of the approach towards
those outside the Jewish covenant. In the first place, though
a person mutilated was forbidden by the Law to enter the
congregation of the Lord (Lev. xxi. 20, Deut. xxiii. 1), a special
blessing is promised (Is. lvi. 3 ff.) on eunuchs who observe the

sabbath law, and there is no reason to suppose that this man was a Gentile. Candace, according to Pliny the Elder, was the hereditary name of the queens of Meroê. The eunuch was evidently driven by his charioteer ; and, as was not unusual, was reading aloud. Philip, by a play on the Greek words (see footnote), asks if he understood what he read, a proof by the way that Luke was using a Greek source.[1] The passage which was being read is quoted *verbatim* from the Septuagint version of Is. liii. 7–8. The Hebrew, which is different, is thus rendered by Moffatt :

> ' dumb as a sheep led to the slaughter,
>   dumb as a ewe before the shearers.
> They did away him unjustly ;
>   and who heeded how he fell,
>   torn from the land of the living.'

We are not informed how Philip interpreted the passage, but only that he preached Jesus from it. This well-known servant chapter of Isaiah is quoted of Christ (Matt. viii. 17, Luke xxii. 32, John xii. 38, Acts iii. 13, 1 Pet. ii. 22, 24, Rom. ix. 16, Heb. ix. 28, Rev. xiii. 8, xiv. 5). Nevertheless, it is rarely, if ever, applied to the Messiah in Hebrew literature.

Ver. 37 is omitted by the best MSS. ; nevertheless, it is an early interpolation or the second century, when it was felt desirable that some confession of faith should be made at baptism. The verse runs : ' And Philip said, If you believe with all your heart, you may. He answered, I believe that Jesus Christ (τὸν Ἰησοῦν Χριστὸν) is the Son of God.' As Mr. G. T. Page truly remarks, Luke could not possibly have written the words, τὸν Ἰησοῦν Χριστὸν.

ix.

1 Meanwhile Saul still breathed threats of murder against the
2   disciples of the Lord. He went to the high priest and

[1] *Basil of Cappadocia*, Ep. 40, quotes the words of the Emperor Julian, ἀνέγνων, ἔγνων, κατέγνων (I read, I understood, I condemned).

asked him for letters to the synagogues at Damascus empowering him to put any man or woman in chains whom he could find belonging to the Way, and bring them to Jerusalem. As he neared Damascus in the course of 3 his journey, suddenly a light from heaven flashed round him; he dropped to the ground and heard a voice saying 4 to him, " Saul, Saul, why do you persecute me? " "Who 5 are you? "* he asked. "I am Jesus," he said, "and you persecute me. Get up and go into the city. There 6 you will be told what you have to do." His fellow- 7 travellers stood speechless, for they heard the voice but they could not see anyone. Saul got up from the 8 ground, but though his eyes were open he could see nothing; so they took his hand and led him to Damascus. For three days he remained sightless, he neither ate nor 9 drank.

* I have deliberately left Κύριε untranslated here, as in xxii. 8 and xxvi. 14, no less than in x. 4. Any English rendering would imply either too much or too little.

There are three accounts of the conversion of Saul of Tarsus. Two are in speeches which Luke attributes to the Apostle, one of which he may have heard, delivered in Hebrew to the Jews from the stairs leading to the fortress of Antonia in Jerusalem (Acts xxii.), the other in Paul's defence to King Agrippa, at which the historian was almost certainly present (Acts xxvi.). These accounts differ in detail, though substantially the story is the same. Three points merit attention : (*a*) the character of Saul's mission ; (*b*) the nature of the vision ; (*c*) the divergences in the different accounts.

(*a*) This is the first time in Acts that the faith in Jesus is known as **the Way.** The implication is that in the eyes, at anyrate of the priesthood of Jerusalem, the disciples had come to be regarded as a distinct sect in Judaism, following a peculiar manner of life. In the Synoptic Gospels those who tempted Jesus are represented as telling him that they knew he taught the 'Way of God' (Mark xii. 14, Matt. xxii. 16, Luke xx. 21). Later in the Acts the word **Way** becomes virtually a synonym for Church (xvi. 17, xix. 9 and 23, xxii. 4, xxiv. 22), in a more or less hostile sense. The expression as used here may mark a crisis in the development of the Faith. Although the word ὁδός (ὁδηγεῖν) would be quite natural in this sense to a Greek, it would be more so to a Jew, as the equivalent of *halakah* (walk or manner of life). The new religion to the priests, who as Sadducees were more concerned with practice than opinion, would be an heretical *halakah*. This alone is later admitted by Paul, when he tells Felix κατὰ τὴν ὁδόν ἣν λέγουσιν αἵρεσιν (which may be rendered, according to what they style an heretical *halakah*, ' I serve the God of my fathers ' (xxiv. 14)). This would fully account for the determination of the Temple authorities to put down Christianity. It should be noticed that Saul had himself requested to be entrusted with the commission to go to Damascus.

Damascus at this time was for the most part a Greek city within the territory of Aretas, the Arabian king. But there is no reason why a Christian church should not have been there from the first. It lay on the route between Jerusalem and Mesopotamia, and Jewish pilgrims were constantly passing through the city, so that from the day of Pentecost the fame of Jesus must have been known. Nevertheless, we have no information of how the gospel was preached there before the conversion of Saul : all we know is that around Damascus was the scene of his earliest activities (2 Cor. xi. 32, Gal. i. 17).

(*b*) The description of the conversion of Saul as an actual happening is confined to Acts. Nowhere does the Apostle, in any of his epistles, allude to the dramatic circumstances attending his submission to Jesus, but only in speeches reported as delivered by him in Acts. Paul, however, but rarely alludes to his conversion. He admits that he was a persecutor, that he had seen the Lord Jesus, that God had revealed His Son in him (1 Cor. ix. 1, Gal. i. 16, 1 Tim. i. 13). As we know he had visions (2 Cor. xii. 1 ff.), we need not doubt that he must have had a remarkable experience, similar to that described by Luke. Whatever this may have been, it changed the whole course of the life of Saul of Tarsus, who became from henceforward a devoted servant of the Christ. The extreme brevity of the Lukan narrative which covers many years in a few words makes it useless to hazard surmises as to the immediate effect of this so called conversion, or to attempt solutions of what, in popular phraseology, may be described as 'the psychological problem.' All that is possible for us is to take the account as it stands, the main points of which are the approach to Damascus, the heavenly light, and the voice of Jesus. To obtain a correct impression of Luke's story it is desirable to give his version of how Paul told it to the mob in the court of the Temple and to King Agrippa.

(I)

xxii.

Now as I neared Damascus on my journey, suddenly about 6 noon a brilliant light from heaven flashed round me. I dropped to the earth and heard a voice saying to me, 7 'Saul, Saul, why do you persecute me?' 'Who are 8 you?' I asked. He said to me, 'I am Jesus the Nazarene, and you are persecuting me.' (My companions saw the 9 light, but they did not hear the voice of him who talked to me.) I said, 'What am I to do?' And the Lord said to me, 10 'Get up and make your way into Damascus; there you shall be told about all you are destined to do.' As I could 11 not see owing to the dazzling glare of that light, my companions took my hand and so I reached Damascus.

(II)

xxvi.

I was travelling to Damascus on this business, with authority 12 and a commission from the high priests, when at mid day 13 on the road, O king, I saw a light from heaven, more dazzling than the sun, flash round me and my fellow-travellers. We all fell to the ground, and I heard a voice 14 saying to me in Hebrew, 'Saul, Saul, why do you persecute me? You hurt yourself by kicking at the goad.' 'Who 15 are you?' I asked. And the Lord said, 'I am Jesus, and you are persecuting me. Now get up and *stand on your* 16 *feet,* for I have appeared to you in order to appoint you to my service as a witness to what you have seen and to the

17   visions you shall have of me. *I will rescue you* from the
People and also *from the Gentiles—to whom I send you,*
18   *that* their *eyes may be opened* and that they may turn *from
darkness to light,* from the power of Satan to God, to get
remission of their sins and an inheritance among those
19   who are consecrated by faith in me.' Upon this, O king
20   Agrippa, I did not disobey the heavenly vision ; I announced to those at Damascus and at Jerusalem in the
first instance, then all over the land of Judaea, and also
to the Gentiles, that they were to repent and to turn to
God by acting up to their repentance.

(c) In some respects the Vision of Saul resembles the
account of the denial of Peter as told in the gospels, with slight
variations. But the four gospel stories are given by different
persons, and the divergences are more easily accounted for
than here, where the same story is told by the same person
under different circumstances. But, if one may hazard the
conjecture, the inconsistencies of Luke make rather for than
against the truth of his narrative. The author of Acts was
present in Jerusalem and Caesarea when the speeches embody-
ing the vision were delivered, and he may actually have heard
both of them. As a companion of Paul he must often have been
told the story. But the accounts of such an experience are
bound to vary in detail when related at different times, and the
Apostle may well have had a confused recollection as to the
less important details of so tremendous a spiritual experience.
That Luke worked up the story which he had heard in this
chapter introducing Paul's work as a minister of Christ is at
least possible.

The word Κύριε which has been omitted from the translation in ver. 5 as liable to mislead, in ver. 10 certainly means
Jesus. The rendering 'Who are you?' scarcely expresses
what a terrified man would have said on seeing a vision of an
unknown person whose presence was accompanied by a bright
light, and who uttered stern words of reproach. Yet if Saul
called him ' Lord ' it would give the impression that he was
using the unpronounceable name of God, which in the Old

Testament is substituted for JHVH. In classical Greek Κύριος is applied to a god, a king, or a master of household. To-day it is the equivalent of ' Sir.' In the New Testament it is often the title of Jesus. The question might be paraphrased, ' Who may you be, my Lord (or sir) ? '

The immediate sequel is twice told.

(I)

ix.

Now there was a disciple called Ananias in Damascus. The 10 Lord said to him in a vision, " Ananias." He said, " I 11 am here, Lord." And the Lord said to him, " Go away to the street called ' The Straight Street,' and ask at the house of Judas for a man of Tarsus called Saul. He is 12 praying at this very moment, and he has seen a man called Ananias enter and lay his hands upon him to bring back his sight." " But, Lord," Ananias answered, " many 13 people have told me about all the mischief this man has done to thy saints at Jerusalem ! And in this city too he 14 has authority from the high priests to put anyone in chains who invokes thy Name." But the Lord said to him, " Go ; 15 I have chosen him to be the means of bringing my Name before the Gentiles and their kings as well as before the sons of Israel. I will shew him all he has to suffer for 16 the sake of my Name." So Ananias went off and 17 entered the house, laying his hands on him with these words, " Saul, my brother, I have been sent by the Lord, by Jesus who appeared to you on the road, to let you regain your sight and be filled with the holy Spirit." In a 18 moment something like scales fell from his eyes, he regained his sight, got up and was baptized. Then he took 19 some food and felt strong again. For several days he stayed at Damascus with the disciples.

(II)

xxii.

" Then a certain Ananias, a devout man in the Law, who had a 12 good reputation among all the Jewish inhabitants, came 13 to me and standing beside me said, ' Saul, my brother, regain your sight ! ' The same moment I regained my

14 sight and looked up at him. Then he said, ' The God
of our fathers has appointed you to know his will, to see
the Just One, and to hear him speak with his own lips.
15 For you are to be a witness for him before all men, a witness of what you have seen and heard. And now, why do
16 you wait ? Get up and be baptized and wash away your
sins, invoking his name.' "

Ananias is never mentioned in the Pauline epistles ; and in
Galatians the Apostle is most careful to assure his converts
that, after his conversion, he consulted with no one, but went
straight to Arabia (Gal. i. 16–17). We know, however, that
Paul was baptized (Rom. vi. 3) ; he assumes as a matter of
course the fact that he had received this sacrament. The
words **I have chosen him,** rendered literally, are poetical, ' he
is a chosen vessel,' an Hebraic expression employed by the
Apostle to denote those whom God has selected as objects of
His mercy or His anger (Rom. ix. 21–23). The idea seems to
be that God chooses a man for His own purpose, as if He
picked a jar from His store at times, either to fill it with
something of infinite value, or to destroy it (2 Tim. ii. 21).
Thus the Apostle compares himself and other messengers of
the gospel to earthenware vessels (σκεύη ὀστράκινα), in which
inestimable treasures are conveyed throughout the world, the
commonness of the material being contrasted with the precious-
ness of the contents (2 Cor. iv. 7). Although Saul was restored
to sight by the laying on of hands, it is significant that in
early days baptism was called φωτισμός, ' enlightenment.'

ix.

20 He lost no time in preaching throughout the synagogues
21 that Jesus was the Son of God—to the amazement of all
his hearers, who said, " Is this not the man who in Jerusalem harried those who invoke this Name, the man who
came here for the express purpose of carrying them all in
chains to the high priests ? "
22 Saul became more and more vigorous. He put the Jewish
residents in Damascus to confusion by his proof that Jesus
23 was the Christ; and the Jews, after a number of days had

elapsed, conspired to make away with him. But their 24
plot came to the ears of Saul, and, although they kept
watch on the gates day and night in order to make away
with him, his disciples managed one night to let him down 25
over the wall by lowering him in a basket. He got to 26
Jerusalem and tried to join the disciples, but they were
all afraid of him, unable to believe he was really a disciple.
Barnabas, however, got hold of him and brought him to 27
the apostles. To them he related how he had seen the
Lord upon the road, how He had spoken to him, and how
he had spoken freely in the name of Jesus at Damascus. 28
He then went in and out among them at Jerusalem,
speaking freely in the name of the Lord ; he also held 29
conversations and debates with the Hellenists. But when 30
the brothers learned that the Hellenists were attempting
to make away with him, they took him down to Caesarea
and sent him off to Tarsus.

The object of this description of events following the conversion of Saul seems to be simply to shew that he began to proclaim Jesus as the Christ at Damascus and, having incurred
the natural resentment of the Jews, was obliged to escape,
and that finally he made his way to Jerusalem. There,
thanks to the good offices of **Barnabas**, he was received by the
Apostles, and addressed himself to the Hellenists. As, however, their enmity made it unsafe to remain not only in Jerusalem but in Judaea, and indeed in Palestine generally, he
embarked at Caesarea, and found refuge in his native Tarsus.
There he remained for some time, till Barnabas went to
Antioch, and, finding that the man he needed for the work
was Saul, fetched him from Tarsus, and began to organize a
church, and an extended missionary campaign. The narrative
of Acts, interrupted by the adventure of Peter (x. 1–xi. 18)
and by the persecution of Herod Agrippa (xii. 1–23), sketches
the days of Barnabas and Saul in ix. 26, xi. 19–30, and xii. 25.
Thus the events of many years are compressed into a few lines.

The extreme brevity with which this period of the development of the Church and the career of Saul is treated, would

make the story in Acts very hard to follow. Fortunately, however, a particlar clue is furnished by the Pauline epistles. From these we learn that years may have passed between the time of Paul's conversion and his joining Barnabas at Antioch. He spent three years in Arabia (Gal. i. 17) before he so much as came to Jerusalem to visit Cephas. He did missionary work in Syria and Cilicia (Gal. i. 21), and did not return to Jerusalem for fourteen years after his first visit. The only other allusion which Paul makes to this period in his life is to his escape from Damascus by being lowered from the city wall in a basket. But even here there is a slight discrepancy. According to Acts the Jews watched the gates, whilst Saul, who had been preaching boldly in the city, lay hid till his disciples contrived his deliverance. But the Apostle's account, as related in his letter to the Corinthians, bears more signs of probability (2 Cor. xi. 32). The city gates were being watched by the governor (*ethnarch*) of Aretas, king of Arabia, and it would appear that Paul had taken refuge in Damascus after causing trouble by his preaching in the neighbouring cities, and was only able to leave it by being let down in a basket from a window on the wall. We can hardly expect the detailed accuracy which some seem to demand when the story of events extending over some years is condensed into about one hundred and thirty Greek words.

31 Now, all over Judaea, Galilee, and Samaria, the church enjoyed peace ; it was consolidated, inspired by reverence for the Lord and by its invocation of the holy Spirit, and so

32 increased in numbers. Peter moved here and there among them all, and it happened that in the course of his tours he came down to visit the saints who stayed at Lydda.

33 There he found a man called Aeneas who had been bed-

34 ridden for eight years with paralysis. "Aeneas," said Peter, "Jesus the Christ cures you ! Get up and make

35 your bed ! " He got up at once. And all the inhabitants of Lydda and Saron saw him, and they turned to the Lord.

36 At Joppa there was a disciple called Tabitha (which may be translated Dorcas, or ' Gazelle '), a woman whose life was

full of good actions and of charitable practices. She 37
happened to take ill and died at this time, and after washing
her body they laid it in an upper room. When the dis- 38
ciples heard that Peter was at Lydda (for Joppa is not far
from Lydda), they sent two men to beg him to " Come on
to us without delay." So Peter got up and went with 39
them. When he arrived, they took him up to the room,
where all the widows stood beside him crying as they
showed him the garments and dresses that Dorcas used to
make when she was with them. Peter put them all out- 40
side; then he knelt down and prayed, and, turning him
to the body, said " Tabitha, rise." She opened her eyes,
and on seeing Peter she sat up. Then he gave her his hand, 41
raised her, and, after calling the saints and the widows, he
presented her to them alive. This became known all over 42
Joppa, and many believed in the Lord.

In ver. 31 the progress of the Church is marked as in ii. 41
and 47, iv. 4, vi. 7. The excitement about Stephen and the
Hellenistic believers had subsided ; the Church was left unmolested, and had evidently established settlements throughout Palestine. It is noteworthy that **Galilee** is here mentioned,
though there is no allusion to any church in that district in
the book of Acts. After the fall of Jerusalem Tiberias in
Galilee became the great centre of Jewish legalism. It is
strange that no Apostle is said to have gone back to preach in
his native land, which had been the chief scene of the activities
of Jesus, though Matthew places the great appearance of
Jesus to his Apostles in Galilee, and in the supplementary
chapter of the Fourth Gospel (John xxi.) Jesus reveals himself
and gives St. Peter his commission by the Sea of Tiberias.
There were no early Christian bishoprics founded in Galilee,
but from early times the Palestinian cities on the Mediterranean were active centres of Christian life.

In viii. 25 we left Peter and John, after their rebuke of
Simon, preaching in the villages of Samaria on their way back
to Jerusalem. Peter now reappears doing the work of an
evangelist in the cities of the ancient Philistine plain. It

would seem that Luke is leading us up to the conversion of the Gentiles in the person of Cornelius by gradual stages : (1) the proselytes at Pentecost (Acts ii.) ; (2) the Hellenists (Acts vi.) ; (3) the acceptance of the gospel by the Samaritans, and (4) by the eunuch of Candace (Acts viii.). Now we have Peter labouring among Jews, but in towns by no means entirely Jewish ; for **Lydda** was later known by the Greek name of Diospolis, and **Joppa,** the nearest seaport to Jerusalem, was only added to the Judaean territory by Jonathan, the brother of Judas Maccabaeus (1 Macc. x. 74-76). It was rebuilt by Pompey, and like other Hasmonaean conquests was taken away from the Jews (Josephus, *Antiq.*, xiv. 4). The districts of **Lydda and Saron** were all only semi-Jewish, and later practically Gentile. In the romance of the so-called Clementines, when Peter encounters Simon Magus, the scene is in the coastal cities of Palestine.

The two miracles wrought by Peter in **Lydda** and **Joppa**, the healing of **Aeneas**[1] and the raising of Dorcas, are related in the style of the gospel narratives. It is to be observed that in the restoration of Dorcas to life Acts follows Mark v. 40 and Matt. ix. 25 in making a parallel between this and the miracle of Jairus's daughter, by telling us that it was performed after all had been put out of the death-chamber, whereas in the Third Gospel the words, ' When we had put them all out ' (Luke viii. 54) are not in the best MSS. The words of Peter, ' **Tabitha, rise,**' and the Lord's words in Aramaic when he raised the daughter of Jairus, ' Tabitha cumi ' (Mark v. 41), are strikingly similar.

ix.

43 In Joppa Peter stayed for some time, at the house of Simon a
x. 1   tanner. Now in Caesarea there was a man called Corne-
2   lius, a captain in the Italian regiment, a religious man, who reverenced God with all his household, who was liberal in his alms to the People, and who constantly
3   prayed to God. About three o'clock in the afternoon he

---

[1] Is this section from a Markan source ? Note the word κράββατον (ver. 34).

distinctly saw in a vision an angel of God entering and
saying to him, "Cornelius." He stared at the angel in 4
terror, saying, "What is it?" He replied, "Your
prayers and your alms have risen before God as a sacrifice
to be remembered. You must now send some men to 5
Joppa for a certain Simon who is surnamed Peter; he is 6
staying with Simon a tanner, whose house stands by the
sea." When the angel who spoke to him had left, he 7
called two of his menservants and a religiously minded
soldier who belonged to his personal retinue, and after 8
describing all the vision to them, he sent them to Joppa.
Next day they were still on the road and not far from the 9
town, when Peter went up to the roof of the house about
noon to pray. He became very hungry and longed for 10
some food. But as they were getting the meal ready, a
trance came over him. He saw heaven open and a vessel 11
coming down, like a huge sheet lowered by the four
corners to the earth, which contained all quadrupeds and 12
creeping things of the earth and wild birds. A voice came 13
to him, "Rise, Peter, kill and eat." But Peter said, 14
"No, no, my Lord; I have never eaten anything common
or unclean." A second time the voice came back to 15
him, "What God has cleansed, you must not regard as
common." This happened three times; then the vessel 16
was at once raised to heaven. Peter was quite at a loss to 17
know the meaning of the vision he had seen; but just
then, the messengers of Cornelius, who had made inquiries
for the house of Simon, stood at the door and called out to 18
ask if Simon, surnamed Peter, was staying there.

This chapter is unique in Acts, and the story is related at
considerable length. Yet though in some respects it appears
to be a free composition of the author, it bears the stamp both
of probability and truth. Peter's vision or dream is just of a
kind which is not uncommonly experienced. Such apparent
absurdities frequently occur in dreams, as most of us can
testify. The immense **sheet** descending from the sky full of
strange animals may seem to us grotesque; but it is not

impossible, and had we seen anything like it in our sleep we should no doubt have wondered just as Peter did whether it had any special meaning for us. It is useless therefore either to criticize the vision or to condemn it as impossible, because to us it appears unworthy of the occasion. The *naïveté* of the tale adds to its charm. There is, as in the accounts of the two miracles in the preceding chapters, a parallelism between the experiences of Peter and those of our Lord. Here Cornelius sends his servants to ask for instruction, just as in the gospels the centurion sends friends to entreat Jesus to heal his sick servant.[1]

Polybius, the Greek historian of Rome (150 B.C.), in his well-known description of the army (Bk. vi. 24) says of the ' centurions,' or, as he also styles them, *taxiarchs*, that they are not expected to be so much ' venturesome seekers of danger, as men who can command, steady in action, and reliable ; they ought not to be over-anxious to rush into the fight, but when hard pressed, they must be ready to hold their ground and die at their posts.' In this way they represented the reliable strength of the army, in whom the common soldiers could trust implicitly. They are always well spoken of in the New Testament, and both the unnamed centurion of the gospel miracle (Matt. viii. and Luke vii.) and Cornelius were serious men, highly regarded by the Jews. As Polybius informs us there were several grades of **captain** or centurion, Cornelius and Julius (Acts xxvii. 1) must have belonged to the higher ranks. The Italian *speira*, or cohort of Cornelius, is, if the legion represents a modern army corps, aptly explained as a **regiment.** The vision which advised him to send for Peter was seen at an hour of prayer in broad daylight. Cornelius evidently was a strict observer of the Jewish worship of God, though his position as an important army officer in Caesarea,

[1] It is to be observed that the first Gentile with whom our Lord came in contact was a centurion—a fact related in the gospels of Matthew and Luke. Strange to say, it is Matthew, not Luke, who records the saying of the Lord, which would be peculiarly applicable to Acts x., 'Many shall come and take their place beside Abraham, Isaac, and Jacob.'

the capital of the province, prevented his openly professing
Judaism. The mention of this devout soldier indicates that
there were Jewish sympathizers in the army.[1] There is no hint
that Cornelius was circumcised after his baptism.

There are certain difficulties connected with this incident,
one being to account for the extraordinary hesitation on the
part of Peter to approach a Gentile, especially when we
recollect his Master's attitude towards the Syro-Phoenician
woman and the centurion, as well as the discourse in Mark vii.
about clean and unclean meats. The explanation is seen in
the sequel (viz. chap. xi.). From Acts vi. we see that at a
very early date there were two communities of believers in
Jerusalem, the 'Hebrews' and the 'Hellenists,' between whom
certain differences existed. These were happily adjusted by
the Hellenists being allowed to appoint their own leaders,
the Seven, the Hebraists remaining under the Twelve, headed
by Peter. In the persecution about Stephen the Hellenists
were driven out of the city, but the Apostles remained
apparently unmolested (viii. 1); and for their devotion to
the observance of the Law were favourably regarded by the
natives of Jerusalem (Acts i. 47, v. 26). To admit heathen
to their society would mean alienating those who were being
increasingly added to the Church from Judaism. We need
not wonder that Peter needed a special vision before he
accepted the invitation of Cornelius to go to a Gentile city
like Caesarea, in which the Jews were numerous, but, as we
learn from Josephus, extremely unpopular, and there openly
to associate with Gentiles. To do so was to take a momentous step needing divine approval; and for this reason Luke
sees fit to introduce the reader to Cornelius by recording two
visions preparing for his conversion.

So the Spirit said to Peter, who was pondering over the vision, 19
"There are three men looking for you! Come, get up 20
and go down, and have no hesitation about accompanying

[1] The messengers of Cornelius were to inquire for Simon, surnamed
Peter (vers. 5, 18, and 32; cf. also Matt. x. 2). It is curious that
Simon should be thus called by a Gentile.

21 them, for it is I who have sent them." Then Peter went down to the men, saying, " I am the man you are looking
22 for. What is your reason for coming ? " They said, " Cornelius, a captain, a good man who reverences God and enjoys a good reputation among the whole Jewish nation, was instructed by a holy angel to send for you to
23 his house and to listen to what you had to say." So he invited them in and entertained them. Next day he was up and off with them, accompanied by some of the brothers
24 from Joppa ; and on the next day he reached Caesarea.
25 Peter was just going into the house when Cornelius met
26 him, fell at his feet, and worshipped him ; but Peter raised
27 him, saying, " Get up, I am only a man myself." Then talking to him he entered the house, to find a large com-
24b pany assembled. (For Cornelius had been expecting him and had called his kinsfolk and intimate friends together.)*
28 To them Peter said, " You know yourselves it is illegal for a Jew to join or accost anyone belonging to another nation ; but God has shown me that I must not call any
29 man common or unclean, and so I have come without any demur when I was sent for. Now I want to know
30 why you sent for me ? " " Three days ago," said Cornelius, " at this very hour I was praying in my house at three o'clock in the afternoon, when a man stood
31 before me in shining dress, saying, ' Cornelius, your prayer
32 has been heard, your alms are remembered by God. You must send to Joppa and summon Simon who is surnamed Peter ; he is staying in the house of Simon a tanner
33 beside the sea.' So I sent for you at once, and you have been kind enough to come. Well now, here we are all present before God to listen to what the Lord has commanded you to say."

* Transposing ver. 24b to its right position between ver. 27 and ver. 28. [W reads, in ver. 25, ' And when Peter drew nigh to Caesarea one of the servants ran before and announced that he had come, and Cornelius jumped up and met him.']

It is noteworthy that in this chapter Jesus does not appear to Peter as might be expected. The medium of communica-

tion here is **the Spirit,** as it is in the story of Philip and the
eunuch in chap. viii. 26 (cf. also xvi. 7, where, however, the
best authenticated reading is ' the Spirit of Jesus ') ; in Acts
xix. 21, xx. 23, the Spirit directs Paul on his journey to
Jerusalem ; Ananias's sin, according to Peter, was a lie to the
holy Spirit.   These passages are significant, a leading idea of
Acts being that the work of the Apostles of Jesus is directed
by God's Spirit, who is described not only as a divine power
but as an actual person.   In Luke's narrative the teaching
appears to be that the work of guiding the Church is that of
the Spirit.   On the other hand, Cornelius also receives the
divine command from an angel who (in ver. 30) appears **in a
shining dress** (cf. Luke xxiv. 4, Acts i. 10).   The word rendered **instructed** also implies that Cornelius had received a
supernatural command : it is used in Matt. ii. 12, Luke ii. 26,
and Heb. xi. 7 in this special sense.   **Joppa** is twenty-eight
miles from Caesarea, and in ver. 30 Cornelius says that Peter
reached that city four days after the angel had told him to
send to Joppa for the Apostle.   The meeting of Peter with
Cornelius, as here related, shews that Luke intends to lay
special stress on its formality.   Peter chose witnesses to
accompany him to Caesarea, and Cornelius invited friends
and relatives to be present at the interview.

Cornelius acted naturally when he prostrated himself at the
feet of Peter.   The word for ' worship ' means an outward
act of reverence : (1) to God ; (2) to a superior being, to an
angel ; (3) to a king or benefactor ; (4) even to one of whom a
favour is being asked.   Peter, having been miraculously
introduced to Cornelius, was naturally an object of worship
to him.

Peter emphasizes the fact, well known to all present, of
the complete isolation of a strict Jew who, by custom, if not
by law, was expected scrupulously to avoid any commerce
with Gentiles, the object of Luke being to stress the extreme
rigidity of the Apostles, who accordingly held themselves
aloof even from the other believers (Acts v. 12, where the
same word for ' join ' is employed).   Peter's words seem to
mean, ' You know that it is contrary to our custom to be

intimate or even to approach an uncircumcised person '—the word alien (ἀλλόφυλος) being applied in the Old Testament to Philistines. In the story of Philip and the eunuch, by the way, which belongs to this section of Acts, the verbs **join or accost** are in the reverse order, ' **Go up and join** (κολλήθητι) **that chariot** ' (viii. 29). All this aloofness somewhat repels the modern reader, and seems alien to the spirit of the gospel, but here and there it is even implied in Jesus, as in the stories of the centurion and of the Syro-Phoenician woman (Matt. viii. and Luke vii., and Matt. xv. and Mark vii.). The object of this narrative is to emphasize the wide gulf which parted an observant Jew even from a Gentile who worshipped the God of Israel and was beloved by the Jewish people.

34 Then Peter opened his lips and said, " I see quite plainly that
35 *God has no favourites,* but that he who reverences Him and lives a good life in any nation is welcomed by Him.
36 You know *the message He sent to* the sons of *Israel when He preached the gospel of peace* by Jesus Christ (who is Lord
37 of all); you know how it spread over the whole of Judaea, starting from Galilee after the baptism preached by John—
38 how *God consecrated* Jesus of Nazaret *with the* holy *Spirit* and power, and how he went about doing good and curing all who were harassed by the devil; for God was with him.
39 As for what he did in the land of the Jews and of Jerusalem,
40 we can testify to that. They slew him *by hanging him on a gibbet,* but God raised him on the third day, and allowed
41 him to be seen not by all the People but by witnesses whom God had previously selected, by us who ate and drank
42 with him after his resurrection from the dead,[1] when he enjoined us to preach to the People, testifying that this was he whom God has appointed to be judge of the living
43 and of the dead. All the prophets testify that, everyone who believes in him is to receive remission of sins through his Name.''

[1] W adds, ' for forty days.'

The address of Peter to Cornelius is peculiarly appropriate to the occasion. It is the first gospel message addressed to Gentiles, and may be contrasted with Peter's speech on the day of Pentecost, the first proclamation of Jesus to Jews. Cornelius is told that God is not like a ruler who has a special favour for any individual among his subjects. He is declared to be ' no lifter up of the face '—a Hebrew phrase to designate a partial judge—but One who disregards nationality and favours only those who do what is right. True, God has by Jesus Christ sent a message of peace to Israel, but not only to Israel, for he (Jesus) is the Master of all men. Peter's hearers, who lived close to Galilee, must have heard of the story which began to be published in the Jews' country **starting from Galilee,** how that on Jesus of Nazareth the Spirit had been poured out when he was baptized by John ; and as a Person specially anointed by God had gone forth as a benefactor of mankind, healing those whom the tyranny of the devil had afflicted with sickness.

This is the only direct allusion to Jesus working miracles in Galilee to be found in Acts, and is especially appropriate to Peter's auditors, and to the locality in which the Apostle was speaking. Jesus must have been well known by repute in Caesarea, and the baptism of John was evidently notorious throughout Palestine. The Greek of this passage is extremely difficult to translate accurately. The words applied to Jesus Christ in ver. 36 do not seem to be in parenthesis unless they are a subsequent addition made for a dogmatic purpose. It would appear that the pronoun $οὗτος$ is emphatic, and that it is part of Peter's declaration, ' This (Jesus) is Master of all men, or all things.' We find the same pronoun repeated in vers. 40 and 43 at the beginning of a sentence, shewing how clearly and unmistakably Peter proclaims Jesus as the centre of his message. It is very significant that Peter admits that the resurrection of Jesus from the dead was only vouchsafed to specially **selected witnesses ;** also the stress he lays upon the fact that those who saw the risen Lord literally **ate and drank with him** (cf. Luke xxiv. 35 and 41, Acts i. 4). The concluding words are eminently characteristic of the other utterances of

93

Peter, who in his speeches insists on the eternal purpose of God to send Jesus to be the Saviour (Acts ii. 31, iii. 20 ; cf. also 1 Pet. i. 10).

The whole address is admirably suited to the occasion. The words, ' You yourselves know,' may well be an appeal to the personal knowledge of his auditors. Granted that these had heard of the great prophet's work in Galilee, they are now told that this Jesus is more than they could have anticipated. Jesus, who appeared in the neighbourhood of Caesarea as a benefactor, has by his resurrection become a Saviour and the coming judge of man. From this it would appear as if the baptism of Cornelius happened soon after the Day of Pentecost, implying that the events recorded in the early chapters of Acts happened within an astonishingly brief period, despite various circumstances which, as has been noticed, seem to require the lapse even of years.

44 While Peter was still speaking, the holy Spirit fell upon all who
45   listened to what he said. Now the Jewish believers who had accompanied Peter were amazed that the gift of the holy Spirit had actually been poured out on the Gentiles—
46   for they heard them speak with ' tongues ' and magnify
47   God. At this Peter asked, " Can any one refuse water for the baptism of these people—people who have received
48   the holy Spirit just as we ourselves have ? " And he ordered them to be baptized in the name of Jesus Christ. Then they begged him to remain for some days.

The holy Spirit's approval was signified by the fact that all Peter's audience felt his influence and manifested his power by ' speaking with tongues.' There is perhaps a conscious parallel to the gift of Pentecost bestowed on the first company of Christians ; but there are no visible tokens of the mighty wind and the tongues like fire. Neither did these Gentile recipients of the Spirit speak in foreign languages, as the members of the first Church are reported to have done in Acts ii. ; but only exercised the *glossolalia* spoken of by Paul in 1 Cor. xiv. In Acts viii. 16 baptism, it is implied, was not the means by which the Spirit was imparted—the laying on of hands by an Apostle was necessary for his bestowal. It is the same in Acts xix. 6, 7, with the disciples of John the Baptist at Ephesus. In this chapter the remarkable fact is that the Spirit fell upon the Gentiles *before* baptism. The doctrine of the sacrament in Acts appears to be very undeveloped. As in Acts viii. and xix. the baptism is said to have been **in the Name of the Lord Jesus.** The only trace of baptism in the name of Father, Son, and Spirit is to be found in Matt. xviii. 19 —the reading being open to question. The gift of the Spirit, however, may not mean more than that the power of God was manifested in these Gentiles by an outward act such as speaking with tongues.

To the ordinary reader of Acts the opening verses of the eleventh chapter may seem no more than a tedious repetition of what has been previously related. Perhaps a critic may perceive in the slight divergences of language from chap. x. the appearance of a fresh source. But those who recognize in the book of Acts a definite historical purpose, rather than an interesting puzzle caused by a confused jumble of authorities, must perceive that what is told us here is of the highest importance to the author. From the sixth chapter onwards Luke sees things increasingly with the eye of an historian to whom the Church is not an ideal community but a human reality. The Twelve are no longer a body, ruling by divine authority, represented by Peter or possibly by Peter and John, but are associated with the brethren, who now, as it were, place Peter himself on trial for the apparent irregularity of his conduct in approaching the Gentiles. The words of the great Apostle are not authoritative but apologetic. He justifies his conduct by a divine revelation, and in the end convinces his hearers. Still, as we shall see in chap. xv., Peter is no longer the chief personage in the church of Jerusalem. Even when he supports Barnabas and Saul he is, at least in a measure, on the defensive ; and from the epistle to the Galatians we should gather that he was sensitive to the least hint that his attitude towards Gentiles might be displeasing to James. These fragmentary notices of the Apostles are scarcely what we should expect, but they are consistent, and bear the impress of truth.

xi.

1 Now the apostles and the brothers in Judaea heard that the
2 Gentiles also had received the word of God. So when Peter came up to Jerusalem,[1] the circumcision party fell
3 foul of him. " You went into the houses of the uncircum-
4 cised," they said, " and you ate with them ! " Then Peter
5 proceeded to put the facts before them. " I was in the town of Joppa at prayer," he said, " and in a trance I saw a vision—a vessel coming down like a huge sheet lowered
6 from heaven by the four corners. It came down to me, and when I looked steadily at it, I noted the quadrupeds of the earth, the wild beasts, the creeping things and the wild
7 birds. Also I heard a voice saying to me, ' Rise, Peter, kill and eat.' I said, ' No, no, my Lord; * nothing com-
9 mon or unclean has ever passed my lips.' But a voice answered me for the second time out of heaven, ' What
10 God has cleansed, you must not regard as common.' This happened three times, and then the whole thing was drawn
11 back into heaven. At that very moment three men reached the house where I was living, sent to me from
12 Caesarea. The Spirit told me to have no hesitation in accompanying them ; these six brothers went with me as
13 well, and we entered the man's house. He related to us how he had seen the angel standing in his house and saying, ' Send to Joppa for Simon who is surnamed Peter ;
14 he will tell you how you and all your household are to be
15 saved.' Now just as I began to speak, the holy Spirit fell upon them as upon us at the beginning ; and I remem-
16 bered the saying of the Lord, that ' John baptized with

[1] W expands this : ' Now Peter had for a long time desired to go up to Jerusalem. And having called the brethren and strengthened them, making much discourse throughout the country, he told them of the grace of God.'

* See Note on next page.

water, but you shall be baptized with the holy Spirit.'
Well then, if God has given them exactly the same gift as 17
he gave us when we believed in the Lord Jesus Christ, who
was I—how could I try—to thwart God?" On hearing 18
this they desisted and glorified God, saying, "So God has
actually allowed the Gentiles to repent and live!"

* Here, as in x. 14, Κύριε is translated. Peter was a Christian, and
the connexion of the Voice with the Spirit is evident from the context.

The circumcision party appear suddenly, and here we have
an unexpected light as to the condition of affairs at Jerusalem.
It would seem that the preaching of Philip to the Samaritans
had caused some distrust among the zealously orthodox
followers of Jesus in Jerusalem, and that Peter and John had
been sent to see what was happening (viii. 4 ff.). Now Peter's
activity in evangelizing Gentiles is a cause of fresh suspicion,
and he is called upon to explain himself. In speaking of οἱ
ἐκ περιτομῆς Luke is obviously employing an expression which
belongs to a date later than the conversion of Cornelius, and
which was used by St. Paul to designate his Jewish opponents
(see Gal. ii. 12) in the same sense as here, though in the
previous chapter (x. 45), as in Col. iv. 11, it means simply
' Jews.' In xv. those who viewed the conversion of the
Gentiles with apprehension are described as ' those of the
Pharisees who had become believers.' The exclusiveness of
the Pharisaic members of the church at Jerusalem is the more
surprising when we recollect that their sect was remarkable for
its proselytizing zeal (Matt. xxiii. 15) ; and they could hardly
hope for success if they refused to enter a Gentile's house.
Luke's object here is evidently to impress Theophilus with
the exclusive character of Judaism and its jealous restriction
of its privileges to those of its own circle.

It is evident that **the six brothers** who had accompanied
Peter to Caesarea were present to defend their action—the
number of the Apostle's colleagues is not given in chap. x.
The reference to the day of Pentecost is evident, as is the
distinction between John's baptism by water and the baptism
of the Spirit, though here the words ' and fire ' recorded in the

gospels do not appear. Yet Luke is anxious to associate the water baptism of John here and elsewhere with spiritual out-pouring. On ver. 18 there is an admirably brief note in Mr. Page's *Commentary*, ' ἡσύχασαν, negative : their opposition ceased ; ἐδόξασαν, positive : their praise began.' The last clause of this verse is noteworthy ; literally, God has given to the Gentiles *the* repentance (observe the article) which leads to life. Here *metanoia* must mean change of heart rather than sorrow for the past.

19 Now those who had been scattered by the trouble which arose over Stephen made their way as far as Phoenicia and Cyprus and Antioch, but they preached the word to none
20 except Jews. Some of them, however, were Cypriotes and Cyrenians, who on reaching Antioch told the Greeks * also
21 the gospel of the Lord Jesus ; the strong hand of the Lord was with them, and a large number believed and turned
22 to the Lord. The news of this reached the church in Jerusalem, and they despatched Barnabas to Antioch.
23 When he came and saw the grace of God he rejoiced, and encouraged them all to hold by the Lord with heartfelt
24 purpose (for he was a good man, full of the holy Spirit and faith). Considerable numbers of people were brought in
25 for the Lord. So Barnabas went off to Tarsus to look for
26 Saul, and on finding him he brought him [1] to Antioch, where for a whole year they were guests of the church and taught considerable numbers. It was at Antioch too that the disciples were originally called " Christians."

* Reading Ἕλληνας with א* A D *, for which Ἑλληνιστὰς seems to have been substituted under the influence of ix. 29.

This marks a new development in the plan of Acts, which is obscured by the present method of dividing the book into chapters. The opening words are practically identical with those in viii. 4, which introduce the labours of the dispersed believers under Philip in Judaea and Samaria. Now the scene

[1] For ' and . . . brought him ' W has ' and having met him he besought him to come.'

shifts to what afterwards became the second capital of the
Faith and the centre of a more extensive evangelization.
Antioch was the chief city of the Hellenic east ; it had been
the seat of the Seleucid empire since its foundation by Seleu-
cius Nicator in 301 B.C. and was the official residence of the
Roman *legatus* of the province of Syria. Its Jewish inhabitants were numerous and influential, and there were many
proselytes. Unlike Jerusalem, Antioch was a busy centre of
commerce within easy reach of the sea and in touch with the
cities of Cappadocia, Syria, and Arabia. The fugitives from
Jerusalem naturally became missionaries of the good news
that in Jesus the promised Messiah had come ; but only, as
might be expected, addressed themselves to their fellow Jews.
This is the one allusion in Acts to unknown and unauthorized
missionary work, which must have been unremittent from the
first. Saul of Tarsus must have been one of the large company
of preachers, as we learn from his letter to the Galatians that
his labours in Syria and Cilicia had been well known before he
publicly presented himself to the church in Jerusalem. These
preachers followed the regular coastal route to Antioch, though
some of them may have crossed to **Cyprus,** which is named first.

In ver. 20 there is a very important variation in the Greek
MSS. Did these natives of Cyprus and Cyrene address themselves to the Hellenes (**Greeks**) or to the Hellenists (Greek-
speaking Jews) ? The documentary authority is so equally
divided that the easier reading would be *Hellenes.* The verse
would then mean that most of the missionaries preached only
to the Jews, but that on reaching Antioch some Cyprians and
Cyrenians proclaimed Christ to the Gentiles, as Peter had done
to Cornelius. This would not imply that they founded a body
of Gentile believers, but that they told their heathen friends
about Jesus.

The more difficult reading is *Hellenists,* due, it is said, to the
influence of ix. 29, where Saul held ' conversations and debates
with (or against) the *Hellenists,*' by whom, as they tried to kill
him, obviously the Greek-speaking Jews are meant. The
inference would then be that the disciples addressed themselves specially to their rivals, the Greek-speaking Jews at

Antioch, for it is by no means certain that the language of the majority of the Syrian Jews was Greek. There is much to be said in favour of either reading ; but upon the whole the former is more probably correct.

The **church** in **Jerusalem** acts in precisely the same manner in sending Barnabas to Antioch as it had done when it sent Peter and John to the city of the Samaritans (viii. 14). In Christian tradition the vigilance of the authorities of Jerusalem is seen in the way James, ' the bishop of Jerusalem,' superintends Peter's work in the Clementine romances. The amiable character of Barnabas is recognized by Luke (for the sense in which the word **good** is here used see Rom. v. 7). **Barnabas** indeed is one of the most attractive characters in the New Testament. He possessed the rare gift of discerning merit in others. Probably inferior in ability to Paul, he was his superior in Christian graces. He seems to have been utterly without jealousy, eager to excuse the faults of others, quick to recognize merit, ready to compromise for the sake of peace. Paul's elevation of character makes him scarcely human, whilst the virtues of Barnabas make him singularly lovable. The Paul of history contributes to the progress of the world, Barnabas and those like him make it endurable to live in. Whilst we admit the greatness of Paul, we cannot forget that Barnabas was the real pioneer of a world-embracing Christianity. The year Barnabas and Saul spent at Antioch resulted in the permanent establishment of that important Church, which became so well known that the inhabitants called its members **Christians.**

One cannot help recalling the fact that Claudius is said later to have expelled the Jews for their constant tumults about Chrestus. This verse may possibly throw light upon the date of Acts, for evidently it was already the common name for the believers, and had been adopted by themselves, as it never was in the New Testament, where it is only used twice elsewhere in the half-jesting words of Agrippa II to Paul (see Acts xxvi. 28 and in 1 Pet. iv. 16 : ' If any of you suffer as (on the charge of being) a Christian,' when the writer uses the word from the standpoint of the Roman law). By the beginning of the second century the Christians called themselves as such with pride.

The word rendered **were called** is used in different senses in the New Testament. Rendered literally it might mean ' transacted business ' under the name of Christians, i.e. were ' commonly known ' henceforward as such. The verse marks the conclusion of a section of the book, and the term Christian makes an impressive finale. Henceforward the records of the brotherhood of believers in Jesus become the history of Christianity.

During these days some prophets came down from Jerusalem 27 to Antioch, one of whom, named Agabus, showed by the 28 Spirit that a severe famine was about to visit the whole world (the famine which occurred in the reign of Claudius). So the disciples put aside money, as each of them was able 29 to afford it, for a contribution to be sent to the brothers in Judaea. This they carried out, sending their contribution 30 to the presbyters by Barnabas and Saul.

The vexed question of the different visits of St. Paul to Jerusalem will be discussed under chap. xv. : here it is enough to say that this is the second recorded in Acts, the first being some time after his conversion (ix. 26). The other points of interest in this passage are : (1) Christian prophecy, and (2) the famine.

(1) In the first book of the Maccabees it is assumed that prophecy had ceased, and that Israel was awaiting the guidance of a faithful prophet (1 Macc. iv. 46, ix. 27, xiv. 41). All direct communication between God and man was considered to be at an end, and if a man felt he had seen a vision, he promulgated his message under the name of some prophet or seer of ancient days ; the Law and its interpreters had taken the place of prophecy. But in the first century of our era the prophets began to reappear. The Baptist was acknowledged to be one ; Jesus was saluted by the people as ' the prophet of Nazareth ' ; impostors arose who claimed to be prophets ; in the Church the prophet ranked next to the Apostle. **Agabus** belonged to this prophetic ministry, and on another occasion

acted in the same symbolic manner as the prophets in the O.T., binding his own hands and feet as a token that Paul would suffer this at Jerusalem (Acts xxi. 11).

(2) He arose in the Christian assembly, and signified that there would be a famine throughout the world, and his prophecy was fulfilled **in the reign of Claudius,** i.e. after A.D. 41. This might imply that Claudius was not emperor when the prophecy was made. But it does not seem necessary to raise perplexities about details where the entire episode is so confusing. All we know is that there were periods of scarcity in the reign of Claudius ; but there is no record of a world-wide famine, such as Luke implies by his use of the word, the same as he uses in describing the edict of Augustus (Luke ii. 1). Josephus relates that there was a famine in Jerusalem when Tiberius Alexander was procurator, and that the poor were relieved by the generosity of Queen Helena of Adiabene. This would be after the death of Agrippa I in A.D. 44, probably about A.D. 48. But according to this section of Acts Barnabas and Saul must have been sent to Jerusalem before or at the time of Agrippa's persecution, A.D. 43–44, the account of which is given in Acts as an interlude between xi. 30 and xii. 25.

There is one point which appears to have been generally overlooked, namely, that in this account of the so-called 'famine visit' Jerusalem is never mentioned except very obscurely in xii. 25 (Barnabas and Saul returned *to* Jerusalem). Now Barnabas and Saul were not sent to Jerusalem, but to Judaea, which in the language of Luke may not always mean even the province, but Jewish Palestine (Luke iv. 44). Those who had been dispersed by the persecution about Stephen had been specially active in preaching along the sea-coast of Judaea ; and those who had reached Antioch would be naturally eager to assist those whom they themselves had converted. The choice of **Saul** to accompany **Barnabas** with the contribution appears strange to us, as he was not likely to be popular in Jerusalem, nor had he taken any active part, so far as we know, in preaching in Judaea.

But apart from all conjecture this notice of the famine and the mission of Barnabas and Saul appears to be an interruption in the general tenor of the narrative. The fitting climax of chap. xi. would be that the disciples were called Christians. Chap. xii. would introduce a fresh topic. It would appear that Luke's object was to assure Theophilus of the harmony at this time existing between Antioch and Jerusalem. He was well aware of the intense interest Paul took later in collecting money for ' the poor saints,' and desired to emphasize it at this point of his history.

The western text has a curious addition to vers. 27–28, reading as follows : ' In those days prophets came down from Jerusalem to Antioch, and there was great exultation, and when we were assembled one of them by name Agabus said,' etc. The possibility of this being a " we " section, and that Luke himself was present on the occasion, has attraction for some (cf. xiv. 22, where the first person plural also occurs). Even assuming, however, that the doubtful reading here is original, neither it nor the ' we ' in xiv. 22 would prove the presence of the author of Acts.

xii.

It was about that time that king Herod laid hands of violence 1 on some members of the church. James the brother of 2 John he slew with the sword, and when he saw this pleased 3 the Jews, he went on to seize Peter. (This was during the days of unleavened bread.) After arresting him he put 4 him in prison, handing him over to a guard of sixteen soldiers, with the intention of producing him to the People after the Passover.

The circumstances related in this chapter are curious and not easy to account for. No explanation is given as to why the persecution of the Church took place, nor how it was that **James the brother of John** was selected for execution. Luke was evidently not well informed on this point, or he was prevented from enlarging upon the death of the first of the Twelve to suffer martyrdom. Strangely enough Matthew and Mark, but not Luke, record the saying of Jesus that James and John the sons of Zebedee should drink of his cup and be baptized with his baptism (Matt. xx. 20, Mark x. 35). The eastern church has perhaps preserved a dim tradition that James and John were martyred together, as in its calendar December 26 is the festival of James and John, whereas in the western John the Divine alone is celebrated on the day following the Saviour's birth. Much as we may desire to know how the protomartyr of the Twelve laid down his life, we have to be satisfied with what the historian has seen fit to tell Theophilus.

From what, however, we learn from Josephus and Philo regarding **Herod** the **king,** the story in this chapter is not surprising. Herod Agrippa, the son of Aristobulus, whom his grandfather, Herod the Great, had put to death in 6 B.C., was brought up in the highest Roman society, and was an intimate friend of Drusus, the son of Tiberius. As a young man he was extravagant and dissipated, and his career was long that of an impecunious adventurer. Tiberius, a very shrewd observer, never trusted Agrippa, whose rise to power and wealth did not begin till the death of the old emperor. Agrippa helped Caligula to succeed Tiberius in the principate, and received the title of king in reward for this service. When Caligula was killed in A.D. 41, Agrippa supported the election of Claudius, by whom he was given practically the whole inheritance of Herod the Great. This Herod, though he spent some time in his northern dominions, preferred to live in Jerusalem, and both Josephus and the later rabbis agree that he did all he could to make himself popular in the city, endeavouring to enclose the northern suburbs by a wall. When a man named Simon tried to exclude the king from the Temple on the ground that he was not a genuine Jew, Agrippa treated him with great moderation (*Antiq.*, xix. 7. 3). The rabbinical tradition is that Agrippa was unwilling to enter the Temple because of his Edomite origin, but that the crowd exclaimed, ' Thou art our brother.' This shews that he was by some regarded as an alien, and that he was exceedingly anxious to be regarded with favour as a most scrupulous Jew. That he should have killed a prominent disciple of Jesus, and have arrested Peter because he saw that **it pleased the Jews,** is by no means improbable.

So Peter was closely guarded in prison, while earnest prayer 5
for him was offered to God by the church. The very 6
night before Herod meant to have him produced, Peter
lay asleep between two soldiers ; he was fastened by two
chains, and sentries in front of the door guarded the prison.
But an angel of the Lord flashed on him, and a light shone 7
in the cell; striking Peter on the side he woke him, saying,
"Quick, get up ! " The fetters dropped from his hands,
and the angel said to him, " Gird yourself and put on your 8
sandals." He did so. Then said the angel, "Put on
your coat and follow me." And he followed him out, not 9
realizing that what the angel did was real, but imagining
that he saw a vision. When they had passed the first 10
guard and the second they came to the iron gate leading
into the city, which opened to them of its own accord;
they passed out, and after they had gone through one
street, the angel immediately left him. Then Peter came 11
to his senses and said, " Now I know for certain that the
Lord has sent his angel and rescued me from the hands of
Herod and from all that the Jewish people were anticipat-
ing." When he grasped the situation, he went to the 12
house of Mary, the mother of John who was surnamed
Mark, where a number had met for prayer. When he 13
knocked at the door of the porch, a maidservant called
Rhoda came to answer it; but as soon as she recognized 14
Peter's voice, instead of opening the door she ran inside
from sheer joy and announced that Peter was standing
in front of the porch. " You are mad," they said. But 15
she insisted it was true. " It is his angel," they said. But 16
Peter kept on knocking, and when they opened the door
they were amazed to see him. He beckoned to them to 17
keep quiet and then described to them how the Lord had
brought him out of prison. " Report this to James," he
said, " and to the brothers." And off he went to another
place.

If the story of the martyrdom of James is only just touched upon, that of the miraculous deliverance of Peter is related in some detail, and seems to shew some knowledge of the city of Jerusalem.[1]   It has been suggested that **the house of Mary** was the *Cenaculum*, where the Last Supper was held, or it may have been the upper room where the Apostles assembled after the Ascension (Acts i. 13).   The traditional scene of the Supper is in the southern part of the modern city.   It is, however, strange that none of the Twelve is mentioned as being in the house of Mary the mother of John ; and we do not again hear of the college of the Apostles in Acts, nor is there any explanation of its disappearance.

The fact is, the entire personnel of the Jerusalem church seems to have changed since the scenes described in Acts i–vi. There is a circle of disciples who seem to have met in **the house of Mary,** presumably a roomy building with a **porch** like that of the palace of the high-priest, in which a girl was stationed at the door to announce visitors.   We find a similar arrangement in 2 Sam. iv. 6 (according to the LXX version), where the porteress is represented as falling asleep, so that the murderers of King Ish-bosheth were able to steal in un-observed.   The leader of the Church now seems to be **James,** who appears without a word of introduction as the head of the brethren.   This James is evidently the same as the ' James the Lord's brother ' of St. Paul, and ' James the brother of Jesus called Christ ' of Josephus.   The episode of the persecu-tion of Herod Agrippa is most difficult to account for or to explain in connexion with the events recorded in Acts, and it is one from which an attempt to draw inferences is, to say the least, precarious.   Of one thing alone can we be certain, namely, that here for the first time in Acts we have a definite date, as Agrippa died in A.D. 44.   From this time Peter vanishes from the scene only to reappear, except in Acts xv., as a somewhat shadowy figure, and again in the Pauline epistles, usually under the name of Cephas (1 Cor. i. 12, iii. 22, ix. 5, xv. 5 ; Gal. i. 18, ii. 9, 11, 14).

[1] After *of its own accord* (in ver. 10) W reads : ' And going out they went down the seven steps leading to the city.'

Now when day broke there was a great commotion among 18
the soldiers over what could have become of Peter.   Herod 19
made inquiries for him but could not find him; so, after
cross-examining the guards, he ordered them off to death.
He then went down from Judaea to Caesarea, where he
spent some time.   As there was a bitter feud between him 20
and the inhabitants of Tyre and Sidon, they waited on him
unanimously and after conciliating the royal chamberlain
Blastus they made overtures for peace, as their country
depended for its food-supply upon the royal territory.
On a stated day Herod arrayed himself in royal robes, 21
took his seat on the dais, and proceeded to harangue
them.[1]   The populace shouted, " It is a god's voice, not a 22
man's ! " and in a moment an angel of the Lord struck 23
him, because he had not given due glory to God; he was
eaten up by worms and so expired.

The word of God spread and multiplied.   24

After fulfilling their commission, Barnabas and Saul returned 25
from Jerusalem, bringing with them John who is surnamed
Mark.

The death of Herod Agrippa is thus related by Josephus :
the king went to Caesarea, which used to be known as Strato's
Tower, and gave a splendid spectacle in honour of Caesar, at
which all the chief personages were present.   On the second
day of the show Herod put on a marvellously woven robe of
silver, which shone wondrously when the rays of the rising
sun caught it.   Thereupon his flatterers cried out, ' Be pro-
pitious ; if we reverenced thee hitherto as a man, from henceforth we acknowledge thee to be more than mortal.'   The
king did not rebuke them, but as he looked up he saw an owl
sitting on a rope, and realized that the bird which had once
been a messenger of good fortune to him now foretold evil.
He was seized with violent internal pains, and told his friends
that he, whom they had saluted as a god, was now about to
depart from life.   He lingered in agony for five days, and died,

---

[1] W adds: He being reconciled to the Tyrians.'   See Ropes's note
on this verse in *Beginnings of Christianity*, iii. 114.

to the great grief of his countrymen, at Caesarea (*Antiq.*, xix. 8. 2). Both the details of the story and the language in which it is related by Luke and Josephus differ, and there is hardly any resemblance between them, with the possible exception of the robe worn by Herod. That one account should depend on the other is hardly credible. The main fact which underlies both, viz. that Agrippa was taken suddenly ill at an important gathering at Caesarea, when the audience with true Oriental flattery acclaimed him as a god, is certain. But the mention of **Blastus** points to an independent source on the part of Luke, whilst the quarrel with Tyre and Sidon is said to have been composed by the submission of the two cities, because they depended on Galilee for their food-supply. That they had done so for centuries is seen in the treaty concluded between Solomon and Hiram (1 Kings vii.). Josephus does not mention this, nor does Luke hint that the display given by Agrippa at Caesarea must have been a heathen one, resembling that described just before at Berytus, where fourteen hundred criminals were made to murder one another, ' in order that they might receive due punishment, and that the peaceful spectators might enjoy a warlike spectacle ' (Josephus, *Antiq.*, xix. 7. 5 and 8. 2). But even the pagan proclivities of Herod did not, as Josephus declares, hinder the Greeks and Syrians from receiving the news of his death with indecent expressions of joy. The disgusting circumstances of Agrippa's death find their counterpart in the account (in 2 Macc. ix. 9) of the fatal illness of Antiochus Epiphanes. Josephus relates much the same of the last days of Herod the Great (*Antiq.*, xvii. 6. 5).

Ver. 24 is the last notice of the progress of the Church, and ver. 25 either belongs to xi. 30 or should commence chap. xiii. The best-supported reading is ' **Barnabas and Saul returned** *to* **Jerusalem**,' which is fatal to the sense of the passage.

xiii.

1 Now in the local church at Antioch there were prophets and teachers, Barnabas, Symeon (called Niger) and Lucius

the Cyrenian, besides Manaen (a foster-brother of Herod
the tetrarch) and Saul. As they were worshipping the 2
Lord and fasting, the holy Spirit said, " Come! set me
apart Barnabas and Saul for the work to which I have
called them." Then after fasting and praying they laid 3
their hands on them and let them go.

Sent out thus by the holy Spirit, they went down to Seleucia 4
and from there they sailed to Cyprus. On reaching 5
Salamis they proclaimed the word of God in the Jewish
synagogues, with John as their assistant.

This is the first mention in Acts of a **local church** with the
possible exception of ix. 31. The community of believers is
represented as an organized body, called by the Gentiles
' Christians,' as a Church distinguished from the Synagogue.
Its leaders are **prophets and teachers.** In chap. xi. 27 it is said
that a prophet came to Antioch from Jerusalem to foretell the
great famine ; but this is the first and only mention of prophets and teachers as recognized ministers (see, however,
I Cor. xii. 28, Eph. iv. 11). The only other Christian prophets named in Acts are Judas and Silas (xv. 32) and Agabus
(xxi. 10), all of whom belonged to the church at Jerusalem.
The word **teacher** is never found elsewhere in Acts. It would
appear as though here Luke was desirous of shewing that the
Christians at Antioch took the momentous step of sending
forth **Barnabus and Saul** by the direct authority of the holy
Spirit ; but it must be remembered that everyone who spoke
or acted under his influence was *ipso facto* a prophet. Of the
five prophets here mentioned, the activity of Barnabas in
Antioch is well known, and, despite the general tradition, he
may perhaps be the real founder of that famous church. Of
Symeon Niger and **Lucius** of Cyrene nothing further is recorded,
although it should be noted that Cyrenian believers had
already preached in Cyprus, and had addressed themselves
to the Hellenes at Antioch (xi. 19-20). **Manaen** was a name
connected with the family of Herod. An Essene so-called
had predicted to Herod the Great as a child that he would be
king of the Jews. Luke was evidently well informed about

the Herod family, and the connexions of its dependents with Jesus and his followers.

The word used for **worshipping** (λειτουργεῖν) is interesting. In Athens it signified the discharge of some costly public duty, such as equipping a ship or furnishing a theatrical exhibition for the public. In the LXX it is used of the duties of a priest serving in the sanctuary, and also of the discharge of the great religious duty of caring for the poor. In the Church the ' Liturgy ' came to signify the service of the Eucharist, hence the Missal is called ' the Divine Liturgy,' and the Breviary, or service book of the hours, ' the Divine Office.' The prophets and teachers of Antioch were called to **set apart Barnabas and Saul** at the time of some solemn period of devotion. The particle after the imperative **set apart** is designed to shew that the command was emphatic. Prayer and fasting are assumed in the early church to be well-nigh inseparable, though there is in the gospel good MS. evidence for the omission of the word fasting in Matt. xvii. 21, Mark ix. 29. The conjunction of the two is only once found in the Pauline epistles (1 Cor. vii. 5— a doubtful reading). The purpose of laying on of hands was here not ordination, but entrusting with a special commission (cf. Acts vi. 6). The gift of the Spirit follows the apostolic laying on of hands in vii. 17, xix. 6.

Antioch is not on the sea ; and the missionaries **went down to Seleucia** in order to embark for **Cyprus**, the native place of Barnabas, largely inhabited by Jews. There were fifteen important cities in the island, but nothing is told us of the work of the Apostles till they reached Paphos. **John** a kinsman of Barnabas (Col. iv. 10) came in a subordinate position. It seems to have been customary, in accordance with gospel precedent, for Christian preachers to travel in pairs, e.g. Peter and John, Paul and Barnabas, Paul and Silas, and for them to be accompanied by some younger men. Timothy, who joined Paul and Silas, is the exact counterpart of John Mark (Acts xvi. 1).

6 They covered the whole island as far as Paphos, where they fell in with a Jewish sorcerer and false prophet called Bar-

Jesus ; he belonged to the suite of the proconsul Sergius 7
Paulus, an intelligent man who called for Barnabas and
Saul and demanded to hear the word of God. But the 8
sorcerer Elymas (for that is the translation of his name)
tried to divert the proconsul from the faith. So Saul (who 9
is also called Paul), filled with the holy Spirit, looked 10
steadily at him and said, "You son of the devil, you
enemy of all good, full of all craft and all cunning, will you
never stop diverting *the straight paths of the Lord ?* See 11
here, the Lord's hand will fall on you, and you will be
blind, unable for a time to see the sun." In a moment a
dark mist fell upon him, and he groped about for someone
to take him by the hand. Then the proconsul believed, 12
when he saw what had happened ; he was astounded at
the doctrine of the Lord.

Paphos, the new as distinguished from the old city, was at
the western end of Cyprus, and apparently the seat of the
government. All commentators note that Luke is accurate
in describing **Sergius Paulus** by his correct title **proconsul,**[1]
especially as Augustus had comparatively recently transferred
Cyprus to the Senate. It is quite in keeping with what is
known of Roman life that **Sergius Paulus** should have a learned
Jew attached to him, and that **Bar-Jesus** should have been a
Magus or **Sorcerer**—one who combined his ' philosophy ' (for
so it would be called) with the exercise of magic or divination.
The difficulty is to discover the meaning of Luke in this
passage. Is there any real parallelism between Peter's contest
between Simon Magus in chap. viii. and Paul's with **Elymas ?**
Simon Magus was a magician whose miracles had made the
people of the city of Samaria declare that he was in some sense
divine. After his baptism he regarded Peter and John as
fellow-magicians, and offered to buy their secret of bestowing
the Spirit. Paul met similar rivals in the sons of Sceva

---

[1] In the A.V. the Greek work for proconsul ($\dot{a}\nu\theta\dot{v}\pi a\tau os$ = ' instead
of the highest ') is rendered *deputy*. In the seventeenth century
this word was used for a representative of the sovereign—e.g. the
' Lord Deputy of the North ' and the ' Lord Deputy of Ireland.'

(xix. 13). But **Bar-Jesus** or **Elymas** did not pose as a rival magician ; he claimed to be a prophet.

Barnabas and Saul had been sent to Cyprus as prophets by their fellow-prophets (xiii. 1). They traversed Cyprus, prophesying in the synagogues that Christ had come. Apparently they were unmolested, as, even if they baptized their converts, that would not separate them from the rest of their Jewish brethren. At Paphos they met a rival prophet **in the suite of the proconsul,** who spoke against the message of salvation which the Apostles were delivering. Thus their opponent is described as a **false prophet.** He is also called a **sorcerer** or worker of magic, but nothing is said of his trying to dissuade the proconsul by any of his arts.

Luke's manner of relation is noticeable. There was with the proconsul a false prophet named Bar-Jesus. But when it comes to the contest Luke writes, **the sorcerer Elymas (for that is the translation of his name).** No explanation is given of the change from Bar-Jesus to Elymas.

The interpretation of Elymas is also perplexing, and was evidently so to the compilers of the western texts, which, with some of the Latin Fathers, spell the name in various ways. Is it conceivable that two distinct accounts of what happened are fused into one ; and that Barnabas and Saul may have encountered a false prophet named Bar-Jesus (not necessarily a patronymic), and also a sorcerer called Elymas or Etoimos, or something like it ? [1] The curse pronounced by Paul on his adversary resembles in some respects Peter's denunciation of Ananias ; only here the punishment is temporary blindness, resembling that of Saul after his conversion when, like Elymas, he sought someone to ' lead him by the hand.' The Venerable Bede's comment is : ' The apostle, remembering his own example, knew that from the darkness of the eye the mind's darkness might be restored to light.'

More stress perhaps was intended to be laid on the victory over the false prophet by the true prophets than on the con-

---

[1] Prof. Burkitt (*Journal of Theological Studies*, iv. 127 f.) thinks that both Elymas and Etoimos (western reading) are variants of the original ὁ λοιμός, i.e. the pestilential fellow.

version of Sergius Paulus ; for the word **believed** may mean, not that the proconsul became a Christian, but that he was convinced of the prophetic office of the Apostles. Anyhow, there is no hint in the New Testament or in Christian tradition of anything like the submission to the gospel of a man of such eminence as any governor of Cyprus must have been. Nor is it probable that Luke, who henceforth consistently uses the name of Paul, intends us to believe that the Apostle dropped his Hebrew for a Roman appellation. The purpose of the change in Acts is to prepare the reader for the work of the Apostle among the Gentiles. Only in the account which Paul gives of his conversion do we find the name of Saul in the last half of Acts, and then in its Hebrew form (xxii. 7 and 13, xxvi. 14). The name Sergius Paulus occurs in the writings of Pliny the Elder, about twenty years later than Acts xiii., and also in Galen, a physician who lived in the third century A.D. The name also appears in the *Fasti* as borne by consuls. The *gens* of the more celebrated Pauli was the Aemilia. The Sergii, however, were also patricians. Sir W. Ramsay thinks there is an inscription testifying to the existence of the family of Sergius Paulus in Asia Minor, which was Christian at a later date.

Setting sail from Paphos, Paul and his companions reached 13 Perga in Pamphylia ; John left them and went back to Jerusalem, but they passed on from Perga and arrived at 14 Pisidian Antioch. On the sabbath they went into the synagogue and sat down ; and, after the reading of the 15 Law and the prophets, the president of the synagogue sent to tell them, " Brothers, if you have any word of counsel for the people, say it." So Paul stood up and motioning 16 with his hand said, " Listen, men of Israel and you who reverence God.

Luke, whether he knew the facts or not, gives us no information about the adventures of Paul and Barnabas after leaving Cyprus. He confines himself to some seventy Greek words in describing how the company of Paul took their adventurous journey into the heart of Asia Minor. The mission reached

Pamphylia, where there were many important cities on the sea-coast, but undertook no evangelistic work in that province. The only place mentioned is **Perga,** on the river Cestrus, about six miles from the sea. From the words **Paul and his companions** (οἱ περὶ τὸν Παῦλον) one may legitimately infer that Paul had become the guiding spirit of the expedition, which may have received recruits in Cyprus. The departure of **John,** who returned to **Jerusalem,** is mentioned without note or comment ; and many explanations of his action have been suggested, no one of which is entirely satisfactory. We learn, however, that Paul strongly resented Mark's desertion (xv. 38). It may be that the prospects of success in Perga were gloomy, and that there was no opening for the gospel in Pamphylia. At anyrate, Paul and Barnabas decided upon what seems to us to have been a desperate enterprise. Abandoning the settled districts they embarked on a journey across a barren and dangerous country, subject to floods from the mountain watercourses, with a bad reputation owing to the prevalence of banditry. At last they arrived at the remote Roman colony of **Pisidian Antioch.** It is possible that, despite the discomfiture of Elymas Bar-Jesus, a formidable Jewish opposition had driven them from Cyprus, and that its emissaries had aroused the prejudices of the people of Perga.

It is remarkable how little is known of the origin and worship of **the synagogue.** These Jewish places of assembly scattered throughout the civilized world are taken so much as a matter of course that such writers as Philo and Josephus rarely mention them. Our Jewish testimony to the Synagogue is comparatively late, although it is not without reason held that some of the prayers and especially the *Eighteen Benedictions* are of great antiquity. Nevertheless, Luke is the first to mention Synagogue services—one at Nazareth, where Jesus addressed the people, and the other **at Pisidian Antioch,** attended by Paul and Barnabas. Jesus, it is said, stood up to read, and was given the book of Isaiah (Luke iv. 17). Having read the passage, ' The spirit of the Lord is upon me,' etc. (Is. xli. 1), he sat down and addressed the people, expounding what he had read. Apparently at Antioch

neither Paul nor Barnabas as strangers were called upon to
read, but were invited to speak **after the reading of the Law
and the prophets.** The reading of the prophets was known as
the *haphtorah,* or ' dismissal,' and concluded the service. It is
suggested that the Apostle took the text from the scripture
lessons ; and as these are of great antiquity it is not impossible that the Sabbath day of the memorable address can
be determined. Unlike Jesus, Paul **stood up,** and with a
motion of his hand bespoke attention. Josephus (*Apion.,*
ii. 40) testifies to the popularity of the Jewish services which
many Gentiles attended on the Sabbath.

The God of this People Israel chose our fathers; he multiplied 17
the people as they sojourned in the land of Egypt and
with arm uplifted led them out of it. For about forty 18
years *he bore with them in the desert, and after destroying* 19
seven nations in the land of Canaan he gave them their
land *as an inheritance* for about four hundred and fifty
years. After that he gave them judges, down to the 20
prophet Samuel. Then it was that they begged for a king, 21
and God gave them forty years of Saul, the son of Kish,
who belonged to the tribe of Benjamin. After deposing 22
him, he raised up David to be their king, to whom he bore
this testimony that ' *In David,* the son of Jessai, *I have
found a man after my own heart,* who will obey all my will.'
From his offspring God brought to Israel, as he had 23
promised, a saviour in Jesus, before whose coming John 24
had already preached a baptism of repentance for all the
people of Israel. And as John was closing his career he 25
said, 'What do you take me for ? I am not He ; no, he is
coming after me, and I am not fit to untie the sandals
on his feet ! ' Brothers, sons of Abraham's race and all 26
among you who reverence God, *the message* of this salvation *has been sent* to us. The inhabitants of Jerusalem 27
and their rulers, by condemning him * in their ignorance,
fulfilled the words of the prophets which are read **every
sabbath**; though they could find him guilty of no crime 28

* See Note on next page.

29   that deserved death they begged Pilate to have him put to death, and, after carrying out all that had been predicted of him in scripture, they lowered him from the gibbet and
30   laid him in a tomb. But God raised him from the dead.
31   For many days he was seen by those who had come up with him from Galilee to Jerusalem ; they are now his
32   witnesses to the People. So we now preach to you the
33   glad news that the promise made to the fathers has been fulfilled by God for us their children, when he raised Jesus. As it is written in the second psalm,

> *thou art my son,*
> *to-day have I become thy father.*

34   And as a proof that he has raised him from the dead, never to return to decay, he has said this : *I will give you*
35   *the holiness of David that fails not.* Hence in another psalm he says,

> *thou wilt not let thy holy One suffer decay.*

36   Of course *David,* after serving God's purpose in his own generation, died and was laid *beside his fathers ; he* suffered
37   decay, but He whom God raised did not suffer decay.
38   So you must understand, my brothers, that remission of
39   sins is proclaimed to you through him, and that by him everyone who believes is absolved from all that the law of
40   Moses never could absolve you from. Beware then in case the prophetic saying applies to you :
41
> *Look, you disdainful folk, wonder at this and perish—*
> *for in your days I do a deed,*
> **a deed** *you will never believe, not though one were to explain it to you."*

---

* The Greek text is difficult. I prefer, as the least radical treatment, Lachmann's proposal to read κρίναντες immediately after ἀγνοήσαντες καί, which at anyrate yields a fair sense.

Whether this is a report of the actual address of Paul in the synagogue, it is of great interest as the first recorded address of the Apostle. It is certainly well suited to the audience as well as to the occasion, breathing the spirit of a very primitive Christianity. To a certain extent it follows the same line as the speech of Peter to the people on the day of Pentecost ; nevertheless, it possesses an individuality of its own. If the speech is a composition put into the mouth of Paul, there is no small skill displayed in the deft employment of Pauline phrases and ideas. In a few verses (17-22) the story of Israel is told from the Exodus from Egypt to the choice of David as king over all the nation. The keynote of this brief survey is God's mercy to Israel, the deliverance of them from captivity, His forbearance or care for them in the wilderness, and His gift of the Promised Land. Next follows the raising up of successive **judges,** the appointment of the great **prophet Samuel,** of **Saul** the king of the people's choice, and finally of **David,** whom God had specially chosen for Israel's guidance. This stress on the Davidic ancestry of Jesus is characteristic of Paul, and finds an echo in the opening words of the epistle to the Romans (Rom. i. 3). Jesus is presented as **a Saviour,** not as the Christ, and what follows is distinctly Pauline. Although Paul never mentions the Baptist in his extant epistles, the introduction of the Forerunner is here eminently appropriate. Israel must be specially prepared for the Saviour, who comes in the fullness of time. Then Paul tells of the death and resurrection of Jesus, like Peter abstaining from aggravating the guilt of the Jews and attributing their crime to **ignorance.** The witnesses of the resurrection were those who had accompanied Jesus from Galilee—and it may be observed that no one is named among those who saw the risen Lord, except his companions in the Galilean ministry. These are still proclaiming that Jesus rose from the dead. In addition there is the testimony of prophecy. Here (33-37) Paul follows Peter almost exactly in asserting that David could not possibly have referred to himself in Ps. xvi., but must have foretold that one of his descendants would never see corruption (cf. ii. 25-31).

Then (38-41) comes the message of the resurrection, followed by a solemn warning. Jesus is the source of forgiveness of sin and of reconciliation to God as the Law as given by Moses could never be (cf. John i. 17). This is the salvation now offered, and those who reject it are in danger of the doom pronounced by the prophets Isaiah and Habakkuk.

No one can fail to observe that Paul is made here to present not the more elaborate Christology of even his earliest epistles, but the primitive doctrine as declared in the speeches of Peter in the very first days of the gospel. There is no proclamation of the power of the Cross and no allusion to its atoning grace. Nothing is said of man's participation in the resurrection, and the word δικαιοσύνη is not employed in the theological sense which is attached to Paul's later use of it in connexion with ' justification.' Jesus is called **Saviour,** but the word ' Christ ' is not found, nor is he termed ' the Son of God.' The discourse is admirably suited to an audience of Jews in a remote town, to whom the facts concerning Jesus were entirely unknown, though they may have heard of the work of the Baptist. The congregation is simply informed that the Jews at Jerusalem had persuaded Pilate to crucify Jesus, whom God had raised from the dead in accordance with what his ancestor David had foretold, thus proving that the risen Jesus was the Saviour for whom Israel was looking—a Saviour, not in a political but in a spiritual sense, through faith in whom we are reconciled to God. There is no hint in this address of eschatology, on which Paul subsequently lays so much stress.

In the study of Acts the historian is constantly perplexed by the absence of chronological information. Here we have no hint as to the length of the missionary journey of Paul and Barnabas. We can only conjecture what time elapsed between their departure from Antioch and their return, when ' they rehearsed all that God had done for them ' to the church of that city (Acts xiii. 1–xiv. 28). The two chapters relating to their labours in Cyprus and Asia Minor may have even covered some years. At anyrate the sermon of Antioch was delivered long before Paul wrote to the Thessalonians ; and we know how, in his later years, the teaching of the Apostle advanced in depth under the influence of his spiritual experiences. At whatever date Acts was written, the book gives an astonishingly convincing picture of the gospel as Paul presented it in his earliest recorded utterance. His speech is not a theological statement, but a gospel of good news.

A few points are worthy of special notice in this speech.
There is an interesting difference in the reading of a single
word in ver. 18 which is also found in the MSS. of the LXX.
In Deut. i. 31 the A.V. has, ' And in the wilderness
. . . the Lord thy God bare thee, as a man doth bear his
son, in all the way that ye went.' One group of MSS. of the
LXX has ' carried them,' which is a literal rendering of the
Hebrew *nas'a* ; the other has ' Suffered their manners ' (or
moods) as the A.V. This last reading is happily rendered
bore with them. The Vulgate translates ' bore their manners.'
The western Latin text has ' carried them.' The Greek words
are almost identical, ἐτροφοφόρησεν (he carried them as a
nurse) and ἐτροποφόρησεν (bare with them). The sense of
the passage seems to require the former word better, as
Paul's meaning seems to be not that God endured the per-
versities of Israel in the wilderness, but that he shewed His
mercy by His care for the people.

**As Paul and Barnabas went out, the people begged to have all 42
this repeated to them on the following sabbath. After 43
the synagogue broke up, a number of the Jews and the
devout proselytes followed them ; Paul and Barnabas
talked to them and encouraged them to hold by the grace
of God. And on the next sabbath nearly all the town 44
gathered to hear[1] the word of the Lord. But when the 45
Jews saw the crowds they were filled with jealousy ; they
began to contradict what Paul said and to abuse him. So 46
Paul and Barnabas spoke out fearlessly. " The word of
God," they said, " had to be spoken to you in the first
instance ; but as you push it aside and judge yourselves
unworthy of eternal life, well, here we turn to the Gentiles !
For these are the Lord's orders to us:** 47
*I have set you to be a light for the Gentiles,
to bring salvation to the end of the earth."*

Luke is careful to point out that Paul's sermon caused no
opposition, but rather was universally applauded. In the

[1] After ' hear,' W reads : ' Paul ; and when he had made much
discourse about the Lord, and when the Jews,' etc.

THE ACTS OF THE APOSTLES

Hellenistic world the Jews welcomed the coming of a Messiah, and were even prepared for such doctrine as Paul had preached. What seems to have provoked them was the interest which the new gospel was arousing among the Gentiles. The conjunction of the words **devout proselytes** is unique in Acts. From the fact that there were three classes of auditors in a synagogue—Jews, proselytes, and worshippers of Jehovah who were still outside the pale of Judaism—there has been a tendency to include the σεβόμενοι or ' devout ' with the non-Jewish worshipper. But in Acts it would seem that the words ' devout ' and ' proselyte ' were interchangeable. Lydia (xvi. 14) and Titius Justus (xviii. 7) are described as ' devout,' but were almost certainly proselytes. The ' devout and honourable women ' in xiii. 50 may have been Gentile sympathizers. Those described at Thessalonica as ' devout ' (xvii. 4) may well have been proselytes. The only use, even of the kindred verb, outside Acts is in the parallel passages (Matt. xv. 9 and Mark vii. 7), when our Lord is quoting Is. xix. 13. Pisidian Antioch had apparently only one synagogue ; but, as at Tiberias (according to Josephus), it may have been a large building capable of containing many of the inhabitants of a small city.

48 When the Gentiles heard this they rejoiced and glorified [1] the word of the Lord and believed, that is, all who had been
49 ordained to eternal life; and the word of the Lord went far
50 and wide over the whole country. But the Jews incited the devout women of high rank and the leading men in the town, who stirred up persecution against Paul and Barnabas
51 and drove them out of their territory. They shook the
52 dust off their feet as a protest and went to Iconium. As for the disciples, they were filled with joy and the holy Spirit.

Without insisting upon all the logical conclusions of the theory of predestination, it cannot be denied that something of the kind is implied in the Old Testament as well as in the New. The prophets taught that if Israel was to be punished as

[1] W reads ' received.'

a nation there was always a ' remnant ' of those who had not
shared in the national apostasy.   These would undoubtedly
be delivered from the coming wrath.   In like manner those who
accepted the gospel were enrolled among the few who were
destined or **ordained to eternal life.**   It is evident that
Pisidian Antioch was the centre of a widespread evangelization of the district by **Paul and Barnabas,** who may have
stayed there some time.   The Jews cannot have been numerous in the little city, as they had to persuade the ladies and
the Gentile rulers that the new teaching was pernicious and
might disturb the peace ; in this way they procured the dismissal of the Apostles.

The fourteenth chapter tells experiences of Christian
missionary work entirely different from those related elsewhere
in Acts.   All the other adventures of the Apostles are in
Jerusalem and in the larger cities.   Paul, for example, afterwards takes ship at one of the great ports, and goes along the
high-roads of the Empire from one important city to another.
As a rule he meets with persecution, but he is not exposed to
disorderly violence.   Where the magistrates are unjust, he is
able to claim the privileges of a Roman citizen.   At Corinth
he teaches in a private house, at Ephesus he hires a lecture-
room.   He selects a great city as a suitable strategic base for
a missionary campaign.   His adventures and perils are many,
but they are those which any advocate of an unpopular cause
might experience in a civilized country ; they resemble to a
certain degree those of the Wesleys in eighteenth-century
England.   But in this chapter the scene is laid in a semi-
barbarous land with towns few and far apart.   The preachers
labour at evangelizing rural districts, places perhaps where it
was not always easy to communicate with people in Greek.
They have to deal with the people of a thinly populated
country, often to escape from furious mobs and conceal themselves as best they could.   There may be something to be said
for the once accepted theory that Paul made a similar missionary journey into the wilder parts of Northern Galatia,
and worked, not among the Greek-speaking people of that

province, but among the Celts, after whom it was called.
Anyhow, Acts xiv. tells us but too briefly of adventures in a
wilder and more romantic atmosphere than is described
elsewhere in the book.

xiv.

1 At Iconium the same thing happened. They went into the
synagogue of the Jews and spoke in such a way that a
3 great body of Jews and Greeks believed. Here they spent
a considerable time, speaking fearlessly about the Lord,
who attested the word of his grace by allowing signs and
2 wonders to be performed by them.* But the refractory
Jews stirred up and exasperated the feeling of the Gentiles
4 against the brothers. The populace of the town was
divided ; some sided with the Jews, some with the apostles.
5 But, when the Gentiles and Jews along with their rulers
6 made a hostile movement to insult and stone them, the
apostles grasped the situation and escaped to the Lycaonian
towns of Lystra and Derbe and to the surrounding country;
7 there they continued to preach the gospel.

* Restoring ver. 3 to what appears to have been its original position
between vers. 1 and 2.

The meaning of the passage is upon the whole plain,
although the first sentence in this translation warns us that
the correct rendering of the Greek is not easy. The A.V.
has, ' And it came to pass that they went both together.' All
the MSS. have practically the same Greek words. These can
be translated in different ways, none of which appears to be
entirely satisfactory. Taken in order the words in English
are, ' It happened in Iconium *according to the same* that
they entered the synagogue.' The Greek of the expression
in italics is κατὰ τὸ αὐτὸ εἰσελθεῖν. The A.V. takes it to
mean ' together ' perhaps in view of Acts iii. 1 (' Now Peter
and John went up together,' ἐπὶ τὸ αὐτὸ ; but these last words
may be added to the concluding verse of chap. ii., as has been
already indicated. A third rendering has also been suggested :
' At Iconium in the same way they (W reads ' he ') went,' etc.

If this is permissible, it would mean that Paul and Barnabas did here exactly what they had done in Pisidian Antioch : they began by entering the synagogue. It is true that they had formally declared that their mission was henceforth to the Gentiles ; nevertheless, they now did as they had done previously and offered the gospel first in the Jewish synagogue (so cf. xvii. 2, where Paul ' as he was accustomed ' went first to the synagogue at Thessalonica).

The A.V. has ' unbelieving,' the R.V. ' disobedient ' for what is here rendered **refractory**. The word means not to ' disbelieve ' but to ' disobey.' The sense seems to be, ' The Jews who refused to submit to the gospel, as delivered by Paul and Barnabas.' The many changes in the western text have the appearance of being made by some who saw the difficulties involved in the passage, and tried to smoothe them over thus : ' But the synagogue rulers of the Jews and the chief men of the synagogue brought persecution against the just men, and exasperated the souls of the Gentiles against the brethren. However, the Lord soon gave peace.' The apparent inconsistency in the narrative which has here suggested a transposition of vers. 2 and 3 is thus avoided. According to this reading, the first preaching **at Iconium** was a success, and instantly aroused the jealousy of the more prominent Jews. But these could not prevail, and the mission was able to preach and work miracles unmolested, till the city was openly divided into two parties. As the situation had then become intolerable, the authorities resolved to have recourse to violence. Who the **rulers** were, whether of the synagogue, or of the city, or of both, is left uncertain, but it is highly improbable that they could have inflicted on Jewish visitors the terrible penalty of stoning. It would seem therefore that Paul and Barnabas got wind of a plot to insult and pelt them, and that they deemed it wise to withdraw. The Jews later made one conspiracy to kill Paul at Jerusalem (xxiii. 12), and another when they tried to induce Festus to send him from Caesarea to be tried by the Sanhedrin (xxv. 3).

The word **apostles** in this section (vers. 4 and 6) is remarkable. Elsewhere in Acts it is only used of the Twelve, or of the leaders of the church of Jerusalem in conjunction with the Elders (xv. *passim*). In his epistles Paul claims he was an Apostle in the fullest sense of the word. Here the title may mean no more than Paul and Barnabas were missionaries sent forth by the church at Antioch (2 Cor. viii. 23).

This difficult little section may assist in part to solve the question as to how Acts was written. Luke was evidently not an eye-witness of what had happened at Iconium, but he may have relied on documentary evidence or have obtained his information direct from Paul. At anyrate he had to condense into a few lines an account of events extending over a considerable period. Everyone who has had experience of historical composition knows that this is a hard task. In attempting to be brief, one is apt to become confused, and often to condense the narrative at the expense of its grammatical construction. It would not be difficult to find similar flaws in many masterly books, and it is no disparagement to Luke to suggest that he may have occasionally, in a comparatively unimportant section like this, expressed himself with some lack of clarity.

The impression produced by Paul at Iconium was deep and possibly more lasting than elsewhere in Asia Minor. In Perga, Troas, even in Ephesus, few if any traditions of the Apostle have survived ; but Iconium is the scene of one of the most graphic legends of the Apostle, that of Paul and the virgin Thecla. The so-called 'Acts of Paul' was the work of a Christian priest in Asia Minor who was, according to Tertullian, deposed about A.D. 160 for writing it (*De Baptismo*, c. 17). Although the story is a species of Christian novel, there are real traits in it, notably the description of Paul's personal appearance : ' A man little of stature, thin haired upon the head, crooked in the legs, of good state of body, with eyebrows joining, and a nose somewhat crooked, full of grace, for sometimes he appeared like a man, and sometimes had the face of an angel.' This points to the fact of a real tradition of the Apostle having survived in Asia Minor. The Apostle is supposed to be escaping from Pisidian Antioch (xiii.) ; nevertheless, he reaches Iconium by the road leading to Lystra.

At Lystra there was a man sitting, who was powerless in his 8
feet, a lame man unable to walk ever since he was born.
He heard Paul speaking, and Paul, gazing steadily at him 9
and noticing that he had faith *enough to make him better,*
said in a loud voice, " Stand erect on your feet." Up he 10
jumped and began to walk. Now when the crowds saw 11
what Paul had done, they shouted in the Lycaonian
language, " The gods have come down to us in human
form! " Barnabas they called Zeus, and Paul Hermes, 12
since he was the chief spokesman. Indeed the priest of 13
the temple of Zeus in front of the town brought oxen and
garlands to the gates, intending to offer sacrifices along
with the crowds. But when the apostles, Paul and 14
Barnabas, heard this they rent their clothes and sprang out
among the crowd, shouting, " Men, what is this you are 15
doing ? We are but human with natures like your own!
The gospel we are preaching to you is to turn from such
futile ways to the living God *who made the heaven, the
earth, the sea, and all that in them is.* In bygone ages he 16
allowed all nations to go their own ways, though as the 17
bountiful Giver he did not leave himself without a witness,
giving you rain from heaven and fruitful seasons, giving
you food and joy to your heart's content." Even by 18
saying this it was all they could do to keep the crowds
from sacrificing to them.

The healing of a lame man **at Lystra** [1] has been compared
with the miracle by Peter and John at the Beautiful Gate of
the temple told in Acts iii. In accounts of restoring lame and
blind persons in the New Testament sometimes stress is laid
on the fact that they were born in that condition. Thus in
John ix. the man healed by our Lord was ' blind from his
birth,' and the lame man in John v. had not walked for thirty-
eight years. Both the cripples in chap. iii. and here were lame
' from their mother's womb.' The object in relating these
miracles is to shew that the disease was beyond the power

---

[1] W has a few touches of vividness, like ' and was in fear ' after
' speaking ' (ver. 9), and ' immediately ' after ' jumped up ' (ver. 10).

of man to cure, and also that the cure was complete. The patient did not merely get better, but was perfectly restored to health (iii. 16). The co-operation of faith naturally aids the cure—and here it is implied that the cripple had become a convert—but this is the only instance in the New Testament of faith being required of the patient, unless we include those who pray Jesus to cure them. When the Master demands or commends the faith of the petitioner, it is when he asks help for another person (the paralytic in Mark ii. 5 ; the centurion in Matt. viii. and Luke vii. ; the Syro-Phoenician woman in Mark vii. 26 ; the father of the epileptic boy in Mark ix. 24, etc.). Paul and Barnabas must already have been known in Lystra, since they had evidently been engaged in evangelizing the country for some time.[1] The miracle evidently convinced the people that these visitors were more than mortal. We are reminded of the beautiful story of Baucis and Philemon, the aged couple whom Zeus and Hermes visited in Phrygia, and to whom they granted as a favour that neither should survive the other (Ovid, *Met.*, viii. 620–724).

It is often said that **Barnabas** was thought to be **Zeus** because of his more dignified appearance ; but we may be content with Luke's explanation that Paul was recognized as **Hermes** because he acted as **spokesman.** Hermes was the recognized interpreter of the gods, in whose name he spoke to men. For the readiness of the heathen to acclaim a man who worked wonders as a god cf. xxviii. 6.

The attempted sacrifice seems to have been a unique experience in the apostolic missions. But the belief that a strange visitor might be a god was by no means unnatural. It has been suggested that the lame man may have been placed at the entrance of **the temple of Zeus** to attract the sympathy of the worshippers, as the cripple in chap. iii. had been at the Beautiful Gate of the Temple. This would amply account for the action of **the priest.** Seeing the man healed in this marvellous manner, it would be assumed that Zeus, with Hermes as his angel, had actually visited his own shrine and worked a miracle of salvation. If what is related took place

[1] W adds, after ver. 7, ' But Paul and Barnabas stayed at Lystra.'

outside the city walls, it is not difficult to imagine what occurred. The shout with which the crowd acclaimed the presence of the gods, unintelligible to the Apostles, would have summoned the priests of the Temple to make instant preparations for the sacrifice, and **the apostles, Paul and Barnabas,** would suddenly discover that the preparations were being made in their honour. That they did not understand the meaning of the frenzied cries of the people is a proof that the gift of tongues was not taken in the later sense that the first preachers were able to communicate with their converts in any language, although the Lycaonians were able to understand them when they spoke Greek. This is a testimony to the fact that many local languages survived in Asia Minor.

St. Jerome, who seems to have possessed remarkable linguistic ability, noticed that the Galatians of Ancyra spoke a language almost similar to that of the Teviri in Gaul. (Stephen of Byzantium, a fifth- or sixth-century writer on geography, says that Derbe was called in Lycaonian Delbe, which means a juniper.) The impassioned disclaimer of Paul and Barnabas as they rushed with their clothes rent to protest against the sacrifice cannot be regarded as one of the speeches in Acts, yet it is of much interest as revealing the sort of argument used to uneducated heathen. As was customary in later times, the preachers' first object must have been to impress their hearers with the truth that God the Creator ought to be the sole object of worship. To the Jews, the message was that Jesus is the Christ ; to the Gentiles, that God is One. God had permitted men for a while to forget this truth (see xvii. 30). At the same time God has never left Himself **without a witness,** since His benevolence and His greatness are revealed in creation (Rom. i. 19, 20). This appeal to natural religion is constantly made by the first preachers of the gospel ; and vers. 15–17 are in themselves an epitome of the earliest method of approach to heathen audiences.

But[1] **Jews from Antioch and Iconium arrived, who won over** 19
      the crowds, and after pelting Paul with stones they

---

[1] W inserts, ' whilst they tarried there and were teaching.'

dragged him outside the town, thinking he was dead.

20 However, as the disciples gathered round him, he got up and went into the town.

21 Next day he went off with Barnabas to Derbe, and after preaching the gospel to that town and making a number of disciples, they turned back to Lystra, Iconium and Antioch,

22 strengthening the souls of the disciples, encouraging them to hold by the faith, and telling them that "we have to get into the Realm of God through many a trouble."

23 They chose presbyters for them in every church, and with prayer and fasting entrusted them to the Lord in whom

24 they had believed. Then they came through Pisidia to

25 Pamphylia, and after speaking the word of the Lord in

26 Perga they went down to Attaleia; thence they sailed for Antioch, where they had been commended to the

27 grace of God for the work they had now completed. On their arrival they gathered the church together and reported how God had been with them, what he had done, and how he had opened a door into faith for the Gentiles.

28 They spent a considerable time with the disciples there.

Lystra was at this time a Roman colony like Philippi, and it may be here noted that, as at Philippi, Paul's troubles were due to one of his few specifically recorded miracles (xvi. 16–23). At both places there seem to have been very few Jews, and the Gentiles (at Lystra instigated by the Jews) seem to have been the aggressors. That the 'stoning' which Paul underwent was the Jewish penalty is scarcely credible. It would have required a regular Hebrew court to sanction it, and it would never have been tolerated in a Roman colony. As at Iconium (xiv. 5) the purpose of the crowd, both Jewish and Gentile, was to insult and stone the Apostles. Here it is obvious that Paul was 'pelted' by a riotous mob, and that he fell down stunned; and, being supposed to be dead, was cast outside the walls. He soon recovered, re-entered the town, and was able to leave for Derbe. One is reminded of the attempts to pelt our Lord with stones in the Temple (John viii. 59), and of the design of the men of Nazareth to hurl him

from the cliff (Luke iv. 29). Neither here nor in the Gospel
is there a hint that a miracle occurred. In recounting his
sufferings for the gospel Paul evidently alludes to Lystra (2
Cor. xi. 25).

It needed no little courage on the part of the missionaries to
return by the same route as they had come, especially as there
was a good road from Derbe to Antioch. That they were able
to revisit the cities from which they had been expelled is
remarkable, but possibly a rumour had spread that Paul had
been killed at Lystra, and there is no suggestion that he and
Barnabas preached or did anything to attract public notice.
Their object was not so much to multiply converts in a
country, where they had evidently been labouring for some
time (xiii. 49, xiv. 6, etc.), as to establish churches by which
the work would be continued. The **presbyters** chosen obviously correspond to the Synagogue officials, and it is advisable
to avoid as much as possible endeavours to make what is said
in Acts into precedents for what we find was afterwards the
rule of the Church. It should not be forgotten that Church
organization at this time must have been very inchoate, however rapidly it may have advanced subsequently. The
appointment or ordination of the elders of the infant
churches is related in language which recalls xiii. 3 : ' When
they had fasted and prayed, they laid their hands upon them.'
The words about opening to the Gentiles **a door into faith** is
characteristically Pauline (1 Cor. xvi. 9, 2 Cor. ii. 12, Col. iv.
13). We are also reminded of the words of the brethren of
Jerusalem when they had heard of the conversion of Cornelius
(xi. 18).

The fifteenth chapter is historically the most difficult in the
whole New Testament, and also one of the most important in
Acts. Luke has in the first place attempted an almost impossible task, namely, to give an account of how it came to
pass that an agreement was reached between the strictly
Jewish party of believers at Jerusalem and the more liberal
and adventurous church of Antioch, as well as how Paul and
Barnabas came to represent two different aspects of mission-

ary activity towards the Gentiles. So strictly was Luke limited in space, that he has told the story in less than seven hundred words. To have related all we desire to know so briefly would have been impossible ; the marvel is that the account as written for Theophilus should be so vivid and interesting, not only to scholars, but to the average reader of Acts to-day. In forty-one verses Luke has related, even with some repetition : (1) how the Pharisaic party in the Church insisted on the circumcision of the Gentiles, and it was agreed to submit the whole question to the mother church of Jerusalem (vers. 1–5) ; (2) how the Apostles and elders met and listened both to Barnabas and Paul, and also to two entirely different but eminently characteristic speeches by Peter and James (vers. 6–21) ; (3) the decision of the assembly embodied in a letter to the church in Antioch, Syria, and Cilicia (vers. 22–29) ; (4) the reception of the letter at Antioch (vers. 30–35) ; and (5) the dispute between Paul and Barnabas (vers. 36–41). Every single one of these five sections has a character of its own and is full of suggestions ; it may be safely affirmed that Luke has performed his difficult task in so masterly a way as to give the entire chapter the stamp of genius.

But it cannot be overlooked that we have also Paul's conflicting account of the circumstances, as told to the Galatians, perhaps the same people whom he had just converted. To enable us to form a judgment on what Luke has related, it is desirable to have before us at least a few extracts from St. Paul's own words as rendered by Moffatt in his version of Gal. i. 15–ii. 13.

The God who had set me apart *from my very birth called* me by his grace, and when he chose to reveal his Son to me, that I might preach him to the Gentiles, instead of consulting with any human being, instead of going up to Jerusalem to see those who had been apostles before me, I went off at once to Arabia, and on my return I came back to Damascus. Then, after three years, I went up to Jerusalem to make the acquaintance of Cephas. I stayed

a fortnight with him. I saw no other apostle, only James
the brother of the Lord. (I am writing you the sheer
truth, I swear it before God!) Then I went to the districts
of Syria and of Cilicia. Personally I was quite unknown
to the Christian churches of Judaea; they merely heard
that ' our former persecutor is now preaching the faith
he once harried,' which made them praise God for me.
Then, fourteen years later, I went up to Jerusalem again,
accompanied by Barnabas; I took Titus with me also.
(It was in consequence of a revelation that I went up at
all.) I submitted the gospel I am in the habit of preaching
to the Gentiles, submitting it privately to the authorities,
to make sure that my course of action would be and had
been sound. But even my companion Titus, Greek
though he was, was not obliged to be circumcised. There
were traitors of false brothers. . . . But we refused to
yield for a single instant to their claims; we were determined that the truth of the gospel should hold good
for you. Besides, the so-called ' authorities ' . . . had no
additions to make to my gospel. On the contrary, when
they saw I had been entrusted with the gospel for the
benefit of the uncircumcised, just as Peter had been for
the circumcised . . . James and Cephas and John gave
myself and Barnabas the right hand of fellowship. . . .
But when Cephas came to Antioch, I opposed him to his
face. The man stood self-condemned. Before certain
emissaries of James arrived, he ate along with the Gentile
Christians; but when they arrived, he began to draw back
and hold aloof, because he was afraid of the circumcision
party. The rest of the Jewish Christians also played false
along with him, so much so that even Barnabas was
carried away by their false play.

It would be impossible to guess by reading Acts that Paul
went to Jerusalem to confer with the leaders of the Church
seventeen years after his conversion, and had evidently spent
a long time in missionary work in Syria and Cilicia. It is
equally difficult to reconcile the two accounts of what hap-

pened at Jerusalem if we assume that Acts xv. describes the same visit as is spoken of by Paul in his epistle. In Acts Paul and Barnabas are represented as deciding to take the question of how the Gentiles were to be received to Jerusalem, where a wise compromise is suggested by James and embodied in an apostolic decree. But in Galatians, Paul represents himself as taking a perfectly uncompromising attitude. He shews very little respect for James, Cephas, or John, who recognize his right to the apostleship of the Gentiles after conferring with him privately. These leaders did not attempt to limit Paul's authority, but gave him a perfectly free hand, recognizing two spheres of missionary activity, the Jewish being committed to Peter and the Gentile to Paul and Barnabas. Nowhere in any of his extant epistles, where he deals with the question of associating with Gentiles, does Paul so much as hint at the decree of the council or the limitations it imposed. Moreover, though in Galatians Peter is said to have gone to Antioch, in Acts the council is represented as sending two delegates, Judas and Silas, without a word about Peter or the bold stand Paul made against him at Antioch. The quarrel of Paul with Barnabas in Acts was due to the apparently trifling question whether Mark should accompany them on their visit to the churches of Asia Minor, whereas in Galatians it is implied that it turned on the whole question of the recognition of the Gentiles in which Barnabas seemed disposed to side with Peter. Finally, in Acts we are told that Paul visited Jerusalem on two occasions before the conference in chap. xv., directly after his conversion (ix. 26), and with alms during a famine (xi. 30).

The utmost ingenuity has been displayed in the attempt to reconcile these discrepancies. Here, however, it may be permitted to assume that the accounts in Galatians and Acts cannot be harmonized.

It is unquestionable that St. Paul's statements in Galatians are to be preferred to those of Luke. In the first place, Paul is writing about his own experiences not long after their occurrence. He makes his statements as it were under oath, calling God to witness that he is telling the exact truth. For this reason alone we should be bound to accept what he says. In addition, the passage in Galatians bears every stamp of veracity. The unexplained appearance of Titus, the obscure allusion to the demand that he should be circumcised, the private interview with the more important leaders, add to the impression that the epistle is a reflexion of the mind of one who is honestly telling the facts, though under great mental agitation.

In Acts we have not the contemporary evidence of what occurred, but an account related by one who could not have been present, and assuredly wrote some years later. Luke's object was probably to tell Theophilus how it was that the Gentiles came to be recognized by the Jewish believers in Jesus. He had to give his information as briefly as possible, and to make it at the same time clear and interesting. To do this he told, as was his wont, his story in a dramatic form. That there was some sort of conference at Jerusalem seems certain ; but that in Acts xv. we have an exact report is doubtful. The speeches by Peter and James are, it is true, highly characteristic of the two men and may represent the substance of what they actually said. They certainly explain the respective attitude of the two in regard to this question. One may venture to add that if Luke seems, here and else-where, to represent the conduct of Paul, it is somewhat different from the impression conveyed by the Apostle's own letters. Though an enthusiastic admirer of his master, the writer of Acts, far from being an indiscriminating panegyrist, shews independence of judgment in describing Paul's motives and actions ; and, at times, he may not have wholly approved of the Apostle's attitude towards the older Apostles at Jerusalem.

xv.

But certain individuals came down from Jerusalem and taught 1
the brothers that "unless you get circumcised after the custom of Moses you cannot be saved." As a sharp dis- 2
pute and controversy sprang up between them and Paul and

Barnabas,[1] it was arranged that Paul and Barnabas, along with some others of their number, should go up to Jerusalem to see the apostles and presbyters at Jerusalem

3   about this question. The church sped them on their journey, and they passed through both Phoenicia and Syria informing the brothers, to the great joy of all, that

4   the Gentiles were turning to God. On arriving at Jerusalem they were received by the church, the apostles and the presbyters, and they reported how God had been with

5   them and what he had done. But some of the believers who belonged to the Pharisaic party got up and said, "Gentiles must be circumcised and told to observe the law of Moses."[2]

I. The preaching of the Christ had already been widespread, and there were communities of believers scattered throughout Palestine, Samaria, **Syria,** and the southern points of Asia Minor, as well as in what was vaguely known as Arabia. Already these often insignificant communities were becoming conscious that they were forming a society of their own, to be known as the Church, and capable of uniting in corporate action. But although the community was almost entirely Jewish, there is no reason to suppose that it did not include **Gentiles.** There is no evidence that Cornelius the centurion was ever **circumcised** ; and, from what Peter is represented as saying, the inference is that he was not. Paul had long been working among the Gentiles to induce them to accept Jesus as their Lord. Still, what he and Barnabas had been doing was probably quite unprecedented. They had worked, possibly for a year or more, in the heart of Asia Minor, where the inhabitants were almost entirely Gentiles, and had established numerous Christian synagogues—if we may use the term— organizing them, and appointing elders to preside. The ques-

---

[1] W adds : ' For Paul said persistently that they should remain as they had believed.'

[2] The text is confused ; another form is, ' But those who charged them to go up to the elders arose saying (some of the sect of the Pharisees who had believed).' Perhaps in the original W text the Pharisees did not appear. See Ropes's note in *Beginnings of Christianity*, iii. 140.

tion then is whether acceptance of Jesus did or did not imply the rise of a new Judaism consisting of synagogues, the members of which were not even proselytes. The demand that these churches should conform to Judaism was not wholly unreasonable, coming from the strict observers of the Law and of the worship of the Temple, who composed the community of believers at Jerusalem. The reception of Barnabas and Paul, accompanied, as we learn elsewhere, by a distinguished Gentile convert named Titus, was evidently cordial, though those Pharisees who were numbered among the believers insisted on making the new converts observe the Law of Moses.

The attitude of the Pharisees towards the first believers is difficult to define. The popular idea for a long time was that they were the chief opponents of Jesus. Now, and not without reason, there has been a reaction in their favour. Nowhere in the Synoptic Gospels are they connected with the condemnation and death of Jesus, except in Matt. xxvii. 62, where they are represented as joining with the priests in asking Pilate to guard the tomb, obviously a later addition to the gospel. In Mark iii. 6 they are said to have united in an unholy alliance with the Herodians to ' destroy ' Jesus, but there is no hint later as to how they attempted to do this. It is only in the Fourth Gospel that they are closely connected with the chief priests as enemies of Jesus, and even then only in John xviii. 3 are they mentioned in the narrative of the passion. In Acts they appear in a favourable light, except where Paul, undoubtedly a Pharisee, acts as a persecutor.

It is remarkable, however, that Jesus, who does not denounce the priesthood nor the Sadducees, is made to pronounce bitter invectives against the perverted legalism of the Pharisees. The very fact that he did so may be accounted for by assuming that his severe language was due to a desire for their conversion. The faults of the Pharisees were precisely those which those who possess them are apt to regard with peculiar complacency—self-righteousness, harshness in judging others, setting a higher value on observances than on acts of kindness, and the like. The Rabbinical teachers themselves were shrewd critics of hypocritical Pharisaism. Making

THE ACTS OF THE APOSTLES

due allowance for all this, the Pharisees were undoubtedly the
representatives of what was best in the Judaism of the first
century. According to Josephus, they were averse to cruel
punishments, and were not as a rule zealots of the type of Saul
before his conversion. They were not so worldly as the Sadducees, and, unlike the Essenes, they mixed freely with their
fellow-men. Their very legalism aimed at helping ordinary
folk to observe the Law. In a word, they had many affinities
with the teaching of Jesus, whose resurrection gave little
offence, as it was a confirmation of their most cherished doctrine. Most of even their disputes with Jesus turned on how
the Law should be kept, on Sabbath observance, fasting,
washing before meals, divorce, paying tribute. Jesus is
recorded to have been a guest in a Pharisee's house, and to
have told the people to obey their rules. Little wonder
therefore that some of the sect embraced the new messianic
belief, especially as, till the second century, Christianity and
Judaism had not formally separated from one another.

6 The apostles and the presbyters met to investigate this question,
7   and a keen controversy sprang up ; but Peter rose and
said to them, " Brothers, you are well aware that from the
earliest days God chose that of you all I should be the one
by whom the Gentiles were to hear the word of the gospel
8   and believe it. The God who reads the hearts of all
attested this by giving them the holy Spirit just as he gave
9   it to us ; in cleaning their hearts by faith he made not the
10 slightest distinction between us and them. Well now,
why are you trying * to impose a yoke on the neck of the
disciples which neither our fathers nor we ourselves could
11 bear ? No, it is by the grace of the Lord Jesus that we
12 believe and are saved, in the same way as they are." So
the whole meeting was quieted and listened to Barnabas
and Paul recounting the signs and wonders God had
performed by them among the Gentiles.

* Omitting τὸν θεόν.

II. The final decision of the question seems to have been in
the hands of a general assembly of the church of Jerusalem,

136

unless the Antiochenes and other believers are included among the ' elders ' or **presbyters.** It is noteworthy that we hear nothing of the Twelve as the ruling body of the Church. The **apostles** are grouped with the elders, and when the church of Jerusalem meets in Acts xxi. they have been supplanted by ' James and the elders.'

The words attributed to **Peter** (W adds ' in the Spirit ') are singularly appropriate to his character as it is consistently represented in the New Testament. They reveal the generous and impulsive nature of the speaker, and from the little we hear of his subsequent conduct shew the Apostle as more ready to come to a decision than to adhere to it. Yet the argument of the speech is remarkably Pauline. For example, we should scarcely expect a man devoted to the Law (x. 14) to speak of it as **a yoke** intolerable to Jews, for the attitude of the pious as reflected in the hundred and nineteenth Psalm is that of intense pride and joy in the Law, nor is there any sign elsewhere in the New Testament that its rules were a burthen to Jewish Christians. To the Gentiles the Law might be intolerable, and Paul, in Gal. v. 1, calls it a ζυγὸν δουλείας, ' a yoke of slavery.' Salvation **by the grace of the Lord Jesus** is also a characteristically Pauline doctrine, and ver. 11 finds an echo in Eph. ii. 8.

The omission of the words τὸν θεόν is a happy conjecture, though unsupported by manuscript authority. It certainly makes the sentence clearer, if one could be convinced that in the New and Old Testaments the word πειράζειν usually means ' to attempt ' (as in Acts xvi. 6, xxiv. 5), and not ' to tempt, or put to the trial.' The conversion of the Gentiles is repeatedly ascribed to God (see xiv. 27, xv. 4). Thus to impose a yoke on the Gentiles whom He had already turned to Himself would be to provoke Him by unduly testing the work He had accomplished.

Whether Luke has recorded the actual events or reported in brief speeches made at a real council may be open to doubt ; but it is not possible to deny the accuracy of the impression he has conveyed. Our author clearly indicates the nature of the point at issue, the controversy which it aroused, and the friendly compromise indicated in the epistle to the Galatians, all of which preceded the apostolic decision. This is arrived at after **Barnabas and Paul** (note the order, for at Jerusalem Barnabas was naturally regarded as the more important person) have related their experiences. Then James proposes a judicious settlement, in which all at the time could concur, although it left some serious issues still open to dispute.

13 When they had finished speaking, James spoke. " Brothers,"
14 he said, " listen to me. Symeon has explained how it was God's original concern to secure a People from among the
15 Gentiles to bear his Name. This agrees with the words of the prophets ; as it is written,
16   *After this I will return and rebuild David's fallen tent,*
      its ruins I will rebuild and erect it anew,
17   *that the rest of men may seek for the Lord,*
      even all the Gentiles who are called by my name,
18   *saith the Lord, who makes this known from of old.* Hence,
19 in my opinion, we ought not to put fresh difficulties in the way of those who are turning to God from among the
20 Gentiles, but write them injunctions to abstain from whatever is contaminated by idols, from sexual vice, from the flesh of animals that have been strangled, and from tasting
21 blood ; for Moses has had his preachers from the earliest ages in every town, where he is read aloud in the syna-
22 gogues every sabbath." Then the apostles and the presbyters, together with the whole church, decided to select some of their number and send them with Paul and Barnabas to Antioch. The men selected were Judas (called Bar-Sabb'as) and Silas, prominent members of the
23 brotherhood. They conveyed the following letter. " The apostles and the presbyters of the brotherhood to the brothers who belong to the Gentiles throughout Antioch
24 and Syria and Cicilia : greeting. Having learned that some of our number,* quite unauthorized by us, have
25 unsettled you with their teaching and upset your souls, we have decided unanimously to select some of our number

* See Note on next page.

and send them to you along with our beloved Paul and 26
Barnabas who have risked their lives for the sake of our
Lord Jesus Christ. We therefore send Judas and Silas 27
with the following message, which they will also give to
you orally. The holy Spirit and we have decided not to 28
impose any extra burden on you, apart from these essential
requirements : abstain from food that has been offered to 29
idols, from tasting blood, from the flesh of animals that
have been strangled, and from sexual vice. Keep clear
of all this and you will prosper. Goodbye.''

* Omitting ἐξελθόντες.

III. As is evident from xii. 17 James is suddenly introduced
without indication as to who he was, and how he came to be
the head of the brotherhood at Jerusalem. It would consequently be assumed that Theophilus, and others for whom
Luke was writing, had no need to be informed about him. Yet,
but for a chance reference in the Galatian epistle, readers of the
New Testament would be at a loss to account for his position.
Still, as we know from Paul that James was the brother of the
Lord, and also from Josephus that he was the brother of the
' so-called Christ,' his pre-eminence in the church of Jerusalem
is only natural. In some respects James is one of the most
interesting characters in the New Testament, although little
is told us concerning him. If the epistle under his name
cannot be accepted as genuine, it at least proves that the
early church appreciated his character, as eminently sensible
and judicious.

The words attributed to James may or may not be an
actual report of what he said, but they are unquestionably
characteristic of the speaker. Notice how he calls Peter by
his original name of Simon in its Hebraic form. **Symeon,** he
says, has related how God at the first (i.e. in the early days
of the gospel, cf. Peter's words ἀφ᾽ ἡμερῶν ἀρχαίων in ver. 7)
shewed regard to take **from among the Gentiles** an Israel to
be called by **his Name.** The famous commentator Bengel
calls the words ' a People from among the Gentiles ' an
' excellent paradox' (*egregium paradoxum*), meaning that till

the coming of the Christ the Gentiles were not God's people
(1 Pet. ii. 2) ; but since then, those who believe are to be
added to the true Israel. The word ἐπεσκέψατο (concern)
occurs thrice in Luke's gospel (i. 68, ii. 76, vii. 16), always in
the sense of God visiting His people. The substantive
ἐπισκοπή is used in the same sense (Luke xix. 44 and 1 Pet.
ii. 12), and Christ is called the ἐπίσκοπος of our souls (1 Pet.
ii. 25). What has been done is in accordance with the prophecy of Amos that the tent (i.e. the abode) of David would
be built anew, as it had been in the person of Jesus his
descendant (Luke i. 32). James quotes the Septuagint
version (that the rest of men, etc.) of Amos ix. 12 instead
of the Hebrew 'that they may possess the remnant of
Edom.'

The decision of James and the council is cast in a legal form,
the interpretation of which is not clear even if the text were
established with certainty. The meaning of the council is
that the Gentiles who turn to God are not to be troubled by
Rabbinical restrictions, but are to be enjoined either (a) to
obey the moral laws of Judaism, or (b) to respect Jewish
scruples.

(a) In favour of the view that the precepts are moral is the
western text : ' But to charge them (the Gentile converts) to
abstain from the pollutions of the idols, and fornication and
blood (murder), and whatsoever they do not wish to be done
to themselves, not to do to others.'

In ver. 29 the sense is the same, with a slight variety of
language : ' To lay on you no further burthen than these
necessary things, to abstain from idol-sacrifices and blood and
fornication and not to do to another what you would not
desire him to do to you.' Now it was a basic principle
of Judaism that three sins—idolatry, murder, and fornication
—were fundamentally opposed to the Law of God. This
principle was adopted by the Christian church, which long held
that it was not in man's power to readmit those guilty of such
sins to communion. The addition of the golden rule to ' do
as we would be done by,' whether stated as by Jesus positively
(Matt. vii. 12), or, as here and by the rabbis, negatively, shews

that the western text regards these precepts as moral and not ceremonial.

(b) On the other hand, there is the more usual version : ' To abstain from the pollution of idols, and fornication, and from what has been strangled and from blood,' a ceremonial injunction, which may be interpreted as advice to be careful not to eat Gentile food which may have been offered to idols, to observe the rules of marriage in Judaism, and not to eat the blood of animals killed by strangulation. If this is so, the meaning of the command would be that the converted Gentiles must observe the food laws in such a way as not to offend Jewish prejudices.

The conclusion of James's speech is very difficult, not so much to translate as to interpret. Although synagogue worship is made quite primitive by the Greek (ἐκ γενεῶν ἀρχαίων) for from the earliest ages, one may be satisfied with understanding the words as meaning no more than ' from of old.' The significance of the rest of the verse must depend on whether the precepts of the proposed decree were intended to be moral or ceremonial. If moral, it is, to say the least, difficult to understand, and the explanations are necessarily more ingenious than satisfactory. But if the purpose of James is to insist on the observance of food laws, he obviously means no more than that Jews are to be found in every city and their prejudice must be respected. (For the reading of Moses in the synagogue we may compare 2 Cor. iii. 15.)

The question of intercourse with Gentiles in the matter of food was indeed a burning one. To share a meal with any person is to enter into some kind of communion with him, and strict Jews carefully avoided such contact with Gentiles or even unworthy Jews. Thus Peter was rebuked for eating with ' men uncircumcised.' At Antioch Paul and Cephas had at first no scruples about eating with their Gentile converts, but this laxity distressed the emissaries of James. Shakespeare aptly describes this Jewish attitude when he makes Shylock say, ' I will buy with you, sell with you . . . but I will not eat with you.'

There was, however, another difficulty besides the racial

prejudice of the Jew. To visit a Gentile's house and to share his meals might involve one in the guilt of idolatry. Any animal food which was served at table might have been part of a beast sacrificed in a heathen temple. As such it was ' food offered to an idol,' and caused anyone who partook of it to have shared in the worship of a strange god. The trouble caused by these scruples is seen in Paul's epistles to the Romans and Corinthians, and they were apparently felt by Gentile as well as Jewish believers ; the Apostle, however, does not refer in any way to the decree of Acts xv. ; nay, rather, he seems to ignore it, by advising the Corinthians to eat what was served at table, and ask no questions.

The difficulty of finding the sin of fornication included among ritual injunctions may have caused the revisers of the western text to omit the word **strangled**, and to add the golden rule, but the confusion between ritual and moral guilt was not always clear in Judaism, or even in Christianity. The earnestness with which Paul insists on sexual purity is in itself a proof that his Gentile converts regarded it as somewhat of an indifferent matter, and not altogether incompatible with the religion they had adopted.

The decree was embodied in a letter to the brethren in **Antioch, Syria, and Cilicia,** but not to Paul and Barnabas's recent converts in Asia Minor. The bearers were two distinguished prophets **Judas and Silas,** and it is noticeable that none of the Twelve except Peter appears throughout the entire business. The assembly, like all later Christian councils, claims to have the authority of **the holy Spirit,** who in the next chapter (xvi. 6 and 7) directs the journey on the mission of Paul and Silas.

30 **When the messengers were despatched, they went down to Antioch and after gathering the whole body they handed**
31 **them the letter. On reading it the people rejoiced at the**
32 **encouragement it brought ; and as Judas and Silas were themselves prophets, they encouraged and strengthened**
33 **the brothers with many a counsel. Then after some time had passed the brothers let them go with a greeting of**

peace to those who had sent them. Paul and Barnabas, 35 however, stayed on in Antioch, teaching and preaching the word of the Lord along with a number of others.

IV. Evidently Luke considered that the matter of the Gentiles was now practically settled, and that it was only necessary to remark that the letter from Jerusalem had been favourably received at Antioch. As is implied in Galatians, there was much discussion as to the future programme of the Church. Parties were formed, emissaries from Jerusalem were coming and going. Apparently—for the western addition about Silas is inadmissible (i.e. ver. 34 in A.V.: ' Notwithstanding, it pleased Silas to abide there still ')—both he and Judas went back to Jerusalem, and Silas returned **to Antioch** to become a fellow-labourer of Paul. But Luke did not see fit to relate the details of a period which was nevertheless of extreme importance in the development of the Church. His object is to hasten on to relate how Paul undertook those momentous missionary journeys by which the western world was opened to the extension of the gospel.

Some days later, Paul said to Barnabas, " Come and let us go 36 back to visit the brothers in every town where we have proclaimed the word of the Lord. Let us see how they are doing." But while Barnabas wanted to take John 37 (who was called Mark) along with them, Paul held that 38 they should not take a man with them who had deserted them in Pamphylia, instead of accompanying them on active service. So in irritation they parted company, 39 Barnabas taking Mark with him and sailing for Cyprus, while Paul selected Silas and went off, commended by the 40 brothers to the grace of the Lord. He made his way 41 through Syria and Cilicia, strengthening the churches.

V. It is perhaps unnecessary to follow the usual practice of commentators by enlarging on this dispute between the two great missionary leaders. Many are disposed to blame Paul for shewing ingratitude to an old friend and benefactor, and to build an elaborate theory on the Apostle's words, ' Even Barnabas was carried away with their dissimulation ' (Gal. ii. 13). It may well be that the council at Jerusalem resulted, as other councils have done, in the sort of compromise which only creates fresh divisions, and that the dispute about taking Mark on another missionary journey was simply an ostensible reason for a quarrel on a matter of principle. But it was not Luke's intention to gratify our curiosity. His object was probably to indicate that Paul and Barnabas did part company, and to introduce us to the second part of his treatise which dealt solely with those missionary enterprises in which Paul was the unique central figure. At this point the Twelve, Peter, Barnabas, and Mark disappear, and figure no more in Luke's history. But from scattered notices in the epistles it is evident that the unrecorded spread of the faith was at least as extensive as the work of the Apostle of the Gentiles.

So ends the first part of Acts. For the information he has given us in the Gospel and Acts i.–xv. Luke has had to depend, as he tells us, upon the tradition of 'eye-witnesses and ministers ' of the word, and doubtless upon certain written sources. From xvi. onwards he is relating many experiences in which he himself bore an active part, most of the actors in which were personally known to him.

Before, however, we enter upon the consideration of the second division of the apostolic record, it may be well to take stock of what we have already learned. The important thing always to remember is that but for Luke we should know nothing whatever about the first generation of the Christian community ; and, so far as we can judge from what has survived, the earliest Christian writers knew little if anything more than we do. They are not able to tell us, apart from legend, anything concerning the work of the Twelve, what churches they founded, or whither they went. They are ignorant concerning the career of Peter and the death of Paul. Barnabas, one of the greatest pioneers of the faith, disappears among the mists of tradition, save for some allusion in Paul's epistles. Even the early Apostolic Acts are no better than romantic stories of impossible miracles. It would be no easy task to reconstruct the early Christian world out of the Pauline letters. When Acts ends about A.D. 62 we have to wait for Eusebius in A.D. 320 for a continuous Church history.

In the first part of Acts Luke has dealt with three main subjects : (*a*) the progress, (*b*) the preaching of Christianity, and (*c*) the organization of the community.

(*a*) There is no attempt to be dramatic in relating what followed the death and burial of Jesus. Yet the restraint of the historian adds to the astonishing character of the events. The Paschal season was over. A new week had begun, and life at Jerusalem became normal once more. The women who had accompanied Jesus from Galilee were unable to find his body, and saw a vision by which they were assured that Jesus had risen. But no one believed them, till two of his friends saw him on the road to Emmaus. There was evidently no attempt to persecute the companions of Jesus, who were able to meet unmolested, and to choose a twelfth Apostle. At the Pentecost, seven weeks after the Crucifixion, Jesus was openly proclaimed to the multitudes at Jerusalem as the Messiah. A large number believed in the good news ; and the Church may be said to have been born under the guidance of the Twelve. The healing of a cripple in the courts of the Temple caused the priesthood to take notice of the movement, and after a few abortive attempts to suppress it, the Church in Jerusalem was left at peace. A violent storm on the day of Pentecost and the sudden cure of a lame man were the only abnormal events which marked this most eventful period in human history. The Resurrection and Ascension had only been witnessed by the immediate friends of Jesus ; but so far as the ordinary life of the Holy City went, the faith which was destined to influence the world began in absolute obscurity.

The believers had become a mixed community of native and foreign Jews, against whom a persecution began on the ground that they were hostile to the Temple and the Law. Expelled, not without bloodshed, from Jerusalem, they began to preach in Samaria and the coast towns of Palestine. The story of this early mission is interrupted by that of the conversion of Saul of Tarsus, and continued by a description of miracles wrought by Peter and his baptism of Cornelius, the first non-Jewish believer. After this the scene changes ; Antioch, not Jerusalem, becomes the centre of interest. From thence, after preaching the gospel in Cyprus, Barnabas and Paul carry the message to the interior of Asia Minor, Gentile churches arise, and their existence is recognized and sanctioned by the Apostolic Church at Jerusalem.

The narrative, making all allowance for the difficulties Luke must have had in condensing it, and even for certain defects in presentation, commends itself to us as a probable report of what occurred. The new message would be expected to spread in this manner, and the stages of its progress are admirably indicated, leading up to the main theme of the rest of Acts—the adventurous carrying of the gospel by Paul into Europe and eventually to Rome.

(*b*) It now remains to determine the character of the message as revealed by the speeches in this part of Acts. Jesus is set forth as the Messiah : (1) because he has risen from the dead, and (2) because all that has happened is in accordance with prophecy. His works as a benefactor to mankind in Galilee are set forth in Peter's words to Cornelius, and the general connexion of Jesus with the entire history of Israel in the defence of Stephen, and in Paul's synagogue speech in Pisidian Antioch. The doctrine as expressed is decidedly primitive, and does not seem to shew the influence of the teaching of St. Paul. Its simplicity is a testimony to the historical insight of the author of Acts.

(*c*) That the followers of Jesus should not from the first have formed themselves into a society, united as they were by common sympathy and devotion to their leader, is hardly conceivable. On this point Luke unmistakably insists, laying the greatest possible stress on the unity of the believers. In the first five chapters the Twelve, with Peter as their head, are the natural and unquestioned rulers of the New Society. In the sixth, by the appointment of the Seven, the principle of the division of labour is recognized ; in the eighth the bestowal of the gift of the Spirit seems to be reserved to the Apostles. Baptism is regarded as indispensable, the Lord's Supper is alluded to more indefinitely. The laying on of hands is the prelude to the undertaking of any special duty or mission. Prophecy is a recognized function, and new communities are entrusted to ' elders.' It is, as has already been remarked, unhistorical to attempt to justify the ecclesiastical arrangements of even very early times by an appeal to the opening chapters of Acts.

In fact, it may be said that Luke has, up to this point, told us but little ; but that what he has related bears the impress of truth, and is assuredly not lacking in interest.

With the sixteenth chapter we enter upon an entirely new phase of the story of Acts, and feel we are in a different atmosphere. The first half of the Acts is intensely Jewish. Even if we do not pay adequate attention to the ingeniously worked-out theory of Dr. Torrey, in which he demonstrates that Luke in the first fifteen chapters used an Aramaic source, we are compelled to confess that, whether his linguistic argument is valid or not, he has correctly sensed the Oriental character of the narrative. The Twelve with Peter and John, the Seven with Stephen and Philip, James, and even Barnabas and Mark, are Hebrews in every respect. The only great utterance of St. Paul reported is a discourse in a synagogue ; and it must never be forgotten that in that early period the great Apostle of the Gentiles was not, in the eyes of his fellow-workers at least, a central figure. One may perhaps suppose that, till he won his crowning triumph by being permitted to approach the Gentiles in his own fashion, Paul was, so to speak, feeling his way towards the assumption of the rôle of the greatest Christian leader and missionary of the primitive church, and that it was not till he had parted from Barnabas and become an unquestioned leader in the diffusion of the gospel throughout the world that his greatness becomes apparent. From that time the story of Acts is almost exclusively that of the Apostle Paul.

With all his Jewish education, and strong sympathy for his ancestral religion, Paul was, in a certain sense, more attracted to the West than to the East. He really found himself in Europe. Like some other eminent Jews, Rome had a strong attraction for him. As a citizen he felt sure of the protection of the Empire ; and with Philo and Josephus he regarded the imperial city as the means by which the peace of the world was secured. When therefore he said, ' I must see Rome,' and wrote to the Christians there, ' I greatly desire to see you,' Paul was expressing a heartfelt wish ; and it is a testimony to the artistic sense of Luke that, having related his adventures and trials, he leaves his hero in his own lodging in the city. If Rome was also the scene of the martyrdom of the Apostle, no place on earth was more suited to witness the triumph of his whole career.

In the ensuing chapters we are given pictures of the work of Paul in five important cities—Philippi, Thessalonica, Athens, Corinth, and Ephesus—each of which is representative of a different phase of Christian activity : in Philippi among Roman colonists ; in Thessalonica, a busy Greek free city ; in Athens, the centre of the culture of the ancient world ; in Corinth, a vigorous commercial port ; and in Ephesus, amid a Hellenized population devoted to an Oriental religion. The pregnant story of the experiences of the Apostle is then related in four brief chapters.

Fewer problems are to be met with in this section of Acts than in the first part, where we were compelled to feel that our guide was not really familiar with many of the facts, and had left much to be explained. Here, however, he is writing from competent knowledge and personal experience, and was an eye-witness of much which he records, especially as he nears the end. Points of difficulty, however, do occur when he seems to be in conflict with what we know of Paul's adventures from his undisputed epistles. These it may be possible to account for if we take into consideration that he may be relating events from a different view-point ; yet we must admit his skill as a narrator, and his evident admiration for St. Paul.

The first five verses of this chapter perhaps belong to the earlier section of the book, especially because the concluding words of ver. 5, which note the increase of the Church, are characteristic of Luke's method of periodically marking the rapid progress of the gospel in its earlier stages. Thus in ii. 47

the Pentecostal section is concluded by the notice that the
Lord was adding daily to the number of the ' saved.' In iv. 4
we have a similar notice appended to the story of the healing
of the cripple in the Temple. In vi. 1 the appointment of the
Seven is prefaced by a notice of the increase of the Church.
Here it is possible that it was Luke's intention to abandon
recording the progress of the Christian community in order to
confine himself to the account of the preaching of Paul. In
this sense the remaining part of Acts may be said to resemble
the gospels, in so far as it is concentrated on a single personality. Paul shares with his Master in the story as told in the
New Testament, in having a biography of his own.

xvi.

He also came down to Derbe and Lystra, where there was a 1
disciple called Timotheus, the son of a believing Jewess
and a Greek father. He had a good reputation among the 2
brothers at Lystra and Iconium ; so, as Paul wished him 3
to go abroad with him, he took and circumcised him on
account of the local Jews, all of whom knew his father had
been a Greek. As they travelled on from town to town, 4
they handed over to the people the resolutions which the
apostles and the presbyters in Jerusalem had decided were
to be obeyed ; and the churches were strengthened in the 5
faith and increased in numbers day by day.

The use of the singular number here and xv. 39-41 is noteworthy. Silas was Paul's companion ; and at Philippi shared
in his sufferings. But, as the visit to **Lystra** and **Derbe** was
Paul's affair, the plural is not resumed till he and Silas were
fulfilling their mission of delivering to the converts the
apostolic decrees.

The choice of **Timotheus** to supply the place of Mark is
evidently regarded as noteworthy, and there are few personages of whom more is told us in the New Testament—2 Tim.
i. 5, iii. 15 ; 1 Tim i. 18, iv. 12, 14, iv. 12 ; 1 Cor. iv. 17 (cf. 1
Tim. i. 2), xvi. 10 ; 2 Cor. i. 19 ; Rom. xvi. 21 ; 1 Thess. i. 3, 6.

The name of Timothy occurs four times elsewhere in Acts, and is joined with that of Paul in the salutations of 1 and 2 Corinthians, Philippians, Colossians, and 1 and 2 Thessalonians. The strange thing is that one who was so constantly with the Apostle, and is alluded to with so much affection and confidence, should have made so little impression upon Christian tradition. Even in the Roman calendar his day (January 24) is one of the minor festivals ; and in the Missal he is not even provided with a special gospel.

The circumcision of Timothy presents a difficulty, especially if Paul carried his point at Jerusalem, and Titus was *not* ' compelled ' to submit to the rite (Acts xv. 28, Gal. ii. 3). But even if the Apostle appears to have been inconsistent, his conduct was in the circumstances justifiable. In the first place Titus was unquestionably a Gentile, whereas Timothy was of mixed parentage, and according to Paul's second letter to him was brought up with a knowledge of the Jewish Scriptures. Again Timothy was destined to be a constant companion of the missionaries, and could not hope to be received in the synagogues they were about to visit unless he were in every respect a Jew. Knowing, moreover, that Paul was regarded with intense suspicion in Asia Minor, we may be sure that if the Jews of Derbe, Lystra, and Iconium knew that he was employing an uncircumcised person as a missionary of the gospel, they would spread the fact throughout the country, thereby increasing the obstacles in the way of evangelization.

6 **They crossed Phrygia and the country of Galatia, the holy
Spirit having stopped them from preaching the word in
7 Asia ; when they got as far as Mysia, they tried to enter
8 Bithynia, but the Spirit of Jesus would not allow them, and
so they passed Mysia by and went down to Troas.**

Luke is evidently either ignorant of the exact route taken by the missionaries, or intentionally relates a long and tedious journey in as few words as possible, being anxious to bring them to Troas, where he himself joined them. The geography is on the whole correct, but there is a curious mixture of racial divisions and Roman provinces, as any rough sketch-map will

plainly shew. Great ingenuity, topographical learning, and
research have been displayed in determining how Paul and his
companions travelled from Iconium to Troas, especially in the
endeavour to determine whether by **Galatia** is meant the
extensive Roman province, or the district occupied by the
Celtic tribe which gave its name to the country. But Luke
gives us no information, and does not mention a single town.
All we can gather is that from an evangelistic point of view
there was nothing done, but that **the Spirit** drove the little
company constantly forward, prohibiting any preaching in
Asia or Bithynia, till they came to a port on the north-west of
the peninsula, from whence Macedonia could easily be reached.
Asia, in the sense of the Roman province, was destined to
become a great centre of primitive Christianity, and **Bithynia**
the scene of one of the earliest persecutions of the Church,
but Luke's object here was to bring Paul to Europe as quickly
as possible.

A vision appeared to Paul by night, the vision of a Macedonian 9
    standing and appealing to him with the words, " Cross to
    Macedonia and help us." As soon as he saw the vision, 10
    we made efforts to start for Macedonia, inferring that God
    had called us to preach the gospel to them. Setting sail 11
    then from Troas we ran straight to Samothrace and on the
    following day to Neapolis. We then came to the Roman 12
    colony of Philippi, which is the foremost town of the dis-
    trict of Macedonia. In this town we spent some days. On 13
    the sabbath we went outside the gate to the bank of the
    river, where as usual there was a place of prayer ; we sat
    down and talked to the women who had gathered. Among 14
    the listeners there was a woman called Lydia, a dealer in
    purple who belonged to the town of Thyatira. She rever-
    enced God, and the Lord opened her heart to attend to what
    Paul said. When she was baptized, along with her house- 15
    hold, she begged us, saying, " If you are convinced I am
    a believer in the Lord, come and stay at my house." She
    compelled us to come.

Luke's object in general is to shew that all missionary work is carried on under the guidance of the Spirit. Philip acts under his inspiration, Peter visits Cornelius after a vision, and Cornelius is moved to send for him by an angel. At Antioch the Spirit commands the prophets to choose Barnabas and Saul. In the same way the holy Spirit prevents Paul preaching in Asia, the 'Spirit of Jesus' hinders him from going to Bithynia, and a mysterious 'man of Macedonia' invites his company to come to his assistance. The writer of the Acts now uses the first person plural, and the rest of the chapter has a special interest as the account of an eye-witness. Luke, as will appear hereafter, has a special interest in itineraries, and carefully notes the places at which he and his friends stopped. The voyage began propitiously, the ship ran before the wind, and within twenty-four hours reached **Neapolis,** a distance of some 150 miles. In Acts xx. 6 the same journey in the opposite direction took five days. The missionaries on landing went straight to **Philippi, the foremost town of the district of Macedonia**—the word **foremost** ($\pi\rho\hat{\omega}\tau o s$) being applied either to its eminence or to its being the first Macedonian city reached by them, Neapolis being considered to belong to Thrace.

Luke is careful to inform us that it was a **Roman colony,** and in the account of what occurred there he shews an accurate knowledge of the condition of a place so described. The colonial system of Rome displays the administrative genius of the people, and was one of the chief means for securing the integrity of their empire. A Roman colony was entirely different from a Greek 'colony' ($\grave{\epsilon}\pi o\iota\kappa\acute{\iota}a$), or a modern settlement in a remote country, in that it was organized by the state, and in no sense a private enterprise, the inhabitants being allotted lands and given homes by the government. A Roman colony was, in fact, a military outpost, constituted as the City in miniature. The people enjoyed the rights of Roman citizenship before the days of the empire, and elected two magistrates, representing the consuls, officially known as *duumviri,* who, however, preferred to be known by the more honourable title of praetors ($\sigma\tau\rho\alpha\tau\eta\gamma o\acute{\iota}$). The pomposity of these petty colonial magistrates caused some amusement to the natives of the imperial city (Cicero speaks of the way in which

the *duumviri* of Capua assumed the dignified name of
' praetors ').

It is possible that Paul's company came to Philippi early in
the week, and finding no Jewish community, waited till the
sabbath, and went to the river, where they might expect to find
any local Jews at prayer. It is doubtful whether the word
προσευχή (a place for prayer) means here a building of any
description, or that the A.V. does not give the correct sense,
' where prayer was wont to be made.' At anyrate only a few
women had met by the little river Gangites, one of whom, a
rich lady from Thyatira in Asia, named Lydia, hospitably
received Paul and his friends in her home. Probably she and
her household were baptized at once. Yet this little informal
gathering of women was the foundation of a church renowned
for its courage, generosity, and truly Christian spirit, for whose
members the Apostle has only praise, gratitude, and love.

Now it happened as we went to the place of prayer that a slave- 16
girl met us, possessed by a spirit of ventriloquism, and a
source of great profit to her owners by her power of fortune-
telling. She followed Paul and the rest of us, shrieking, 17
" These men are servants of the Most High God, they proclaim to you the way of salvation ! " She did this for a 18
number of days. Then Paul turned in annoyance and told
the spirit, " In the name of Jesus Christ I order you out of
her ! " And it left her that very moment. But when her 19
owners saw their chance of profit was gone, they caught
hold of Paul and Silas and dragged them before the magistrates in the forum. Bringing them before the praetors 20
they declared, " These fellows are Jews who are making an
agitation in our town ; they are proclaiming customs which 21
as Romans we are not allowed to accept or observe ! " The 22
crowd also joined in the attack upon them, while the
praetors, after having them stripped and after ordering
them to be flogged with rods, had many lashes inflicted on 23
them and put them into prison, charging the jailer to keep
them safe. On receiving so strict a charge, he put them 24
into the inner prison and secured their feet in the stocks.

The story of Paul's adventures at Philippi, despite the difficulties which it raises, bears every trace of probability. A modern physician might declare that the girl was insane. To her contemporaries she seemed to be inspired by Apollo. Her utterances were so remarkable that she had been purchased and exploited, and proved a profitable investment to her owners. The presence of the missionaries drove her into a sort of frenzy, as that of Jesus had the demoniacs in Galilee. Doubtless she had listened to the preaching, and to their great annoyance **followed** them, constantly **shrieking** that they were **servants of the Most High God** (cf. Luke viii. 28—the Gadarene demoniac). Paul exorcised **the spirit,** and the girl became sane, thereby being no longer a source of profit. No hint is given of her having become a convert ; the story is only related because of its sequence.

The accusation made by the girl's owners is skilfully framed and suited to prejudice both the praetors and the people against Paul and Silas : (1) these men are causing trouble in the town ; (2) being **Jews** to begin with ; (3) they are teaching our people to observe **customs** ; (4) which they have no business to do, as we are **Romans.** (1) Nothing is said of the healing of the girl ; it is merely a general charge that Paul and his companions are a public nuisance. (2) As Jews, they belong to an unpopular and despised class—this would incite the mob. (3) The practices (not doctrines) they are advocating are illegal for our people. (4) Being Romans we have the right to resent their presence. One is reminded of the Methodist persecutions in the eighteenth century in England, mob violence, and stupid or prejudiced magistrates. **The praetors** probably never gave the missionaries any opportunity for defence. They handed the accused over to the police, who plied their **rods** and drove **them into prison.** The proceedings seem to have been conducted with brutal informality, and all may have happened in a very short time. It is quite possible that here Luke relates what he saw.

25 **But about midnight, as Paul and Silas were praying and singing
26   to God, while the prisoners listened, all of a sudden there**

was a great earthquake which shook the very foundations of the prison ; the doors all flew open in an instant and the fetters of all the prisoners were unfastened. When the 27 jailer started from his sleep and saw the prison-doors open, he drew his sword and was on the point of killing himself, supposing the prisoners had made their escape; but Paul 28 shouted aloud, " Do not harm yourself, we are all here ! " 29 So calling for lights he rushed in, fell in terror before Paul and Silas, and brought them out (after securing the other 30 prisoners).* " Sirs," he said, "what must I do to be saved ? " " Believe in the Lord Jesus Christ," they said, 31 " and then you will be saved, you and your household as well." And they spoke the word of the Lord to him and to 32 all in his house. Then he took them at that very hour of 33 the night and washed their wounds and got baptized instantly, he and all his family. He took them up to his 34 house and put food before them, overjoyed like all his household at having believed in God.

* Adding τοὺς λοιποὺς ἀσφαλισάμενος with D and the (Harklean) Syriac version.

Luke could not have witnessed what actually happened in the prison, and he may have so related events as to dispose the reader to imagine a scene more imposing and miraculous than circumstances warrant. A small place like Philippi probably had a somewhat primitive house of detention, with the simplest methods for securing the prisoners. Earthquakes were not infrequent, and the clumsy doors may easily have been unhinged even by a slight shock. Paul and Silas were singing praises to God in the darkness and the prisoners were listening to them. Doubtless, as the Apostles are represented to have done after being beaten in the Sanhedrin (Acts v. 41), they rejoiced at having suffered in the Name of Jesus.

The jailer's conduct is more naturally described than the earthquake. The man was thoroughly frightened by the shock, which cannot have been considerable, as the prison was evidently not seriously damaged. A western reading says that he secured the other prisoners and took Paul and Silas into his house. His baptism and that of the whole **family** has a very primitive touch about it. Contrary to the practice of the later church, no preparation whatever seems to be needed. The eunuch in Acts viii. was at least a proselyte, and it was the same with Lydia. But **the jailer,** unlike Cornelius, was not even a worshipper of the God of Israel, and yet **he** was **baptized** with **all his family** without any preparation (because he desired it).

35 When day broke, the praetors sent the lictors with the message,
36   " Release these men." The jailer repeated this to Paul. " The praetors," he said, " have sent to release you. So
37   come out and go in peace." But Paul replied, " They flogged us in public and without a trial, flogged Roman citizens ! They put us in prison, and now they are going to get rid of us secretly ! No indeed ! Let them come here
38   themselves and take us out ! " The lictors reported this to the praetors, who, on hearing the men were Roman citi-
39   zens, became alarmed ; they went to appease them and after taking them out of prison begged them to leave the
40   town. So they left the prison and went to Lydia's house, where they saw the brothers and encouraged them ; then they departed.

What follows can cause no difficulty except to commentators. To the plain reader nothing happened except what might be expected. It did not need an earthquake, as the western text asserts, to convince the *duumviri* of Philippi that they had acted foolishly in maltreating two Jewish visitors on an absurd accusation by interested persons. Lydia their hostess was a person of some consideration, and the Jewish community in Macedonia might well make complaints to the provincial governor that two rabbis had been treated with contumely. The magistrates acted as might have been expected of such persons, and curtly ordered the jailer to release his prisoners, hoping thus to end the matter. But to their horror they discovered that they had involved themselves in what might prove serious litigation. The men they had insulted were **Roman citizens !**

We may wonder why Paul and Silas did not make this known when brought before the praetors. Two good reasons suggest themselves—they had no opportunity, the whole business being tumultuary, or they received their ill-treatment, rejoicing at the fact that it was for the sake of their Master : Paul, according to his own statement (2 Cor. xi. 25), was thrice beaten by the lictors, and five times by the Jews. It may be asked, Why did he assert his citizenship when Claudius Lysias ordered him to be examined under the lash (Acts xxii. 24) ? The answer is obvious. The Jewish scourging was a discipline not needlessly cruel; the *fasces* of the lictors were doubtless painful and degrading to submit to, but not dangerous to life. But the Roman *flagrum* (μάστιξ) was a diabolic instrument of torture, and Paul knew that if he were submitted to its infliction he would probably be killed, and pleaded his rights as a Roman to save his life. But doubtless Paul and Silas had another reason for insisting on the Philippian officials making them an abject apology. It would save their adherents who remained in the city, at least for a time, from brutal outrage.

In chapter xvii. the progress of the Christian gospel in two cities of the empire is now related. Each place had its own peculiar characteristic. Thessalonica was a large commercial centre, with a numerous and turbulent Jewish population, and a disorderly mob. Athens, on the contrary, was the intellectual centre of the Roman world. In each of these cities the artistry of Luke is manifested by his sketches of the progress of the mission. It is worth remarking that, whereas at Philippi and Thessalonica, where the gospel was subjected to opposition and persecution, flourishing churches were founded, at Athens, where Paul suffered no annoyance, no success followed his mission. One is bound to admire the skill with which the different episodes in every town are introduced. In no single place are the conditions the same. Luke has undertaken the difficult task of describing the missionary work of Paul in the fewest possible words. The result is that, if he has left much the reader would like to know practically unnoticed, and sometimes condensed the events of months and even years within the limits of one or two verses, he has given a series of brief sketches admirably selected to depict the varied conditions of the towns throughout the Roman Empire, in which there was no drab uniformity, each having characteristics of its own. In the modern world different cities, in the same country at anyrate, are much alike ; but in the first century there was an amazing variety not merely in appearance, but in constitution, government, and the temper of the populace. Corinth was no more like Ephesus than Athens resembled Philippi.

xvii.

1 Travelling on through Amphipolis and Apollonia they reached
2 Thessalonica. Here there was a Jewish synagogue, and Paul as usual went in ; for three sabbaths he argued with
3 them on the scriptures, explaining and quoting passages to prove that the messiah had to suffer and rise from the dead, and that " the Jesus I proclaim to you is the messiah."
4 Some were persuaded and threw in their lot with Paul and Silas, including a host of devout Greeks and a large number
5 of the leading women. But the Jews were aroused to jealousy ; they got hold of some idle rascals to form a mob and set the town in an uproar ; they attacked Jason's house in the endeavour to bring them out before the
6 populace, but as they failed to find Paul and Silas they haled Jason and some of the brothers before the politarchs, yelling, "These upsetters of the whole world have come
7 here too! Jason has welcomed them! They all violate the decrees of Caesar by declaring someone else called
8 Jesus is king." Both the crowd and the politarchs were
9 disturbed when they heard this ; however, they let Jason and the others go, after binding them over to keep the peace.

Towards the conclusion of the previous chapter Luke vanishes from the scene. The first person plural by which he makes his presence known disappears when Paul and Silas are thrown into prison. Probably he remained at Philippi, to reappear at the same place some years later (Acts xx. 5). But even if the writer of Acts was not actually present at Thessalonica, the narrative is characteristically Lukan.

Apparently Paul and Silas delayed as little as possible till they reached **Thessalonica** by way of the Egnatian road which took them through **Amphipolis and Apollonia,** their object being to make as their centre a city from which the gospel could be diffused throughout Macedonia (cf. 1 Thess. i. 8). In the synagogue Paul is represented as **arguing,** not necessarily preaching, but acting as a rabbi in discussing **the scriptures;** for a synagogue was not so much a preaching-house as a school, in which education was carried on by discussion. The verb διελέξατο here employed has the same meaning as our word dialogue, and instruction was carried on as in a catechism by question and answer. Luke represents Paul's teaching as exactly analogous to that of our Lord on the walk to Emmaus, when he told Cleopas and his companion that, as the Christ, he must suffer in accordance with the Scripture, and taught them, ' Beginning with Moses and the prophets ' (Luke xxiv. 25–27). Paul is represented as insisting on the same thing to Agrippa II (Acts xxvi. 22–23).

The result of Paul's teaching was the foundation of a church, consisting of Jews, Greeks (who had been worshippers of the true God, like Cornelius, the word translated **devout** being a technical term), and of many of **the leading women** of the city, the Greeks and women being in the majority. **The Jews** (as in xiii. 50), furious at the defection of many possible proselytes and great ladies, on whose influence and liberality they relied, raised a serious tumult by inducing the idlers who were loafing in the market-place (A.V. ' lewd fellows of the baser sort ') to mob the house of **Jason,** the host of the missionaries. As **Paul and Silas** could not be found, they arrested **Jason** and brought him before the city magistrates.

Philippi, as we have seen, was a colony ruled by Roman officers. Thessalonica was a free city with a government of its own entrusted to what we should call a corporation of borough magistrates. These bore the title of **politarchs** (rulers of the city), and were naturally anxious to preserve the autonomy granted by Rome. The accusation was skilfully framed. Jason, it was said, had received into his house men who were causing trouble throughout the empire. So well organized was the Jewish community that rumours of the disturbing character of the Christian propaganda had probably already reached Thessalonica from Asia, and the magistracy would be naturally prejudiced against possible breakers of the peace. Nothing was said about religion, but a serious charge of disloyalty to the emperor was preferred. Jesus himself, according to Luke, had been somewhat similarly accused of forbidding people to pay tribute to Caesar, because, being the Messiah, he was himself king of Israel (Luke xxiii. 2). In the Fourth Gospel the Jews tell Pilate that if he releases Jesus he is no friend of Caesar ; for by proclaiming himself a king (John xix. 12) he had defied the *imperium* of Rome. Pilate, it is true, treated the charge as ridiculous, as did the Thessalonian magistrates ; but it had important consequences later. For the kingdom of Messiah meant not merely Jewish nationalism, but world domination.

It must be remembered that, although Augustus and his successors posed at Rome as no more than leading citizens of the Republic, in the East they were ' kings,' not as the Herods and others who were so called, but as the ancient rulers of Assyria, Babylon, Persia, and even the Seleucid monarchs. In the eyes of the Orientals the head of the Roman state was known as βασιλεύς ; and, though the English equivalent for this is **king**, it really meant an emperor in the modern sense of the word. The preachers of the gospel were accused of trying to secure allegiance to one whom they claimed to be the true World Ruler.

Our knowledge of what happened at Thessalonica is supplemented by two short letters of Paul to the local church. These were written very soon after the Apostle had left the city. Without entering into details or questions of exegesis, the following points may be noticed in the Thessalonian epistles. (1) The persecution endured by Paul was felt by the whole Church. (2) Thessalonica became a centre of evangelization.

(3) Not only ' devout ' Greeks joined the Church, but those who had previously been idolaters. (4) At Thessalonica we are informed for the first time of Paul's practice of working for his living that he might not be chargeable to his converts. The Philippians, however (Phil. iv. 15), insisted on sending money to the Apostle. (5) The Gentiles seem to have persecuted the converts. (6) Paul tried to return, but ' Satan ' hindered him. (7) Some sort of ministry had been established. (8) Paul urged his new church to be an industrious society. (9) The Apostle's preaching from his letters may be inferred to have been largely eschatological, but no suggestion of this appears in Acts.

Then the brothers at once sent off Paul and Silas by night to 10 Beroea. When they arrived there, they betook themselves to the Jewish synagogue, where the people were more 11 amenable than at Thessalonica ; they were perfectly ready to receive the Word and made a daily study of the scriptures to see if it was really as Paul said. Many of them 12 believed, together with a large number of prominent Greeks, both women and men. But when the Jews of 13 Thessalonica heard that Paul was proclaiming the word of God at Beroea as well, they came to create a disturbance and a riot among the crowds at Beroea too. The brothers 14 then sent off Paul at once on his way to the sea, while Silas and Timotheus remained where they were. Paul's escort 15 brought him as far as Athens and left with instructions that Silas and Timotheus were to join him as soon as possible.

Beroea was an unimportant town, not on the great Egnatian road, and some sixty miles f.om Thessalonica. There **Paul and Silas** met with some success. They went into the **synagogue** and found **the people amenable** to argument in the words of Luke, in the A.V. ' more noble than those in Thessalonica.' The adjective is εὐγενής, which is twice used in the N.T. to imply high birth (Luke xix. 12, 1 Cor. i. 26). Here it is the equivalent of the Latin *generosus* (nobly born), both signifying the qualities supposed to be attached to high birth. Perhaps

the best English rendering would be 'liberal,' in the sense of
free from prejudice, in contrast with the bigotry of the Thessalonian Jews. These good people listened to the arguments for
Jesus being the Christ adduced by the missionaries (cf. xvii. 2),
and verified them by daily examination of the Scriptures.
What happened is exactly analogous to what is recorded in
xiv. 19. **The Jews of Thessalonica** got wind of Paul's preaching in Beroea and stirred up the people. Evidently, as the
Apostle's danger was great, his faithful friends would not leave
him till he reached **Athens,** whether by land or sea we are not
clearly informed. (A western reading adds that he was
unable to preach in Thessaly.)   Silas and Timothy were left
to follow as best they could.   A church was founded in
Beroea, and one of its citizens named Sopater accompanied
Paul later on his final journey to Jerusalem (xx. 4).

16 While Paul was waiting for them at Athens, his soul was irri-
17 tated at the sight of the idols that filled the city. He
argued in the synagogue with the Jews and the devout
proselytes and also in the market-place daily with those
18 who chanced to be present. Some of the Epicurean and
Stoic philosophers also came across him. Some said,
"Whatever does the fellow mean with his scraps of learning?" Others said, "He looks like a herald of foreign
deities" (this was because he preached 'Jesus' and 'the
19 Resurrection'). Then taking him to the Areopagus they
asked, "May we know what is this novel teaching of
20 yours? You talk of some things that sound strange to us;
21 so we want to know what they mean." (For all the
Athenians and the foreign visitors to Athens occupied
themselves with nothing else than repeating or listening
to the latest novelty.)

In these verses Luke shews himself not so much an historian
as a consummate artist, his object being to lead the reader
on to the contemplation of Paul's speech on Mars Hill. The
description of the Apostle's vexation at beholding so many
evidences of idolatry is a fitting preface to a diatribe against
the unreasonableness of image worship. His **daily** encounters

in the **market-place** with chance strangers prepares us for the academic character of the coming discourse ; for Paul was evidently considered as a philosopher visiting the city. The **Epicureans** and **Stoics** are introduced because their peculiar doctrines are going to be discussed. Finally, the idle, garrulous, and inquisitive **Athenians** shew the sort of audience the Apostle was about to address. We are prepared to hear a great speech, leading, however, to no great result.

The *mise en scène* is admirably depicted. The *Agora*, or market-square, of Athens lies on the south-east of the Acropolis, and due south of **the Areopagus,** or hill of Mars. A disputant like Paul may in his conversations have drawn together knots of inquisitive students. There were various opinions about him. Some called him a seed picker (σπερμό-λογος, the name of a bird), a word aptly paraphrased in the translation above. Others thought he was preaching a new religion—**foreign deities,** such as Socrates had been accused of introducing. All must have considered the Apostle, to use a modern term, somewhat of a ' crank ' ; but at anyrate no one could converse with him and deny that he was an interesting personality. So the crowd in the Agora must have invited Paul to accompany them to the **Areopagus,** and give a formal address—there is no suggestion that the religious court was held or that the speaker was on his trial.

All this is very natural and excellently told, but two points are difficult. One is the extreme irritation which Paul is represented to have felt on beholding the idolatry of Athens. It is not as if he had been a Jew brought up in Jerusalem and suddenly transplanted to a city like Athens full of statues, temples, and works of art. Paul had seen many cities, all of which were in this sense full of idols. Nor were idols worshipped in Athens more than elsewhere, since by this time the city had become a show-place to students and tourists. Elsewhere Paul shews little Jewish fanaticism against images ; indeed, he tells the Corinthians ' there is no such thing as an idol in the world.' Even when he writes to the Romans, and declares that the heathen were punished for their refusal to know God by what was revealed in nature to be, by falling into the folly of supposing that He was like to corruptible man or even animals and reptiles, he seems to be thinking rather of the gods of Egypt than of the statuary of Athens.

The second difficulty is whether the speech was composed or compiled by St. Luke, or is an epitome of what St. Paul said on the occasion. It is undeniably of great importance as the earliest Christian ' apology ' to the Greeks.

22 So Paul stood in the middle of the Areopagus and said, " Men of Athens, I observe at every turn that you are a most religious people. Why, as I passed along and scanned 23 your objects of worship, I actually came upon an altar with the inscription

TO AN UNKNOWN GOD.

Well, I proclaim to you what you worship in your ignorance. *The God who made* the world *and* all *things in it,* 24 he, as Lord *of heaven and earth,* does not dwell in shrines that are made by human hands ; he is not served by 25 human hands as if he needed anything, for it is he who *gives* life and *breath* and all things to all men. All nations 26 he has created from a common origin, to dwell all over the earth, fixing their allotted periods and the boundaries of their abodes, meaning them to seek for God on the chance 27 of finding him in their groping for him. Though indeed he is close to each one of us, for it is in him that we live 28 and move and exist—as some of your own poets have said,

' WE TOO BELONG TO HIS RACE.'

Well, as the race of God, we ought not to imagine 29 that the divine nature resembles gold or silver or stone, the product of human art and invention. Such ages of 30 ignorance God overlooked, but he now charges men that they are all everywhere to repent, inasmuch as he has 31 fixed a day on which *he will judge the world justly* by a man whom he has destined for this. And he has given proof of this to all by raising him from the dead."

The situation of the Areopagus is admirably suited to the occasion. The hill is a low rock just below the Acropolis, and

Paul probably spoke to his audience facing the noblest monuments of Greek art and the most revered objects of Hellenic religion. It is in full view of the Parthenon, and of the statue of Athena with her gleaming spear, the light of which, when caught by the rising sun, was the first object the mariner saw on approaching Athens. The old religion in its glory and the new religion, represented by an insignificant-looking Jew, so to speak, confronted one another, and the great struggle between the Faith and the cults of the ancient world was in this way inaugurated.

The opening words of Paul are marked by a courteous compliment to his hearers. ' Gentlemen **of Athens,** I can see **you are a most religious people.'** The translation ' too superstitious ' in the A.V. is misleading, though the word ' fearing demons ' is used in this sense ; in the '' Characters '' of Theophrastus the ' superstitious man ' is one who is in constant fear of the unseen world. But in Acts xxv. the substantive *deisidaimonia* is used of Judaism when the procurator Festus told the Jewish King Agrippa that Paul was accused by the Jews in matters of ' their own superstition,' meaning to be as polite as possible to his royal visitor. ' For as I was going through your city and inspecting the monuments of your religion, I found an **altar with the inscription to an Unknown God.'** The critical eye of the great Christian scholar, St. Jerome (fourth century), perceived a fallacy here. There were at Athens altars to ' unknown gods ' but not to ' the ' or to **' an ' unknown God.** But Paul implies that on careful inspection he found a single altar thus dedicated, which may well have escaped the notice of those who had written about Athens. It is even possible that this altar may have been dedicated to the God of Israel, whose name was never mentioned. His next words, ' Whom therefore ye **worship** without knowing I now declare **to you,'** are thoroughly in keeping with the tone of ancient Christian apologists, who consistently strove to maintain that the true God whom they proclaimed was He whom mankind had always unconsciously adored. Or, to put it otherwise, that monotheism was no innovation but the natural religion of the human race. Here

St. Paul in the first century and Tertullian more than a hundred years later are in complete accord.

This God, maker and Lord of heaven and earth, **does not dwell in shrines that are made by human hands.** That God made all things is fundamental to Judaism and Christianity alike, and few educated Greeks would question the last clause, since all were agreed that the Supreme Being cannot be localized. At the same time popular religion of every description endeavours to do this, and the shrine or inner temple was believed to be the special home of the deity ; even the Holy of Holies in the Temple of Jerusalem testifies to this, nor is the idea absent from every form of Christian piety. This sentiment is an echo of Stephen's speech (vii. 48). The word ' hand-made ' or ' manufactured ' is applied in the New Testament to the circumcision of the flesh (Eph. ii. 11) and to the Tabernacle on earth as contrasted with that in heaven (Heb. ix. 11). In the LXX the plural signifies idols.

No Jew would deny that all men had a common ancestor, although their prejudices were strongly in favour of religious exclusiveness. The argument here is as follows. As a creation of God, man has **a common origin,** yet national divisions have been of old God's ordinance. This is the Hebrew idea (see Deut. xxxiii.) of the seventy nations of the world. Hellenism again had grasped two truths : (1) the Epicurean schools held that God needs nothing at man's hands, and inferentially that worship by gift and sacrifice is needless ; and (2) in Stoicism, the truth, that all of us are sons of God, was declared by the poets Aratus and Cleanthes. As such we cannot think that our common Father and Maker is comparable to any image, however skilfully made and designed. Yet men had always been seeking for God, though blindly as one groping for something in the darkness. These days are now over. **God** has **overlooked** man's errors and mistakes, and now invites all to ' turn ' to Him (for so the word μετανοεῖν ought to be interpreted here, and not by **repent**). God has now appointed **a day on which He will judge the world by a man whom He has** proclaimed His representative **to all** humanity **by raising him from the dead.**

But on hearing of a ' resurrection of dead men,' some sneered, 32
while others said, " We will hear you again on that subject." So Paul withdrew from them. Some men, how- ³³
ever, did join him and believe, including Dionysius the ³⁴
Areopagite, a woman called Damaris, and some others.

The mention of a resurrection appeared to be ridiculous to
some of Paul's audience, whilst others politely expressed a wish
to hear him again. It is strange that of the few who joined
Paul one, **Dionysius the Areopagite,** had an extraordinary
hold on Christian tradition, being the only name connected
with the Apostle which seems seriously to have interested
the early church. The historian Eusebius (A.D. 320) mentions
him twice (*H.E.*, iii. 4 and iv. 23), and says he was bishop of
Athens. His name is attached to certain mystical writings of
the sixth century, and later he was declared to be the Apostle
of France, sent there by Pope Clement I and martyred in Paris
on Montmartre. Chrysostom, in his book *On Priesthood*, says
that **Damaris,** or Damalis, was his wife.

The question whether the speech at Athens was really
delivered by St. Paul is still open. Its value cannot be disputed. The strongest argument in favour of its Pauline origin
is that, what was evidently in the eyes of the author a magnificent speech, should have failed to convince the audience. Did
any so-called apology for the faith ever make a Christian ?

After leaving Athens, Paul, though most anxious to return
to the churches he had founded in Macedonia, went unaccom-
panied by his friends to Corinth, not then the ancient and
famous city of antiquity which had been destroyed by the
Romans in 146 B.C., but a new town built by Caesar in 46 B.C.
Its importance in the days of the Apostle was due to the fact
that it was a commercial centre of the trade between Italy and
the East, and contained a floating population in touch with
the two main divisions of the Roman world, its merchandise
being conveyed overland from the western port of Lechaeum
to the eastern one at Cenchreae, the city itself being a natural
meeting-place of the traders of Italy and of the Asiatic

provinces. On going to Corinth, Paul, possibly unwittingly, inaugurated a new departure in his missionary activity by coming into contact with Rome.

It would appear that the Apostle was in great straits when he reached Corinth, and that his meeting with Aquila and Priscilla was providential because they not only provided him with the means for maintaining himself by his manual labour, but proved most valuable assistants in his evangelistic work.

xviii.

: After this Paul left Athens and went to Corinth. There he came across a Jew called Aquila, a native of Pontus, who had recently arrived from Italy with his wife Priscilla, as Claudius had ordered all Jews to leave Rome. Paul
3 accosted them, and as he belonged to the same trade he stayed with them and they all worked together. (They
4 were workers in leather by trade.) Every sabbath he argued in the synagogue, persuading both Jews and Greeks.
5 By the time Silas and Timotheus came south from Macedonia, Paul was engrossed in this preaching of the word,
6 arguing to the Jews that the messiah was Jesus. But as they opposed and abused him, he shook out his garments in protest, saying, "Your blood be on your own heads! I am not responsible! After this I will go to the Gentiles."
7 Then he removed to the house of a devout proselyte called
8 Titus Justus, which adjoined the synagogue. But Crispus the president of the synagogue believed in the Lord, as did all his household, and many of the Corinthians listened,
9 believed, and were baptized. And the Lord said to Paul in a vision by night, ' *Have no fear,* speak on and never stop,
10 *for I am with you,* and no one shall attack and injure
11 you; I have many people in this city.' So he settled there for a year and six months, teaching them the word of God.

The connexion of Paul with **Aquila and Priscilla** was particularly close ; thrice he mentions the wife first, and always calls

her Prisca (Rom. xvi. 3, 1 Cor. xvi. 19, 2 Tim. iv. 19). The
pair accompanied the Apostle as far as Ephesus when he was
on his way to Syria, and there remained, meeting with Apollos,
whom they instructed about the baptism of Jesus. They send
their salutations from Asia (1 Cor. xvi. 19), and their names
stand first with the highest praise in the salutations appended
to the epistle to the Romans (xvi. 3–5). In 2 Timothy (iv. 19)
the Apostle sends his salutation to ‘ Prisca, Aquila, and the
household of Onesiphorus.’ According to these statements
Aquila was a native of Pontus, who had made his way from one
of the most easterly provinces of Asia Minor to Rome, and
when expelled from the city had crossed the Adriatic to
Corinth with his wife. There they met with Paul, established
themselves in business, and continued in the city for a considerable time. Thence they accompanied Paul to Ephesus,
and remained there whilst Paul went to Palestine, but they do
not seem to have stayed to await his return. Whether they
went back to Rome is not certain ; but they may well have
done so, though much depends upon the salutations in Rom.
xvi. being an integral part of the epistle, or really intended for
Ephesus. According to 2 Timothy, the genuineness of which
letter is open to doubt, Aquila and Priscilla were again at
Ephesus towards the close of the life of the Apostle.

Various questions arise concerning this interesting couple :
that they were of some social importance there is little doubt,
otherwise they could hardly have travelled so extensively and
established businesses which enabled them to employ assistants. (1) The first thing we naturally ask is the nature of
their occupation. Σκηνοποιός is a difficult word. It is
rendered ‘ tent-maker ’ in the A.V. In the Vulgate there is no
attempt to translate the word, which is rendered *scenofactoriae
artis*. One Latin MS. has *lectari* (*lectarii*)—makers of
couches. The rendering workers in leather, found in some
Latin versions, is open to the alleged objection that this was
considered to be an unclean trade, and consequently one not
likely to be chosen by a family of strict Pharisees, like Paul's.
Paul is popularly called a ‘ tent-maker ’ ; and there we must
leave it. It seems that the Apostle was no mere artisan, but

that his family, at least, possessed some means. There is nothing improbable, if his father were wealthy, that the son should learn the practical part of his business. In the first place, as it was in the middle ages, every employer of labour knew how to make the article he dealt with as well if not better than any of his craftsmen ; and in the second it was customary for every Jewish father to teach his son a trade.

We do not know the circumstances under which Aquila and Priscilla left Rome. Suetonius, who wrote two generations later, relates that **Claudius** expelled the Jews for tumults raised at the instigation of Chrestus (*impulsore Chresto*). We have no means of knowing who Chrestus was, nor can we say positively that Suetonius was thinking of Jesus Christ. The Jews, we learn from Josephus and Tacitus, were a frequent cause of trouble in the city, and were often ordered to leave it. But as there are estimated to have been 30,000, we may be fairly sure they did not all quit Rome, and absolutely certain that, when the reason for their dismissal was forgotten, they silently resumed their residence. Aquila and Priscilla may have had good reasons for leaving and not going back. This raises another point : were they already believers before they met Paul ? There is no hint that they were converted or baptized at Corinth. Consequently there must have been at this early date a church in Rome.

12 But when Gallio was proconsul of Achaia the Jews without exception rose against Paul and brought him up before the
13 tribunal, crying, " This fellow incites men to worship God
14 contrary to the Law." Paul was just on the point of opening his lips to reply, when Gallio said to the Jews, " If it had been a misdemeanour or wicked crime, there would be
15 some reason in me listening to you, O Jews. But as these are merely questions of words and persons and your own Law, you can attend to them for yourselves. I decline to
16 adjudicate upon matters like that." And he drove them
17 from the tribunal. Then all [the Greeks] caught hold of Sosthenes the president of the synagogue and beat him in front of the tribunal ; but Gallio took no notice.

Till recently there was no evidence that **Gallio** was **proconsul of Achaia** except a casual hint of Pliny the Elder that he had been there. Now, however, an inscription at Delphi has conclusively proved that he was appointed by Claudius in A.D. 52. He must have arrived there in the later spring, a year and a half after Paul's coming. Gallio was the elder brother of Seneca, the philosopher and statesman, who according to Christian tradition corresponded with St. Paul. The acquittal of the Apostle by Gallio's decision that the prosecution had no case was of importance. The charge was more subtle than might at first sight appear. At Thessalonica Paul had been declared to have taught what amounted to treason (*maiestas*), an accusation too absurd for the magistrates seriously to entertain. Gallio, on the other hand, was asked to adjudicate on the question whether Paul's preaching had not put him outside the pale of Judaism, and of the toleration granted to that religion by Roman law. But Gallio was too good a lawyer to listen to such a charge, and ordered the court to be cleared. The Greeks, delighted at the rebuff of the Jews, assaulted **Sosthenes,** the synagogue-ruler, probably Paul's chief accuser, **and beat him.** Gallio **took no notice.** According to the A.V. and R.V. he ' cared for none of these things ' ; not, as used to be assumed, because he was indifferent to religious impressions, but because, as a judge, it was not his business. Paul was not even asked to speak in his own defence. As for the beating of Sosthenes, one addition in the text is that Gallio pretended not to see it.

After waiting on for a number of days Paul said goodbye to the 18
brothers and sailed for Syria, accompanied by Priscilla and
Aquila. (As the latter was under a vow, he had his head
shaved at Cenchreae.) When they reached Ephesus, 19
Paul left them there. He went to the synagogue and
argued with the Jews, who asked him to stay for a while. 20
But he would not consent ; he said goodbye to them, telling 21
them, " I will come back to you, if it is the will of God."
Then, sailing from Ephesus, he reached Caesarea, went up 22
to the capital to salute the church, and travelled down to

23   **Antioch. After spending some time there he went off
on a journey right through the country of Galatia and
Phrygia, strengthening the disciples.**

In this section we have a very hurried description of events
which must have covered at least several months. **Cenchreae**
was the eastern port on the Isthmus of Corinth. It is not
certain, from the words ' having **shaved his head**,' whether
Paul or Aquila had taken a vow. We know, however, that
on a subsequent occasion Paul was discharging a vow in
the Temple of Jerusalem (xx. 26) when he was attacked
by his enemies. Why Luke, who is evidently not well acquainted with the circumstances of this part of Paul's career,
mentions this apparently unimportant detail we know not,
unless it were to shew that he or his friend were observant
Jews. It is to be noticed that after his departure from
Corinth Paul is no longer accompanied by Silas and Timothy.
Silas disappears altogether, but, when Paul wrote to the
Corinthians from Ephesus (1 Cor. xvi. 10), he tells them to
expect a visit from Timothy, whose name appears in the salutation of 2 Corinthians, written after Paul had left Ephesus.

The compression of the narrative here is remarkable. Paul
evidently attached great importance to his visit to Syria, as he
refused to stay at Ephesus, though entreated to do so. On his
outward passage by sea and his return by land he must have
covered at least 1,500 miles. Yet Luke dismisses this long
journey in a few words, either because he did not know any
details, or because he did not think that it was necessary to
inform Theophilus. All he relates of the voyage is that the
Apostle landed at **Caesarea**, Stratonis, and thence went up and
saluted the Church. The addition **to the capital** is felicitously
ambiguous because Caesarea not Jerusalem was the seat of the
government, and we cannot be sure that Paul visited the Holy
City, though it is probable that he did so.

Of the return to Ephesus by land nothing is related save
that Paul, still apparently alone, traversed the entire length of
the peninsula of Asia Minor, and on the way visited the
churches of **Phrygia and Galatia**. Stress has been laid on the

fact that he traversed this particular district ; but as Luke has seen fit to tell us nothing of this long journey or of Paul's purpose in quitting Ephesus to go up and salute the Church, we can only surmise what happened, and why he undertook a journey which certainly occupied many months and possibly more than a year. That it was attended by much hardship cannot be questioned.

There came to Ephesus a Jew called Apollos, who was a native 24 of Alexandria, a man of culture, strong in his knowledge of the scriptures. He had been instructed in the Way of 25 the Lord and he preached and taught about Jesus with ardour and accuracy, though all the baptism he knew was that of John. In the synagogue he was very outspoken at 26 first ; but when Aquila and Priscilla listened to him, they took him home and explained more accurately to him what the Way of God really meant. As he wished to cross 27 to Achaia, the brothers wrote and urged the disciples there to give him a welcome. And on his arrival he proved of great service to those who by God's grace had believed, for 28 he publicly refuted the Jews with might and main, showing from the scriptures that the messiah was Jesus.

This is a remarkable section, being the only one in the later part of Acts in which St. Paul's is not the principal figure. This and the first paragraph of chap. xix. introduce an otherwise unexpected episode into the history of the early church, without which we could have formed no idea of the influence of the Baptist after the ministry of Jesus. Yet, although there is no mention of John in the New Testament, outside the gospels and Acts, nor in the so-called Apostolic writings, great stress is laid on the connexion of John and Jesus in both the Synoptists and the Fourth Gospel. Here, however, we learn that the two baptisms persisted side by side, possibly in rivalry, though the disciples of John apparently accepted Jesus as the Messiah.

The important Jewish colony of **Alexandria** only contributed one name, that of **Apollos**, to the record of Luke. Like so many other notable characters in Acts, Apollos is not conspicuous in Christian legend, although, to judge from the First Epistle to the Corinthians, he played no small part in the evangelization of their city.

That **Apollos** (or Apollonius) was a native of Alexandria may be significant, as that city was the chief centre of an important phase of Judaism. As Jerusalem represented the Law and the cultus, and Antioch the Hellenic aspect of world-embracing Judaism, so Alexandria stood for Judaism imbued with the philosophy of Greece. For this reason Apollos is supposed by some to have been the writer of the epistle to the Hebrews with its Pauline teaching coloured by the allegorism of Alexandria. He had been a disciple in the school of the Baptist, and had evidently learned that John was the forerunner of one mightier than he. Thus the teaching of Apollos concerning Jesus, so far as it went, was accurate (**he taught,** ἀκριβῶς). But to all appearances the new Christian movement had escaped his notice, and it was certainly late in reaching Alexandria. **Aquila and Priscilla** heard him in the synagogue, and at once realized the power his message would have, if only he understood the true significance of what he was endeavouring to teach. They consequently explained to Apollos **the Way of God** more perfectly, and, finding that he was going to Corinth, commended him to the infant community there, with the result that he gave a powerful impulse to the spread of the gospel, even though the factious character of the inhabitants tried to make him the head of a party. All the same, the Apostle regarded him as a most useful ally, and could say, ' Paul planted and Apollos watered ' (1 Cor. iii. 6).

All things considered, the story of St. Paul's work at Ephesus is not among the best part of the narrative of Acts, though this chapter concludes with a most dramatic account of the great riot in the theatre. There are hints, however, that the period of Paul's sojourn at Ephesus was one of great activity, and this increases regret that the two incidents which Luke has seen fit to relate—the baptism of the disciples of John and the contest with magic—are comparatively so uninteresting to us.

It was when Apollos was in Corinth that Paul,[1] after passing 1
through the inland districts, came down to Ephesus.
There he found some disciples, whom he asked, "Did you 2
receive the holy Spirit when you believed?" "No,"
they said, "we never even heard of its existence." "Then," 3
said he, "what were you baptized in?" "In John's
baptism," they replied. "John," said Paul, "baptized 4
with a baptism of repentance, telling the people to believe
in Him who was to come after him, that is, in Jesus."
When they heard this, they had themselves baptized in the 5
name of the Lord Jesus, and after Paul laid his hands on 6
them the holy Spirit came upon them, they spoke with
'tongues' and prophesied. They numbered all together 7
about twelve men.

After traversing the upper district of provincial Asia Paul
reached Ephesus. There he found twelve disciples of the
Baptist who had become believers, but had not as yet received
the Spirit. What Luke proceeds to tell us is not like the story
of Apollos, nor is it entirely Pauline in tone. The brief record
is full of difficulties regarding the nature and doctrine of primitive baptism. These ' disciples ' were presumably believers in
Jesus as the Messiah, and had sealed their faith by accepting a
baptism. But according to most of the notices in Acts,
apostolic baptism was accompanied by the gift of the holy
Spirit (ii. 38 at Pentecost ; viii. 13, Simon Magus believed and
was baptized by Philip, but the holy Spirit was bestowed by
Peter and John ; x. 44, the Spirit came at the words of Peter,
before baptism ; xvi. 15 and 33, Lydia and the jailer were
baptized, but nothing is said of the holy Spirit. The same
is true of the Ethiopian, viii. 38). Paul's question (literally)
' Did you as believers receive a holy Spirit ? ' and the reply,
' We never heard that there is a holy Spirit ' (note the omission
of the articles) are both ambiguous. When you believed must
mean, when you believed in Jesus. Confession of Jesus as

---

[1] ' But when Paul desired of his own counsel to go to Jerusalem, the
Spirit told him to return to Asia ; and ' (W).

THE ACTS OF THE APOSTLES

Messiah was apparently immediately accompanied by some sort
of baptism. But John, as Paul remarks, could not baptize for
anything but remission of sins after confession, on the ground
that the age of the Messiah was at hand. May we suppose
therefore that the disciples of John accepted Jesus as the
Messiah without discontinuing the baptism of their Master, or
formally joining the Church ? Taking into account the late
date of the Fourth Gospel, it would appear that a Baptist sect
continued long after the foundation of the Church of Christ
(John ii. 22 ff.) ; but that it was decreasing as the influence of
Jesus increased. The persistence of the school of the Baptist
is an interesting, but not easily explained, phenomenon in the
development of early Christianity. Paul's explanation of the
nature of the baptism of John increases the difficulty. ' **John
baptized, telling the people to believe in** the Coming One,
namely, **Jesus,**' but this his hearers had already done. The
baptism **in the name of the Lord Jesus** (cf. viii. 16) which
followed raises the question : If there was *one* baptism (Eph.
iv. 5), were these followers of Jesus on earth, who later entered
the Church, rebaptized ? Note that in giving the holy Spirit
by the imposition of his hands Paul exercised the same
apostolic authority as that of Peter and John in Samaria
(viii. 15).

Finally, we must ask ourselves whether the doctrine of the
Spirit and Baptism here implied is that of St. Paul. In
him the Spirit is the bestower of power to believers, sometimes miraculous, hortatory, prophetic, or administrative
(1 Cor. xii. 8 ff.), elsewhere bearing ' fruits ' in the form
of the Christian virtues (Gal. v. 22). But in connexion
with baptism—a word very rare in the Pauline epistles (only
in Rom. vi. 4 and Eph. iv. 5)—the Spirit signifies the new life
which those who are Christ's receive (Rom. vi. 4, Col. ii. 12).
In Acts the Spirit at baptism here and elsewhere is manifested
by speaking with ' tongues ' and prophesying.

8 Then **Paul entered the synagogue and for three months spoke
out fearlessly, arguing and persuading people about the
9 Reign of God. But as some grew stubborn and disobedient,**

decrying the Way in presence of the multitude,[1] he left
them, withdrew the disciples, and continued his argument
every day from eleven to four* in the lecture-room of
Tyrannus. This went on for two years, so that all the 10
inhabitants of Asia, Jews as well as Greeks, heard the
word of the Lord.

* The words ἀπὸ ὥρας πέμπτης ἕως δεκάτης (D, etc.) are probably
original.

The words **spoke out fearlessly** are a rendering of the equivalent Greek verb applied to Apollos (xviii. 26). This is always
used in a good sense in Acts, of giving the Christian message
without reservation. At Ephesus, as at Corinth, there was a
formal separation from the synagogue (xviii. 7). Here Paul
seems to have hired a room in which to deliver his message.
From his address to the elders of Miletus the Apostle seems to
have plied his craft in order to maintain himself and his companions (xx. 34). The interesting addition **from eleven to four**
(literally, ' from the fifth to the tenth hour ') found in the
western text may have been omitted, because it was not
understood that workers were at leisure in that part of the
day. The Greek for **lecture-room** is the equivalent of the
English ' school.' This word σχολή means leisure, and came
to signify the place where men spent the hour of recreation in
mutual discussion. When the Jews refused to listen to him in
the synagogue (ἠπείθουν, cf. xiv. 2), he and his disciples hired
a place where they could discuss matters, in this school of
Tyrannus. The work at Ephesus continued **for two years** or
perhaps three (xx. 31), and was evidently fruitful. As we
learn from his epistles, Paul was frequently in danger from his
Jewish opponents, but many cities of **Asia** were evidently
evangelized, although the words **all the inhabitants** may savour
of exaggeration. At anyrate the province became the great
centre of primitive Christianity, though the records, outside
Acts, give but little credit to the work accomplished by Paul.

God also worked no ordinary miracles by means of Paul; 11
 people even carried away towels or aprons he had used, and 12

[1] W adds ' of Gentiles.'

13 at their touch sick folk were freed from their diseases and
evil spirits came out of them. Some strolling Jewish
exorcists also undertook to pronounce the name of the
Lord Jesus over those who had evil spirits, saying, "I
14 adjure you to the Jesus whom Paul preaches!" The
seven sons of Sceuas, a Jewish high priest, used to do this.
15 But the evil spirit retorted, "Jesus I know and Paul I
16 know, but you—who are you?" And the man in whom
the evil spirit resided leapt at them, overpowered them all,
and belaboured them, till they rushed out of the house
17 stripped and wounded. This came to the ears of all the
inhabitants of Ephesus, Jews as well as Greeks; awe fell
on them all, and the name of the Lord Jesus was magnified.
18 Many believers would also come to confess and disclose
19 their magic spells; and numbers who had practised magic
arts collected their books and burned them in the presence
of all. On adding up the value of them, it was found
that they were worth two thousand pounds.

The opening words of this section recall the description of
the miracles wrought by Peter and the Apostles in Jerusalem
(v. 12 ff.), and the vagueness of both passages seems to indicate
that Luke was equally in the dark as to what happened in these
cities; for nowhere else in this part of Acts does he speak in so
indiscriminate a manner of constant miracles. Here alone
does he relate that Paul cast out evil spirits, and, in describing
the adversaries of the Apostle, calls them exorcists, a word not
found elsewhere in the New Testament, although those who
cast out demons later became such an order in the Church.
Two things may be noticed as characteristic of this section:
(1) the purely physical character of some of the miracles;
(2) the use of the name of Jesus as having magical power.

(1) Cures wrought by the passing shadow of Peter (v. 15),
or by garments worn by Paul are possible; and 'miracles' of
this description are not unknown in mediaeval, and even in
modern, times. But these cannot be classed among those
wonders which are proofs of divine grace. Except the beautiful story of the woman, who with simple faith touched the hem

of the Lord's garment, there is nothing like this in the miracles of Jesus, which in the Fourth Gospel are called ' signs.' The record of these wonders is of interest to us rather as illustrative of the credulity of the age than as serving the purpose of edification. They seem to foreshadow the period at which such material objects as the relics of the saints were believed efficacious in benefiting Christians.

(2) The power of Jesus' name is recognized throughout the New Testament ; miracles, especially the casting forth of demons, are wrought by it (Matt. vii. 22, Mark ix. 38, etc., Acts iii. 6, xvi. 18). The Name is a power to which all in heaven and earth must bow (Phil. ii. 9, 10), and it was, not unnaturally, employed for purely magical purposes by the sons of **Sceuas** or Sceva,[1] whose use of it produced an effect but to their detriment ; for the spirit made the possessed man turn on them in insane fury and drive them away **stripped** of their garments and **wounded.** The result of this was a crusade against magic of every description. A public conflagration of the literature on the subject, which reminds us of the burning of objects of luxury at Florence in the fifteenth century due to the preaching of Savonarola, ensued. The value of the books was estimated at five myriad drachmas (50,000), roughly estimated in our translation at £2,000 or $10,000.

Hitherto this chapter has provided more interest to the critic than edification to the reader. Luke has given a condensed narrative of what he may have known only by hearsay. Now he relates an experience of Paul's which he may well have learned from the Apostle ; the account of this riot in the theatre of Ephesus is among the most brilliant bits of word-painting in Acts.

Thus did the word of the Lord increase and prevail mightily. 20
After these events Paul resolved in the Spirit to travel through 21

---

[1] The seven ' sons of Sceva ' may have been, not brothers, but members of a guild of exorcists. The text of Westcott and Hort is : ' overpowered both of them,' as if two only had made the attempt. The word rendered in A.V. and R.V. ' chief priest ' means here no more than what we might render ' archpriest.' Sceva is a Latin name.

Macedonia and Achaia on his way to Jerusalem. "After

22 I get there," he said, "I must also visit Rome." So he
despatched two of his assistants to Macedonia, Timotheus

23 and Erastus, while he himself stayed on awhile in Asia. It
was about that time that a great commotion arose over the

24 Way. This was how it happened. By making silver
shrines of Artemis a silversmith called Demetrius was the

25 means of bringing rich profit to his workmen. So he got
them together, along with the workmen who belonged to
similar trades, and said to them : "My men, you know

26 this trade is the source of our wealth. You also see and
hear that not only at Ephesus but almost all over Asia this
fellow Paul has drawn off a considerable number of people
by his persuasions. He declares that hand-made gods are

27 not gods at all. Now the danger is not only that we will
have our trade discredited but that the temple of the great
goddess Artemis will fall into contempt and that she will be
degraded from her majestic glory, she whom all Asia and

28 the wide world worship." When they heard this they were
filled with rage [1] and raised the cry, "Great is Artemis of

29 Ephesus ! " So the city was filled with confusion. They
rushed like one man into the amphitheatre, dragging along
Gaius and Aristarchus, Macedonians who were travelling

30 with Paul. (Paul wanted to enter the popular assembly,
31 but the disciples would not allow him. Some of the
Asiarchs, who were friends of his, also sent to beg him not

32 to venture into the amphitheatre.) Some were shouting
one thing, some another; for the assembly was in confusion, and the majority had no idea why they had met.

33 Some of the mob concluded it must be Alexander, as the
Jews pushed him to the front. So Alexander, motioning
with his hand, wanted to defend himself before the people;

34 but when they discovered he was a Jew, a roar broke from
them all, and for about two hours they shouted, "Great is

35 Artemis of Ephesus ! Great is Artemis of Ephesus ! " The
secretary of state then got the mob calmed down, and said

[1] W adds here, 'they ran into the street' (ἀμφοδος = Lat. *in campum*).

to them, "Men of Ephesus, who on earth does not know
that the city of Ephesus is Warden of the temple of the
great Artemis and of the statue that fell from heaven ? All 36
this is beyond question.   So you should keep calm and do
nothing reckless.   Instead of that, you have brought these 37
men here who are guilty neither of sacrilege nor of blasphemy against our goddess.   If Demetrius and his fellow 38
tradesmen have a grievance against anybody, let both
parties state their charges ; assizes are held and there are
always the proconsuls.   Any wider claim must be settled 39
in the legal assembly of the citizens.   Indeed there is a 40
danger of our being charged with riot over to-day's meeting; there is not a single reason we can give for this disorderly gathering."   With these words he dismissed the 41
assembly.

Paul's plan of visiting **Macedonia and Achaia** and then of
going to **Jerusalem** and finally visiting **Rome** is practically the
preface to the remainder of Acts, in the same way as the order
in which the disciples' mission is given by the Lord introduces
the scope of the entire book (i. 8).   At Ephesus began the most
important period of the literary activity of the Apostle, and
for his experiences at this period one must refer to his two
letters to Corinth and the epistle to the Romans.   The riot
was another matter.

It is remarkable that in the account of the affair of Demetrius Paul, though the principal object of attack, does not
appear.   As at Philippi (xvi.), the cause of the hostility of the
heathen was financial.   **Demetrius** appealed to the pocket of
the workmen and to the piety of the people of Ephesus (ver. 27).
Diana or **Artemis** of the Ephesians was not the virgin huntress
of Greek mythology, but an Oriental deity representing the
fecundity of nature.   Her presence was believed to be attested
by a meteorite which had fallen from the sky, and her temple
was one of the wonders of the world.   The city enjoyed the
honour of being the keeper of her shrine (νεοκόρος).   Probably
her festival was being celebrated at this time in the month
dedicated to her name (Artemision=March ; see 1 Cor. xvi. 8).

If so, the occasion was well chosen, for the people were keeping holiday and the city was crowded with visitors. The account falls into three sections : (1) The speech of Demetrius (23–28) ; (2) the scene in the theatre (29–34) ; and (3) the speech of the town clerk or scribe of the city (35–41).

(1) The trade in **shrines** or images of the sanctuary which people were accustomed to purchase had probably fallen off. Not only the Ephesians but the provincials of Asia had been so perverted by the mission of Paul and his friends that there was no sale for these objects of devotion. Demetrius appealed to popular sentiment. Not only was Paul's preaching bad for trade, but for religion itself. If it were allowed to continue, the reverence for the goddess, worshipped not only in Asia but throughout the empire, would be diminished. The indignant auditors of Demetrius raise the cry of **Great is Artemis** which reverberated throughout the city.

(2) A great multitude rushed into the vast theatre of **Ephesus,** where an informal meeting was held. Two Macedonian companions of Paul were haled before it, and the Jews were seriously alarmed that they might be implicated in the charge of defaming the goddess. Paul, with his natural impetuosity and fearlessness, was anxious to go before the public authorities (εἰς τὸν δῆμον) in defence of his friends, but was restrained by **his disciples,** who doubtless would have been unable to persuade him, had not some of the **Asiarchs** sent a message to warn him not to enter the theatre. These Asiarchs or representatives of the cities of the province were too important to be disregarded. They were appointed annually, and were supposed to preside over the worship of Rome and the Emperor. The office was highly honourable and, like some of the magistracies of Rome, entailed great expense ; that Paul should have made friends of such exalted personages is remarkable. At anyrate, as the Asiarchs of Ephesus presided over the theatre, their advice amounted to a command. The scene was one of utter **confusion. The Jews** tried to put forward a certain **Alexander** as their spokesman, but he was howled down by the mob. A characteristic touch is given by Luke, who says the majority had no idea what it was all about.

(3) After two hours of tumult a high official of the city, **the secretary** (γραμματεύς), managed to obtain a hearing. His speech has been skilfully condensed, and is full of point. He conciliated his audience by pointing to the absurdity of supposing that their **great** goddess could be injured by any propaganda : her position was too assured for that. The men Gaius and Aristarchus (ver. 29) had been guilty of no crime ; and here it may be noticed that the Jewish law wisely, if incorrectly, interpreted Deuteronomy's prohibition, ' Thou shalt not curse the gods,' etc., as prohibiting scurrilous abuse of heathen deities. The whole meeting was irregular ; and if Demetrius and his fellows had **a grievance** the courts were open to them if they thought fit to bring an action. This prudent address reveals the liberty enjoyed by the great cities of the empire, which were free to administer their own affairs, but were held responsible for any **disorderly** outbreaks.

This is the beginning of one of the most interesting sections of Acts. The author is on familiar ground, and has a personal knowledge of what he has to tell ; instead of presenting his material, as heretofore, in a series of pictures, he gives a more or less connected narrative. His design is also apparent. He relates with detail two memorable journeys he took in company with the Apostle—one to Jerusalem, culminating in Paul's arrest and imprisonment, the other to Rome, the climax being that after a most perilous voyage the Apostle arrived at Rome and taught in his own house for two years unmolested. In the journey from Troas to Jerusalem Luke has evidently in mind the story of how Jesus went up from Galilee to the Holy City to meet death. This he has told in the Gospel with especial care, devoting a large part of his short treatise to the subject, and lavishing on it the most notable parables and miracles of the greatest significance, many of which are peculiar to this Gospel. The same is in a lesser degree true of his story of the itinerary of Paul, which is characterized by a speech (to the Elders of Ephesus at Miletus), by the raising from the dead of the boy Eutychus, as well as by one of the most affecting farewell scenes in the Bible. The account of the arrest of the Apostle in the Temple and what follows is dramatic in the extreme. In these chapters St. Luke is at his best.

XX.

1 When the tumult had ceased, Paul sent for the disciples and encouraged them; he then took leave of them and went his

2 way to Macedonia. After passing through the districts of Macedonia and encouraging the people at length, he came

3 to Greece, where he spent three months. Just as he was on the point of sailing for Syria, the Jews laid a plot against him. He therefore resolved [1] to return through Mace-

4 donia. His company as far as Asia consisted of Sopater of Beroea (the son of Pyrrhus), Aristarchus and Secundus from Thessalonica, Gaius of Derbe, Timotheus, and

5 Tychicus and Trophimus from Asia. They went on to

6 wait for us at Troas, while we sailed from Philippi, after the days of unleavened bread, and joined them five days later at Troas. There we spent seven days.

The opening verses are, as are some other records of events in which Luke was not actively engaged, sketchy and unsatisfactory. Here, however, we have the Pauline epistles to fill up some of the details, as no information is given in Acts of what Paul did on his long journey from Ephesus through **Macedonia** to Greece. One would have expected to find Achaia (the name of the province) rather than **Greece** or Hellas, and it is only from the epistle to the Romans that we learn the purpose of the journey, viz. to convey to Jerusalem an apparently large sum of money for the relief of the poor ' saints.' Paul, as we know, devoted much time and attention to the question of raising money in the Greek cities for the benefit of the community in Jerusalem. He instructed the Corinthians to make weekly contributions for the purpose ; and he takes most careful precautions to prevent any suspicion that he had in any way mishandled the money which might have been entrusted

---

[1] W has, ' the Spirit told him.'

to him (1 Cor. xvi. 1–4, 2 Cor. viii. 16–ix. *ad fin.*). The affair of this collection may seem trivial to us, but in St. Paul's eyes it was of the highest importance. It emphasized the essential unity of the infant Church, at a time when the division between Jewish and Gentile Christians was becoming increasingly imminent. At least it shewed the Apostle's practical desire to help his Jewish fellow Christians and to bind the Hellenistic believers by bonds of sympathy closer to their brethren in Jerusalem.

The fact of **a plot** being hatched by **the Jews** to kill Paul, which prevented his sailing direct to **Syria** and forced him to travel a long way round by land, is noteworthy. If we may judge from 1 Cor. xvi. 5 ('I am going to make a tour through Macedonia'), it is probable that he had intended to sail to Corinth by the more direct route, and was for some reason, probably owing to a similar plot, compelled to take a more devious one. This is confirmed by the incidental note in 2 Cor. i. 8–9, where the Apostle implied that his life was in great danger. This is one of the 'undesigned coincidences,' as Paley calls them, between Acts and Paul's letters, which seem to be written in complete independence of one another.

The circumstance that Paul travelled in so large a **company,** which was apparently able to regulate its movements at pleasure, and that there is no hint of any preaching the gospel on the way, may be accounted for by supposing that his companions appeared as delegates of different cities carrying a large sum of money to Jerusalem. This need not have attracted any particular attention. We know from Josephus that a vast cortege attended the bringing of the temple tax to Palestine from Parthia, and that Jews should be bringing their contributions thither would be expected. **Troas** was evidently the rendezvous of Paul's party, and here Luke signifies his presence by using the first person plural : **They went on to wait for *us* at Troas.**

On the first day of the week we met for the breaking of bread;   7
    Paul addressed them, as he was to leave next day, and he
    prolonged his address till midnight (there were plenty of 8

9 lamps in the upper room where we met). In the window
sat a young man called Eutychus, and as Paul's address
went on and on, he got overcome with drowsiness, went
fast asleep, and fell from the third storey. He was picked
10 up a corpse, but Paul went downstairs, threw himself upon
him, and embraced him. "Do not lament," he said,
11 "the life is still in him." Then he went upstairs, broke
bread, and ate; finally, after conversing awhile with them
12 till the dawn, he went away. As for the lad, they took
him away alive, much to their relief.

It is a remarkable fact that in the entire Bible there are so
few stories of the raising of the dead. There are the stories of
Elijah and the widow of Sarepta, of Elisha and the son of the
woman of Shunem (in 1 and 2 Kings), the daughter of Jairus
in the Synoptic Gospels, the widow's son at Nain, recorded by
Luke, Dorcas and Eutychus in Acts. The raising of Lazarus
in St. John's gospel belongs to a different category. This is
not a ' mighty work ' but ' a sign,' incapable of any rational-
ized explanation, but a proof to those who accept it that
Jesus Christ can and will restore the dead to life. The other
stories of resuscitation are remarkably similar, and the parallel
between them is most instructive. Elisha, for example, hears
that a lad has died of sunstroke. He orders Gehazi to lay a
staff on the child's mouth ; as this had no effect the prophet
comes himself, casts his body on the supposed corpse, to which
warmth and life returned (2 Kings iv. 18 ff.). Jesus, on his
way to heal the daughter of Jairus, is told the girl is dead. He
is taken into a room full of mourners. He thrusts them out
and declares the maid is not dead but asleep. In the presence
of parents and his disciples he revives the child (Luke viii. 40,
etc.). Peter does much the same with Dorcas, using practically the same words as are recorded of Jesus by Mark (Acts
ix. 40). Eutychus falls and is taken up as dead. Paul,
however, will not admit this. He says **The life is still in him,**
having ascertained the fact by embracing the body. Before
he leaves the assembled disciples, the boy is brought in alive
and presumably uninjured.

Now it is well known that the symptoms of actual death are not always easy to determine, and that mistakes easily occur. Both Jesus and Paul admit this ; nor can we uphold the miraculous power of either by questioning their veracity.[1]

The description of the Christian assembly at Troas is very interesting. It was (a) **on the first day of the week,** (b) at night, (c) in an upper chamber, (d) with **many lamps,** (e) Paul discoursed at great length, (f) after Eutychus had been restored to life he went up and took food, (g) conversed for some time, and then departed. Each point needs separate discussion, the question being, How far does it all bear on the early Liturgy of the Church ?

(a) The earliest mention of **the first day** as being connected with a Christian assembly is in 1 Cor. xvi. 2, where St. Paul suggests that on that day a collection should be made for the poor at Jerusalem. In the book of Revelation John says he was ' in the spirit on the Lord's day ' (Rev. i. 10), which may be assumed to be Sunday, though this is not expressly stated. By the beginnings of the second century it is evident from the letters of St. Ignatius that the Jewish Sabbath was succeeded by the Christian ' Lord's day.' Another reason, however, may here be suggested. Paul and his friends could not, as good Jews, start on a journey on the Sabbath ; they did so as soon after it as was possible, viz. at **dawn** on the ' first day '—the Sabbath having ended at sunset.

(b) That before undertaking so important a journey Paul should have spent the night with his converts at Troas in prayer is of course natural, and so persistent was the habit of holding Christian devotions at night that in the Breviaries the Psalms are arranged in *nocturns*. The night service here culminated probably in a eucharistic meal, the purpose being declared to be ' to break bread."

(c) The ' upper chamber ' is here, and in the opening

---

[1] Philostratus, in his *Life of Apollonius of Tyana*, relates how the sage raised a girl from the dead, and appends this remark : ' Now whether he detected some spark of life in her . . . or whether life was really extinct . . . neither I myself nor those who were present could decide.'

chapters of Acts, rendered by the Latin *caenaculum* = dining-room, a large room at the top of the house, used as a place for entertaining guests. From the first the wealthier believers threw their houses open for assemblies of the brethren.

(*d*) The mention of **lamps** has led to the assumption that even at this early date they had some ritual significance. Undoubtedly lights have played an important part in worship for ages ; and in the Christian church from a very early date were considered to have a spiritual significance. But this must not be unduly pressed here. Perhaps one may regard it as a proof that this memorable service is recorded by one actually present who remembered every detail. The western text for *lampades* reads *hypolampades*, which may signify ' apertures ' or windows.

(*e*) We must recall Justin Martyr's well-known description of a Christian service about A.D. 150. It consisted of two main divisions, one preliminary, devoted to reading of scripture and exhortation, followed by a solemn participation of bread and wine, which had already become a ritual act, rather than a meal, as here implied. But even here we have an outline of the structure of the Divine Liturgy in every branch of the Christian church, namely, instruction and prayer, followed by a Eucharist.

(*f*) What the exact meaning of **broke bread and ate** is cannot be particularly determined. The Greek for the word rendered ' ate ' is γευσάμενος, i.e. tasted or partaken of food. The ' breaking of bread ' is the special means by which the risen Lord made himself known to the disciples at Emmaus, and Luke must have thought of the Last Supper when he described the farewell discourse and meal St. Paul partook of at Troas. We may suppose that the breaking of bread was eucharistic, and that it was here followed by a regular meal preliminary to the departure of the Apostle.

(*g*) The meal Paul evidently spent in friendly converse with his companions. The word ὁμιλεῖν, though in modern language connected with a homily or sermon, here obviously means not a set address, but familiar interchange of thought.

Now we had gone on beforehand to the ship and set sail for 13
Assos, intending to take Paul on board there. This was
his own arrangement, for he intended to travel by land.
So when he met us at Assos, we took him on board and 14
got to Mitylene. Sailing thence on the following day we 15
arrived off Chios ; next day we crossed over to Samos, and
[after stopping at Trogyllium] we went on next day [1] to
Miletus. This was because Paul had decided to sail past 16
Ephesus, to avoid any loss of time in Asia ; he wanted to
reach Jerusalem, if possible, by the day of Pentecost.

It is noteworthy how careful Luke is to mark the stages of
every journey he took with Paul—from Troas to Philippi, from
Troas to Jerusalem, from Caesarea to Rome. It is perhaps
permissible to pass by the details, interesting as they are, and
to come to the address to the elders of Ephesus at Miletus, one
of the most beautiful utterances of Paul recorded in Acts, and
actually heard by the author. It is important to notice that
henceforward the speeches of the Apostle are all apologetic,
justifying his conduct here to the leaders of an important
church, and later to Jewish and Roman audiences.

From Miletus he sent to Ephesus for the presbyters of the 17
church. When they came to him, he said, "You know 18
quite well how I lived among you all the time [2] ever since I
set foot in Asia, how I served the Lord in all humility, with 19
many a tear and many a trial which I encountered owing
to the plots of the Jews, how I never shrank from letting 20
you know anything for your good, or from teaching you
alike in public and from house to house, bearing my
testimony, both to Jews and Greeks, of repentance before 21
God and faith in our Lord Jesus Christ. Now here I go to 22
Jerusalem under the binding force of the Spirit. What will
befall me there, I do not know. Only, I know this, that in 23
town after town the holy Spirit testified to me that bonds
and troubles are awaiting me. But then, I set no value on 24
my own life as compared with the joy of finishing my course

[1] W reads, 'in the evening.'
[2] W adds, 'three years and more.'

and fulfilling the commission I received from the Lord Jesus
25   to attest the gospel of the grace of God. I know to-day
that not one of you will ever see my face again—not one
of you among whom I moved as I preached the Reign.
26   Therefore do I protest before you this day that I am not
27   responsible for the blood of any of you ; I never shrank
28   from letting you know the entire purpose of God. Take
heed to yourselves and to all the flock of which the holy
Spirit has appointed you guardians ; shepherd *the church of*
29   *the Lord* which *he has purchased* with his own blood. I
know that when I am gone, fierce wolves will get in among
30   you, and they will not spare the flock ; yes, and men of
your own number will arise with perversions of the truth
31   to draw the disciples after them. So be on the alert,
remember how for three whole years I never ceased night
32   and day to watch over each one of you with tears. And
now I entrust you to God and the word of his grace ; he is
able to upbuild you and give you your *inheritance* among
33   all the *consecrated*. Silver, gold, or apparel I never
34   coveted; you know yourselves how these hands of mine
provided everything for my own needs and for my com-
35   panions. I showed you how this was the way to work
hard and succour the needy, remembering the words of the
Lord Jesus, who said, ' To give is happier than to get.' "
36   With these words he knelt down and prayed beside them
37   all. They all broke into loud lamentation and falling upon
38   the neck of Paul kissed him fondly, sorrowing chiefly
because he told them they would never see his face again.
Then they escorted him to the ship.

If we had an epistle of Paul to the Ephesians belonging to
this period, the present letter being somewhat later, it would
possibly be somewhat like parts of 2 Corinthians, in which the
Apostle has to reply to several misrepresentations. For this
speech implies that the situation in the church of Ephesus
was complicated by the constant machinations of Jews and
converts hostile to Paul. Otherwise he would not have been
so eager to assert his disinterestedness or maintain the integrity

of his teaching. The eminently pastoral tone which distinguishes this address reminds the reader of the epistles to Timothy and Titus, as do many of the phrases employed. Nevertheless, there are indications that the elders of Ephesus needed warnings against the misrepresentations to which Paul had been exposed, and he does not seem quite sure of the fidelity of all of them.

Paul reminds the Ephesian elders of his life among them, his sorrows (**with many a tear** is characteristic), and **the plots** against him by **the Jews.** He recalls his teaching both in **public** and private to both Jews and Greeks (again Pauline), urging them to turn to God and have **faith in the Lord Jesus Christ.** He further declares that he is going up to Jerusalem bound by the Spirit (cf. Gal. ii. 2, where he and Barnabas went there ' by revelation '), not knowing what his fate would be save that everywhere the Spirit bore witness that it would result in his imprisonment. But he cared not for this, provided he might finish his **course** (cf. 2 Tim. iv. 7) with joy, and bear testimony to the **gospel of the grace of God** (24). Paul knows full well that the Ephesians will never see him again (this may be a proof that Luke was ignorant of Paul's having visited Ephesus after his captivity, according to 1 Tim. i. 3). He then calls them to judge whether he is not guiltless of **the blood of anyone,** as he has kept nothing of **the purpose of God** back from them.

After this he warns his hearers of troubles to come. The enemy is at hand ; like **wolves** they will devour **the flock** or Church of Christ, over which the presbyters or elders have been appointed overseers by the Spirit (note that **the holy Spirit** commissions men to special offices, as in xiii. 4, 2 Tim. i. 6-7). The elders are warned not only of outside enemies (the wolves) but of men of their own body, who will teach false doctrine and **draw** away disciples. The elders are here called bishops, *episcopoi,* a word the meaning of which is the exact equivalent of overseers, though here well rendered as **guardians,** namely, of the ' flock ' of Christ. Paul, in writing to the Philippian church, addresses the ' bishops and deacons ' (Phil. i. 1). Except in the Pastoral epistles, the word is not found in the

New Testament, save that Christ is called the *episcopos* or guardian of our souls (1 Pet. ii. 25, where it is coupled with the word ' shepherd '). In the very difficult passage—**the church of the Lord which he has purchased with his own blood,** the word **purchased** recalls the substantive analogous to it which is used in 1 Pet. ii. 9, ' a people who belong to God ' (literally for God's possession). The idea is that of the Church as God's ' Israel.' The redemption of the Church **by the blood** of God is hard to explain, and the alternative reading ' the Lord's blood ' does not make the difficulty less. Westcott and Hort, who read ' God,' thought that possibly the original of what follows is ' by the blood of his own Son.' For the rest, Ephesus, as we learn from the message to the Church in the Apocalypse (Rev. ii. 1 ff.), was troubled by heresy, and from Colossians and Ephesians we gather that there was some sort of Gnosticism prevalent in the province of Asia. Here, however, it seems probable that the real trouble was with Jews or Judaizing Christians.

Now the exhortation to the presbyters or elders begins. They are to be vigilant, and to remember the **three whole years** that Paul has been with them (but cf. Acts xix. 8 and 10). He reminds them how he had maintained himself by his own labour, as he wrote to the Corinthians (1 Cor. ix. 12), and concludes with the beautiful but elsewhere unrecorded saying of Jesus : ' It is more blessed to give than to receive.'

xxi.

1 When we had torn ourselves away from them and set sail, we made a straight run to Cos, next day to Rhodes, and thence
2 to Patara ; as we found a ship there bound for Phoenicia,
3 we went on board and set sail. After sighting Cyprus and leaving it on our left, we sailed for Syria, landing at Tyre,
4 where the ship was to unload her cargo. We found out the local disciples and stayed there for seven days. These disciples told Paul by the Spirit not to set foot in Jeru-
5 salem ; but, when our time was up, we started on our journey, escorted by them, women and children and all, till

we got outside the town.   Then, kneeling on the beach,
we prayed and said goodbye to one another.   We went on 6
board and they went home.   By sailing from Tyre to 7
Ptolemais we completed our voyage ; we saluted the
brothers, spent a day with them, and started next morning 8
for Caesarea, where we entered the house of Philip the
evangelist (he belonged to the Seven, and had four un- 9
married daughters who prophesied).   We stayed with him. 10
While we remained there for a number of days, a prophet
called Agabus came down from Judaea.   He came to us, 11
took Paul's girdle and bound his own feet and hands, saying, " Here is the word of the holy Spirit : ' So shall the
Jews bind the owner of this girdle at Jerusalem and hand
him over to the Gentiles.' "   Now when we heard this, we 12
and the local disciples besought Paul not to go up to
Jerusalem.   Then Paul replied, " What do you mean by 13
weeping and disheartening me ?   I am ready not only
to be bound but also to die at Jerusalem for the sake
of the Lord Jesus."   As he would not be persuaded, we 14
acquiesced, saying, " The will of the Lord be done."
After these days we packed up and started for Jerusalem, 15
accompanied by some of the disciples from Caesarea, who 16
conducted us to the house of Mnason, a Cypriote, with
whom we were to lodge.   He was a disciple of old standing.

The account of this journey is interesting, because it gives
an idea as to how a company of travellers voyaged from port
to port and chartered passages on different merchant vessels.
At **Patara** they ceased creeping, as they had done, along the
west coast of Asia Minor, and put out into the open sea for
Tyre.   For Luke and his companions, except Paul, this
voyage was a new experience ; and the fact that **Cyprus** was
pointed out to them (ἀναφάναντες, *lit.* ' having made Cyprus
rise up out of the sea ') is characteristically mentioned.   The
ship unloaded her cargo **at Tyre,** where Paul was warned by
the disciples through the Spirit not to go to **Jerusalem.**   Here,
as in the journey section of the gospel, the Apostle, like his
Master, fully realizes the dangers which await him, with the

difference that Jesus warns his disciples of what would happen, while Paul is warned not to go by disciples ; and by a prophet not to enter the Holy City.

The two verses 8 and 9 throw much light on the condition of the early church, especially when we recollect that this chapter must be an authentic record of one who was actually present. The points to be severally noted are indicated by the words : (1) **Philip the evangelist,** (2) ' one of **the Seven,**' (3) ' four daughters virgins ' (**unmarried,** Moffatt) who prophesied.

(1) The mention of Philip takes us back to the narrative of Acts viii. 40 (' While Philip found himself at Azotus, where he passed on, preaching the gospel (i.e. *evangelizing*) in every town, till he reached Caesarea '). Here he evidently had made his home, and was known as **the Evangelist.** Does this imply that Philip was as such an official in the Church, or is it no more than an allusion to his past and present labours in preaching the gospel ? In Eph. iv. 11 there are five orders of persons endowed by the Spirit with gifts for the edification of his Church—apostles, prophets, **evangelists,** shepherds (A.V. pastors), and teachers. Timothy is enjoined to fulfil his duties as a minister by discharging the work of an *evangelist*. Philip seems to have gained the title by having been the earliest recorded preacher of the gospel outside Jerusalem. It was but natural that **Caesarea** should be already an important Christian centre, with the most active of the Seven as a resident, as well as the household of Cornelius, the first Gentile convert (Acts x.).

(2) **He belonged to the Seven.** This may throw some light on the real meaning of Acts vi., and solves the difficulty of reconciling the description of the Seven as administrators of charitable funds with the appearance of their leaders Stephen and Philip as active propagators of the faith. It is more likely, as has been already suggested, that the Seven were the leaders of the Hellenistic Jewish community. If so, the mention of Philip at Caesarea, the capital of the districts of Judaea and Samaria, may mean that his position in regard to the Christians was somewhat analogous to that of James in Jerusalem, and that he filled rather the position of a ' bishop '

than a ' deacon,' namely, as the leading man in the Caesarean church.

(3) St. Luke alone of the N.T. writers mentions women as exercising the gift of prophecy. In the Infancy-narrative Anna is described as a prophetess (Luke ii. 36), and the *Magnificat* of the Blessed Virgin is a prophetic utterance (i. 46 ff.). The **daughters** of Philip are mentioned in Euse-bius's *History* as living with their father at Hierapolis in Asia Minor. Philip was doubtless a strict observer of the Law, and it is remarkable that the allusion to his four inspired daughters being virgins is evidently made to his credit, although it was considered the duty of a Jewish father to dispose of his daughters in marriage at an early age. Except that, according to a very obscure passage in 1 Cor. vii. 27 ff., some Christians abstained from marriage because of the imminence of the end of all things, no merit is elsewhere attached to a celibate life. The ' virgins ' in the Apocalypse are men guiltless of carnal sin. Here, however, at this very early date we have Jewish women apparently devoted to virginity, the precursors of the Christian ' virgins ' of a later period.

Agabus the prophet has already appeared as coming from Jerusalem to Antioch (Acts xi. 28). His symbolical act of binding his **feet and hands** in token of the fate of Paul at Jerusalem is characteristic of the prophets of the Old Testament. The word ' We packed up ' (ἐπιεκευασάμενοι) is rendered in the A.V. ' we took up our carriages,' in the sense of luggage, as in 1 Sam. xvii. 22, ' and David left his *carriage* ' (i.e. what he was carrying to his brothers), etc. This preparation for departure **for Jerusalem** seems to imply that the travellers were carrying a considerable fund to relieve their poorer brethren. **Mnason** the **Cypriote** was evidently one who had been a Christian from the first, and is introduced to shew that the original converts were favourable to Paul, whose arrival was expected and provided for.

The brothers welcomed us gladly on our arrival at Jerusalem. 17
    Next day we accompanied Paul to James ; all the presbyters 18
    were present, and after saluting them Paul described in 19

20 detail what God had done by means of his ministry among the Gentiles. They glorified God when they heard it. Then they said to him, "Brother, you see how many thousands of believers there are among the Jews, all of

21 them ardent upholders of the Law. Now, they have heard that you teach all Jews who live among Gentiles to break away from Moses and not to circumcise their children, nor

22 to follow the old customs. What is to be done? They

23 will be sure to hear you have arrived.* So do as we tell

24 you. We have four men here under a vow; associate yourself with them, purify yourself with them, pay their expenses so that they may be free to have their heads shaved, and then everybody will understand there is nothing in these stories about you, but that, on the contrary,

25 you are guided by obedience to the Law. As for Gentile believers, we have issued our decision that they must avoid food that has been offered to idols, the taste of blood, flesh of animals that have been strangled, and sexual vice."

26 Then Paul associated himself with the men next day; he had himself purified along with them and went into the temple to give notice of the time when *the days of purification* would be completed—the time, that is to say, when the sacrifice could be offered for each one of them.

* Omitting [$\delta\epsilon\hat{\iota}\ \pi\lambda\hat{\eta}\theta os\ \sigma v\nu\epsilon\lambda\theta\epsilon\hat{\iota}v$] and [$\gamma\dot{\alpha}\rho$].

This passage is difficult to explain in detail, and does not seem to be in accord with the explanation of the law in Num. vi. in the Mishna. Its purport is sufficiently plain. Paul has been accused of lax teaching in regard to the Law. To refute this calumny he is advised to discharge his vow in company with some poor men who could not find the money necessary for the completion of their own. To defray the expenses of such persons was a popular act of Jewish piety (cf. Josephus, *Antiq.*, xix. 16. 1, where Agrippa I paid the expenses of Nazarites). James seems to have acted, much as he did at the Council of Jerusalem, the part of a reasonable man anxious to effect a compromise. His advice was wise in so far as it was intended to conciliate the Jewish believers in Jerusalem, but resulted in a deplorable attack on Paul which no one could have foreseen. To understand what happened it is necessary to understand a little of the topography of the Temple.

The Temple Hill, called by the Rabbis ' the Mountain of the House,' was a large square on a plateau which formed the north-east side of the city. This square was strongly built and fortified, and was surrounded on three sides by colonnades or porches. On the top of these was a flat roof, from which the Roman sentries were able to look down and give warning in the event of disturbances. On the northern side was the formidable castle of the Antonia, used as barracks, and approached by a staircase. Any person might enter the square, and the porticoes were used by teachers of the Law. On the western side (though the exact site is indeterminate) stood the Temple buildings, a series of courts leading up to the great altar and the holy place. Around these buildings, which were approached by steps, was a series of stones, warning Gentiles that they passed this boundary at their peril, since no one but a Jew might enter the Temple. We must realize this in order to understand the nature of the riot.

The seven days were almost over when the Asiatic Jews, catch- 27 ing sight of him in the temple, stirred up all the crowd and laid hands on him, shouting, " To the rescue, men of 28 Israel! Here is the man who teaches everyone everywhere against the People and the Law and this Place! And he has actually brought Greeks inside the temple and defiled this holy Place! " (They had previously seen Trophimus 29 the Ephesian along with him in the city, and they supposed Paul had taken him inside the temple.) The whole city 30 was thrown into turmoil. The people rushed together, seized Paul and dragged him outside the temple ; where- upon the doors were immediately shut. They were 31 attempting to kill him, when word reached the commander of the garrison that the whole of Jerusalem was in confu- sion. Taking some soldiers and officers, he at once rushed 32 down to them, and when they saw the commander and the soldiers they stopped beating Paul. Then the commander 33

came up and seized him ; he ordered him to be bound with a couple of chains, and asked " Who is he ? " and " What
34 has he done ? " Some of the crowd roared one thing, some another, and as he could not learn the facts owing to the uproar, he ordered Paul to be taken to the barracks.
35 By the time he reached the steps, he had actually to be carried by the soldiers on account of the violence of the
36 crowd, for the whole mass of the people followed shouting,
37 " Away with him ! " Just as he was being taken into the barracks, Paul said to the commander, " May I say a word
38 to you ? " " You know Greek ! " said the commander. " Then you are not the Egyptian who in days gone by raised the four thousand assassins and led them out into
39 the desert ? " Paul said, " I am a Jew, a native of Tarsus in Cilicia, the citizen of a famous town. Pray let me speak
40 to the people." As he gave permission, Paul stood on the steps and motioned to the people. A great hush came over them, and he addressed them as follows in Hebrew.

Hitherto every accusation brought against Paul had failed and been dismissed as ridiculous. Now one far more serious and plausible was advanced, which could not be ignored, and might result either in his immediate death at the hands of an infuriated mob, or on a criminal charge which would oblige the Romans to pronounce a capital sentence. The Asiatic Jews had evidently followed him to Jerusalem and raised an outcry that in his teaching he had insulted the Temple (cf. the charge brought against Stephen, Acts vi. 13), and introduced a heathen into its precincts.

From the standpoint of literature the description of the scene of the riot in the Temple is a masterpiece. It is so vivid that not only do we feel convinced that the writer himself witnessed it, but we ourselves seem to realize it as though we had been actually present. The Asiatic Jews having seen Paul in the city with **Trophimus** of Ephesus inferred, perhaps deliberately, that the Apostle had brought a heathen within the precincts of the *Soreg* or barrier around the Holy House. Thereupon they raised the cry " **Men of Israel, to the rescue,**" etc. This was sufficient to collect a crowd of fanatical Jews from every part of the city, and Paul was hustled out of the Temple into the court of the Gentiles. Thereupon the priests, to avoid the risk of further profanation, closed the building. The tribune or **commander of the garrison** in the Antonia, hearing that all Jerusalem was in confusion, came down from the fortress with his soldiers and officers, evidently in strong force, and charged into the mob, who thereupon ceased to beat Paul ; the commander arrested him, put him in chains, and inquired the reason for the tumult. As the replies were contradictory and the mob was becoming dangerous, the soldiers were ordered to bring Paul into their camp and he was **carried** up **the steps** to the Antonia to protect him from the infuriated populace.

In the midst of this wild confusion, the Apostle, who preserved his calmness, asked the commander permission to address him. The fact that he spoke in Greek was a cause of astonishment, since Paul, torn and dishevelled as he was, could hardly have passed for an educated man. Besides, the tribune inferred that he had arrested a most dangerous fanatic, a (Jewish) native of Egypt, who had brought an army of assassins (*sicarii*, or dagger-men) against Jerusalem, and after being repulsed by the procurator Felix with the assistance of the citizens, as we learn from Josephus (*Antiq.*, xx. 8. 6), had made good his escape. Paul, however, declared himself to be a citizen of Tarsus, and obtained leave to address the people from the steps. There was evidently a dignity about the Apostle, who impressed the crowd by a gesture of his hand and in the midst of a great silence spoke **in Hebrew.**

Hebrew, or the Hebrew dialect, is generally supposed to be Aramaic, a view confirmed by the use of such words in the New Testament as ' Talitha-cumi,' ' Maranatha,' ' Abba,' etc. In the days of the New Testament Hebrew was a language known only by the learned, and a kindred tongue, now known as Aramaic, had become the *lingua franca* of non-Greek-speaking inhabitants of the Eastern Roman world. Josephus employed it in writing to the inhabitants of the farther east, to whom he sent an account of the Jewish war. Parts of the

Bible—the narrative in Daniel, the letter in Ezra, a verse of Jeremiah—are in this language, which was known to our ancestors as ' Chaldee ' or ' Syriac.' Not long after the days of St. Paul, Aramaic paraphrases of the Scriptures began to appear. The Apostle's auditors doubtless understood Greek, but were more appreciative when he addressed them in their mother-tongue.

This and the four succeeding chapters are occupied by Paul's defence against the serious charge that he had profaned the Temple by introducing Trophinus the Ephesian within its forbidden precincts. Much of the narrative is legal in tone, the object being to shew that the Jews, the ruling class in Jerusalem, the Roman officials, and the native King Agrippa II, were unable to find any real foundation for the charges of Paul's enemies. Consequently, this section of the Acts, though probably of the highest interest to Theophilus, for whom Luke was writing, is of less importance to the modern reader than the rest of Acts, as few passages in it are spiritually or even dogmatically suggestive, whereas those in the earlier part of the book are of great value in enabling the reader to determine the character of the gospel proclaimed and the institutions of the primitive church.

xxii.

1 " Brothers and fathers, listen to the defence I now make
2 before you." When they heard him addressing them in
3 Hebrew they were all the more quiet. So he went on. " I am a Jew, born at Tarsus in Cilicia, but brought up in this city, educated at the feet of Gamaliel in all the strictness of our ancestral Law, ardent for God as you all are to-day.
4 I persecuted this Way of religion to the death, chaining and
5 imprisoning both men and women, as the high priest and all the council of elders can testify. It was from them that I got letters to the brotherhood at Damascus and then journeyed thither to bind those who had gathered there and
6 bring them back to Jerusalem for punishment. Now as I

neared Damascus on my journey, suddenly about noon a
brilliant light from heaven flashed round me. I dropped 7
to the earth and heard a voice saying to me, ' Saul, Saul, 8
why do you persecute me ? ' ' Who are you ? ' I asked.
He said to me, ' I am Jesus the Nazarene, and you are persecuting me.' (My companions saw the light, but they did 9
not hear the voice of him who talked to me.) I said, 'What 10
am I to do ? ' And the Lord said to me, ' Get up and make
your way into Damascus ; there you shall be told about all
you are destined to do.' As I could not see owing to the 11
dazzling glare of that light, my companions took my hand
and so I reached Damascus. Then a certain Ananias, a 12
devout man in the Law, who had a good reputation among
all the Jewish inhabitants, came to me and standing beside 13
me said, ' Saul, my brother, regain your sight ! ' The
same moment I regained my sight and looked up at him.
Then he said, ' The God of our fathers has appointed you to 14
know his will, to see the Just One, and to hear him speak
with his own lips. For you are to be a witness for him 15
before all men, a witness of what you have seen and heard.
And now, why do you wait ? Get up and be baptized and 16
wash away your sins, invoking his name.'

When I returned to Jerusalem, it happened that while I was 17
praying in the temple I fell into a trance and saw Him 18
saying to me, ' Make haste, leave Jerusalem quickly, for
they will not accept your evidence about me.' ' But, 19
Lord,' I said, ' they surely know it was I who imprisoned
and flogged those who believed in you throughout the
synagogues, and that I stood and approved when the blood 20
of your martyr Stephen was being shed, taking charge of
the clothes of his murderers ! ' But he said to me, ' Go; 21
I will send you afar to the Gentiles——' '' Till he said 22
that, they had listened to him. But at that they shouted,
'' Away with such a creature from the earth ! He is not
fit to live ! ''

The speech delivered from the steps is undoubtedly a condensed report of what the author may actually have heard ;

the fact that it terminates so abruptly and yet so naturally is an additional argument for its genuine character. That it was listened to with patience by a mixed multitude of priests and lay worshippers in the Temple is very significant. St. Paul's auditors could not complain of the way he began to address them, and seem to have received his account of his vision with interest. They had, in fact, no objection to offer to one who preached Jesus as revealing himself to man ; for still, as in chaps. ii.–v., the believers were not unpopular in Jerusalem, and their leader James was generally respected. It was not incredible to many that he might not after all be the Christ and return to redeem Israel. Furthermore, the delegates of the churches, headed by Paul, were bringing money to the city to relieve the distressed, and had been favourably received. It was only when Paul declared that he had a mission **to the Gentiles** that the crowd became excited, and the favourable impression which he had created was lost in a torrent of indignant fanaticism.

Another noteworthy point in Paul's speech is the account he gives of his conversion. This differs in detail from that of Luke in chap. ix. and from the description of his vision in Acts xxvi. It may be due to different sources being employed, though it is not easy to separate those of chaps. xxii. and xxvi. Taking into account that the details are somewhat different, but that the vision is evidently the same, tentative explanations are alone possible. It may be that Luke had received the first account in chap. ix. by tradition, and that he, after his wont, gave the story his own interpretation, as he does in the case of the narratives he found in the Marcan gospel. It is quite likely that he actually heard the two speeches, and that Paul gave two separate versions of his momentous spiritual experience. We all know how liable anyone is who retells the same story to vary the details, and this especially is true of a vision which made a profound impression. This, as has been said previously, would be no disparagement of the general accuracy of Acts, nor would it prove the fictitious character of what Luke describes. It rather confirms our opinion that the writer was the more honest, because he was in trifling matters somewhat inconsistent. Less plausible but equally possible is it that Luke tried to avoid repeating himself in the three accounts in order to make his narrative more readable. Any attempts to harmonize the narratives or to explain away their difficulties on the assumption that Scripture must necessarily be inerrant in details of no great significance, are bound to prove unsatisfactory.

The noteworthy points in the speech are these. Paul was educated in Jerusalem **at the feet of Gamaliel.** Gamaliel I (or Gamliel) is a very elusive personage, despite the importance attached to him in N.T. and rabbinical tradition. He appears to represent the ripest fruit of rabbinic wisdom and moderation (v. 34). Curiously, his name does not occur in the writings of Philo nor of Josephus, nor does Paul mention him in his epistles, although some other passages in his letters remind us of this speech (cf. Phil. iii. 4 ff.). The word **ardent** means zealous, a term of commendation (see note on i. 17).

This Way (of religion) is an expression not found in the Pauline epistles. But Christianity was called ' the Way ' from a very early time, and in the sub-apostolic age, ' the Way of Life ' (see note on xix. 23).

It is difficult to say who **the high priest** was at any particular time, as the office was constantly given to different people. That Ananias (xxiii. 2) was present at this very tumultuary gathering is most improbable.

The mention of the other **Ananias** who restored Saul to sight and urged him to be baptized is significant and appropriate, the object being to indicate that the best Jews who strictly observed the Law approved of Paul at the time of his conversion.

That Paul was warned by a vision **in the Temple** to leave Jerusalem is not in accordance with what Luke relates in his account of the circumstances in ix. 26–30.

It is evident that Paul's offence, in the eyes of those who heard him, was not that he preached that the risen Jesus was about to return as the Messiah, but that he was undermining the foundations of the legalism of the national religion by endeavouring to make it acceptable to the rest of mankind.

The principles of Judaism were felt to be safeguarded by rendering it difficult for Gentiles fully to accept them, whereas Paul was labouring to make entrance into the fold of Israel easy.

23 They yelled and threw their clothes into the air and flung dust
24 about, till the commander ordered him to be taken inside the barracks and examined under the lash, so as to find
25 out why the people shouted at him in this way. They had strapped him up, when Paul said to the officer who was standing by, " Are you allowed to scourge a Roman citizen
26 —and to scourge him without a trial ? " When the officer heard this, he went to the commander and said to him, "What are you going to do ? This man is a Roman
27 citizen." So the commander went to him and said, " Tell me, are you a Roman citizen ? " " Yes," he said.
28 The commander replied, " I had to pay a large sum for this
29 citizenship." " But I was born a citizen," said Paul. Then those who were to have examined him left him at once alone ; even the commander was alarmed to find that Paul was a Roman citizen and that he had bound him.
30 Next day, as he was anxious to find out the real reason why the Jews accused him, he unbound him, ordered the high priests and all the Sanhedrin to meet, and brought Paul down, placing him in front of them.

The narrative is here resumed with much descriptive power. We realize the frenzied crowd of excitable Jews, shouting, waving their clothes, and darkening the air with their dust, the perplexity of the commander, who, perhaps not understanding what was being said, hurried Paul into the soldiers' quarters in the Antonia, and resolved to torture him with the awful *flagellum* in order to ascertain the truth. And now Paul for the second time claimed his privilege as a Roman citizen. It has been already indicated that scourging as a torture (Vulg. *torqueri*) meant, if not death, at least crippling for life (see the explanation of xvi. 22), and as he was being stretched out for the torment he asked whether it was lawful to scourge a Roman citizen. Why he had not previously declared himself is difficult to explain, but hitherto he had been content with

saying he was a Jew of Tarsus : it was only in an extremity
that he claimed the privilege of citizenship. It is also perplexing to understand how his claim could have been instantly
admitted, though we know he had relatives in Jerusalem who
could have substantiated his statement, and might have
prosecuted the commander had he proceeded to extremities.
Anyhow, that officer instantly perceived that he had placed
himself in a very difficult position. Despite the popular
modern idea that Paul was only an humble maker of tents,
there are several indications that his relatives were people of
consideration and influence.

xxiii.

With a steady look at the Sanhedrin Paul said, " Brothers, I 1
have lived with a perfectly good conscience before God
down to the present day." Then the high priest Ananias 2
ordered those who were standing next Paul to strike him
on the mouth. At this Paul said to him, " You white- 3
washed wall. God will strike you! You sit there to judge
me by the Law, do you ? And you break the Law by
ordering me to be struck !" The bystanders said, "What! 4
would you rail at God's high priest ? " " Brothers," said 5
Paul, " I did not know he was high priest " (for it is
written, *You must not speak evil of any ruler of your
people*). Then, finding half the Sanhedrin were Sadducees 6
and the other half Pharisees, Paul shouted to them, " I am
a Pharisee, brothers, the son of Pharisees! It is for the
hope of the resurrection from the dead that I am on trial ! "
When he said this, a quarrel broke out between the Phari- 7
sees and the Sadducees ; the meeting was divided. For 8
while the Sadducees declare there is no such thing as
resurrection, angels, or spirits, the Pharisees affirm them
all. Thus a loud clamour broke out. Some of the scribes 9
who belonged to the Pharisaic party got up and contended,
" We find nothing wrong about this man. What if some
spirit or angel has spoken to him ? " The quarrel then 10
became so violent that the commander was afraid they
would tear Paul in pieces; he therefore ordered the troops

II to march down and take him from them by force, bringing him inside the barracks. On the following night the Lord stood by Paul and said, " Courage! As you have testified to me at Jerusalem, so you must testify at Rome."

The report of Paul's trial before the Sanhedrin bears many traces of genuineness. His speech was interrupted from the first, and he escaped condemnation by the none too creditable stratagem of setting his judges by the ears. This is not the sort of incident which one would expect in the laudatory biography of a saint ; it is to the credit of the author that he has recorded it.

The speech opens with a Pauline phrase, which is literally, ' I have been a good citizen of God's state ($\pi\epsilon\pi o\lambda\acute{\iota}\tau\epsilon\upsilon\mu\alpha\iota$; cf. Phil. i. 27, ii. 20) to this day.' The high-priest orders those near to smite Paul on the mouth for his presumption. Thereupon the Apostle retorts that God will smite him as a ' whited wall.' The bystanders complain of this insult to God's high-priest, whereupon Paul apologizes on the ground that he did not know that he had spoken so rudely to so great a dignitary. Some have supposed that this was due to the Apostle's short or imperfect sight : it is, however, more probable that, as he had only been a few days in Jerusalem, he had no knowledge as to who was the high-priest. Luke says here that his name was Ananias ; but when one tries to find out from Josephus at what time this man (? Ananias the son of Nebedaeus) was in office, it is not an easy task. Paul's quotation of Ex. xxii. 28 is interesting. The English of the whole verse is, ' Thou shalt not revile the gods (the great men) nor speak ill of the ruler of thy people.' Josephus explains the first clause as a prohibition against insulting pagan deities (*Antiq.*, iv. 8. 10, and *Apion*, ii. 33). Paul applies the last clause to the high-priest and expresses regret for what he had said. But the meeting soon became so hostile that, as he had appealed to the commander as a Roman, so now he claimed the support of his friends the Pharisees. He had been accused of a gross violation of the Law, and his best refutation of the calumny was to declare that he belonged to the Pharisaic brotherhood. As a member of this society, it was incredible that he could have been guilty of such a breach of the Law as to have introduced a Gentile into the Temple ; and in addition, his preaching was the same as theirs in regard to the belief that the dead would rise.

Now we learn from Acts that the priests of the Temple arrested the disciples when they began to preach ' through Jesus the resurrection of the dead.' Apparently they did so because they regarded the doctrine as dangerous to the peace of the city, by encouraging a belief in a miraculous deliverance of Israel from the Roman yoke. The denial of such a resurrection was regarded by the Sadducees as the best means of maintaining the *status quo.* This made them and the wealthy priesthood hostile to the new preaching ; they opposed the followers of Jesus, because they regarded them as liable to excite the passions of the multitude. The Pharisees, on the other hand, held firmly to a belief that the dead would rise, and consequently were in sympathy with the Church in this respect. When therefore Paul exclaimed, ' **I am a Pharisee,**' etc., and declared that he was there because of ' **the hope of the resurrection,**' the Pharisees in the Sanhedrin rallied to him with one accord.

This gives us a clue to the significance of the chapter, which is in some respects very perplexing. The contending parties were not the Jews and the believers in Jesus, but the Pharisees as opposed to the Sadducean priesthood. On hearing that Paul was one of them and preached a resurrection of the dead, the Pharisees declared not only that he was guiltless, but possibly also inspired. Suppose **an angel or a spirit has spoken to him !** That Jesus was to bring about the resurrection was not the point at issue. The belief in a resurrection was the crucial matter, as all Pharisaic principles hinged upon this. Still, it is no use to attempt to acquit Paul entirely of blame for trying to save himself by dividing the contending parties in the Sanhedrin, nor did he deny in his speech before Felix that he may have been in the wrong in so doing. Josephus tells us but little about the Pharisees, though he was a member of their sect. On the Sadducees he is even less satisfactory.

as also are the rabbinical writers, who are not very clear even about their denial of a resurrection. As regards the Temple-worship they were more particular than their rivals. Angels play a greater part in popular than in orthodox Judaism. One may add that Josephus dwells on the merciful disposition of Pharisaism.

12 When day broke, the Jews formed a conspiracy, taking a solemn oath neither to eat nor to drink till they had killed
13 Paul. There were more than forty of them in this plot.
14 They then went to the high priests and elders, saying, "We have taken a solemn oath to taste no food till we have
15 killed Paul. Now you and the Sanhedrin must inform the commander that you propose to investigate this case in detail, so that he may have Paul brought down to you.
16 We will be all ready to kill him on the way down." Now Paul's nephew heard about their treacherous ambush; so
17 he got admission to the barracks and told Paul. Paul summoned one of the officers and said, "Take this young man to the commander, for he has some news to give him."
18 So the officer took him to the commander, saying, "The prisoner Paul has summoned me to ask if I would bring this young man to you, as he has something to tell you."
19 The commander then took him by the hand aside and asked him in private, "What is the news you have for
20 me?" He answered, "The Jews have agreed to ask you to bring Paul down to-morrow to the Sanhedrin, on the
21 plea that they * propose to examine his case in detail. Now do not let them persuade you. More than forty of them are lying in ambush for him, and they have taken a solemn oath neither to eat nor to drink till they have murdered him. They are all ready at this moment, awaiting your
22 consent." Then the commander dismissed the youth, bidding him, "Tell nobody that you have informed me of
23 this." He summoned two of the officers and said, "Get ready by nine o'clock to-night two hundred infantry to march as far as Caesarea, also seventy troopers, and two

* See Note on next page.

hundred spearmen.'' Horses were also to be provided, on 24
which they were to mount Paul and carry him safe to
Felix the governor. He then wrote a letter in the following 25
terms. '' Claudius Lysias, to his excellency the governor 26
Felix: greeting. This man had been seized by the Jews 27
and was on the point of being murdered by them, when I
came on them with the troops and rescued him, as I had
ascertained that he was a Roman citizen. Anxious to find 28
out why they accused him, I took him down to their Sanhedrin, where I found he was accused of matters relating to 29
their Law but not impeached for any crime that deserved
death or imprisonment. I am informed a plot is to be laid 30
against him, so I am sending him to you at once,† telling
his accusers that they must impeach him before you.
Farewell.'' The soldiers, according to their instructions, 31
took Paul and brought him by night to Antipatris. Next 32
day the infantry returned to their barracks, leaving the
troopers to ride on with him. They reached Caesarea, 33
presented the letter to the governor, and also handed Paul
over to him. On reading the letter he asked what province 34
he belonged to, and finding it was Cilicia he said, '' I will
go into your case whenever your accusers arrive,'' giving 35
orders that he was to be kept in the praetorium of Herod.

* Reading either μέλλοντες with the Latin, Syriac, Sahidic, and
Ethiopic versions, or μελλόντων (אᵉ, Chrysostom, and some minu-
scules).

† Reading ἐξαυτῆς instead of ἐξ αὐτῶν.

Taking a solemn oath is the purport of the original, but
the Greek is more forcible, meaning that the conspirators
bound themselves by an *anathema*, by which they declared
that they would accomplish their end or suffer themselves to
be accursed of God. The word is doubled in ver. 14 to give
greater emphasis to the tremendous character of their oath.
It meant ' devoted to absolute destruction '—such as in
ancient religion was pronounced on a town (Jericho—Josh.
vi. 17), or a people (Amalek—1 Sam. xv. 3).

Nephew, or in Greek ' sister's son.' In the A.V. Mark is called ' sister's son to Barnabas,' but a different word, ἀνέψιος, is used (Col. iv. 10).

Some MSS. of a western type add that Claudius Lysias feared the Jews would slay Paul, and that he himself would be accused of bribery.

We must now consider what Luke has told us ; perhaps it may be permissible to read between the lines of his very brief narrative. Paul's appearance before the Sanhedrin had brought about a contention between the popular party of the Pharisees and the aristocratic and priestly faction of the Sadducees. Much as the Apostle was disliked for his opinions by the Asiatic Hellenists, it by no means follows that he was an unpopular person in Jerusalem. In the first place, he was the head of a deputation bringing a large contribution to assist the poor. Further, the leader of the Christians in the city was James, the Lord's brother, who, as we learn from Josephus, and later from Hegesippus, was greatly respected for his thoroughly Jewish piety. Again he had, as a disciple of the revered Gamaliel, the support of the Pharisees, who had acquitted him in the Sanhedrin ; and his murder would have been the signal for a riot against the priestly rulers, which might have endangered the peace of the Holy City. At all costs, therefore, Claudius Lysias had to see that Paul was protected, till the Roman government could decide as to his innocence or guilt.

In the second place it must be remembered that at this time the whole of Palestine was a scene of sedition and disorder. Armed banditti were perpetrating outrages in the name of patriotism in every district, despite the vigour of Felix's administration. Every day the *sicarii* or assassins were murdering Jews whom they suspected of pro-Roman or heretical sympathies (Josephus, *Antiq.*, xx. 8. 5). Upon the whole the narrative of Paul's treatment by the Roman officials is a testimony to the excellence of the provincial administration under Claudius and Nero. Had Claudius Lysias been an incompetent or corrupt official, he might have connived at Paul's death by giving him an incomplete escort, instead of taking every precaution for his safety. Paul's escort consisted of infantry, cavalry, and auxiliary, i.e. non-legionary troops, the uncertain word rendered **troopers** being only found here.

The letter of Claudius Lysias bears every trace of being genuine ; it is the sort of report an officer who had acted at first hastily would write. The account of what happened is business-like, terse, and misleading ; instead of bringing his soldiers to deliver Paul, on hearing he was **a Roman citizen,** he had mistaken the Apostle for an Egyptian rebel, and had been on the verge of putting him to the torture. **Antipatris** is forty-two miles from Jerusalem, which could scarcely have been accomplished in a night by a mixed force of infantry and cavalry. From **Antipatris** to Caesarea the country was open, unlike the hilly and treacherous country of Central Palestine.

The first question asked by Felix as to Paul's native province was a purely formal one. According to Luke it seems to have been similar to that put when Jesus was brought before Pilate. **The praetorium of Herod** (A.V. ' judgment-hall,' R.V. ' palace ') is perhaps designedly ambiguous, since it is capable of many explanations. The word is of course Latin, and is connected with *praetor*, which in Greek is rendered στρατηγός. It signifies : (1) the general's tent or headquarters in a Roman camp ; (2) the residence of a governor or prince, as here and in Mark xv. 16 ; (3) a spacious villa ; (4) the *praetorium* or camp of the praetorian cohorts in Rome (Phil. i. 3, with Bishop Lightfoot's note on the passage).

Felix had been appointed procurator in A.D. 52-53, and had therefore been a long time in Palestine. He was the brother of Pallas, the unpopular minister of Claudius, and has gone down to posterity with the character of one of the worst of men. This is not the impression Luke's narrative would convey, but we have the testimony of Josephus, Tacitus, and Suetonius.

According to Josephus, Felix was appointed as successor to Cumanus, and under both these procurators things in Palestine were increasingly critical. The land was full of brigands and marauders, and there were constant murders by the *sicarii*.

Felix suppressed disorder with a heavy hand ; and, when the revolt of the Egyptian broke out, he was assisted by the citizens in defeating him under the walls of Jerusalem. He was considered an accomplice to the murder by the *sicarii* of Jonathan, the virtuous chief priest, and also is recorded to have sent some priests to Rome to answer charges made against them. Further mention is made of his having induced Drusilla, sister of Herod Agrippa II, to desert her husband the King of Emesa and become his wife. There are two accounts of Felix, one in the *War* written before A.D. 80, the other in the *Antiquities* produced about A.D. 90. In the last-named work the crimes of Felix are mentioned. It is impossible to ascertain the precise date of these events by a perusal of Josephus, but it is fairly certain that Felix received his appointment about A.D. 53. The only thing of which we can be absolutely certain is that Paul and Luke were in Palestine in the days of Felix.

Tacitus wrote after Josephus, and as the main part of his *Histories* dealing with this period is lost we are in the dark as to his knowledge of Palestinian affairs. In his earlier work, the *Annals*, Tacitus says that Felix, the brother of Pallas, governed Samaria, Cumanus and Judaea ; he declares that the two combined in fomenting strife between the Jews and Samaritans with a view to their personal profit, making out of the quarrel a means for robbing the country. Quadratus, the governor of Syria, interfered by naming a commission to investigate the scandal, and made Felix one of the judges to try Cumanus (*Ann.*, xii. 54). In the *Histories* (v. 9) Tacitus indulges in one of his unforgettable epigrams, that Felix exercises ' royal power with the disposition of a slave ' ; he further makes the strange mistake of thinking that Felix's wife Drusilla belonged to the imperial family, hinting that this disreputable freedman was by his marriage a relation of the Emperor Claudius. The malice of this remark inclines us to doubt the accuracy of Tacitus's information.

In Suetonius, a later contemporary of Tacitus, whose sketches of the emperors are rather literary gossip than serious history, Felix appears in the light of an active military adventurer, who successively married no less than three queens (*Claudius*, xxviii.).

If Luke wrote before Josephus, he is our earliest authority, and as this part of Acts is more or less the work of an eye-witness, his account of Felix is of the utmost importance.

xxiv.

Five days later down came the high priest Ananias with some 1 elders and a barrister called Tertullus. They laid informa- tion before the governor against Paul. So Paul was sum- 2 moned, and then Tertullus proceeded to accuse him. " Your excellency," he said to Felix, " as it is owing to you that we enjoy unbroken peace, and as it is owing to your wise care that the state of this nation has been improved in every way and everywhere, we acknowledge all this with 3 profound gratitude. I have no wish to weary you, but I 4 beg of you to grant us in your courtesy a brief hearing. The 5 fact is, we have found this man is a perfect pest ; he stirs up sedition among the Jews all over the world and he is a ringleader of the Nazarene sect. He actually tried to 6 desecrate the temple, but we got hold of him. Examine 8 him for yourself and you will be able to find out about all these charges of ours against him." The Jews joined in 9 the attack, declaring that such were the facts of the case. Then at a nod from the governor Paul made his reply. 10 " As I know you have administered justice in this nation for a number of years," he said, " I feel encouraged to make my defence,

The Jews employed heathen advocates ; one named Irenaeus was apparently hired to plead the cause of the Herod family in Rome before Augustus, when the will of Herod the Great was in dispute (Josephus, *Antiq.*, xvii.).

The account of the trial of Paul before Felix is a model report. Condensed as the speeches for the prosecution and defence are, they give all the necessary points, and leave noth-ing to be desired. Tertullus opens with a compliment **to Felix** in order to win the goodwill of the judge. The allusion to the quietude of the time was particularly well timed, as the Jews of Jerusalem had co-operated with Felix in suppressing the insurrection of ' the Egyptian ' (xxi. 38 ; Josephus, *Antiq.*, xx. 8. 6). Paul is declared to be (1) a nuisance (λοιμός—happily rendered **a perfect pest**) and a revolutionary, who has stirred up riots among the Jews in all parts of the Empire ; (2) as a ringleader of the faction of **the Nazarenes** ; (3) and one who **tried to desecrate the Temple.** Every point here must have told, as the accusations were admirably framed to convince Felix.

(1) Whatever may have been his faults, this procurator had waged ceaseless war on revolutionary movements. At Thessalonica Paul and his friends had been accused of disturbing the Empire, and Felix could not afford to tolerate such people.

(2) Paul was the leader of a dangerous faction, here only in the New Testament called **the Nazarenes.** In later time it was used as a term of reproach, instead of the word Christian. Jesus is called the Nazarene by his enemies (Matt. xxvi. 71, etc. ; Acts vi. 14), and was popularly so known (Acts ii. 22, iii. 6, etc.). Nazarenes may have been the popular name of the new ' sect ' in Palestine during the days of Felix before the outbreak of the war. As the burning question in Jewry was that of the resurrection of the dead, one may perhaps boldly hazard the conjecture that all who were expecting an immediate messianic deliverance accompanied by a resurrection were more or less united against the Sadducean priesthood ; and when Paul boldly claimed to be a Pharisee and a believer in the Resurrection, he had a great deal of sympathy from the popular party in Jerusalem.

(3) Tertullus's remark that Paul had **tried to desecrate the Temple** is extremely significant. Perhaps he was too good a lawyer to assert that Paul had committed sacrilege by introducing Trophimus, the Ephesian, into the precincts, because he knew the charge could not be maintained. But it is noteworthy that throughout the New Testament the persecutors were invariably the Sadducean hierarchy of the Temple. Thus

Jesus was condemned by the priests chiefly on the charge of
defaming the Temple, and Stephen for saying that Jesus
would destroy it. It would seem as though messianism and
the doctrine of a resurrection were abhorrent to the Temple
rulers, because both connoted a visitation of the sanctuary by
God (cf. Mal. iii. 1).

Tertullus speaks in the name of his clients, **but *we* got hold
of him.** The rest of the sixth verse and the following verse
in the A.V. are omitted, as the MS. authority is not sufficient
for their retention. Nevertheless, the words, ' And would
have judged him according to our law. But the chief captain
Lysias came and with great violence took him away out of our
hands, commanding his accusers to come to you,' are extremely
apt, giving the misleading impression that Paul would have
had a fair trial when the mob dragged him out of the Temple
but for the untimely interference of Claudius Lysias. If he
actually said these words, Tertullus certainly scored a point,
as he shewed that Claudius Lysias had no business to interfere
in the matter of the observance of the laws of the Temple.

because it is not more than twelve days, as you can easily 11
ascertain, since I went up to worship at Jerusalem.
They never found me arguing with anyone in the temple 12
or causing a riot either in the synagogue or in the city ;
they cannot furnish you with any proof of their present 13
charges against me. I certainly admit to you that I 14
worship our fathers' God according to the methods of
what they call a ' sect '; but I believe all that is written in
the Law and in the prophets, and I cherish the same hope 15
in God as they accept, namely that there is to be a resurrection of the just and the unjust. Hence I too endeavoured 16
to have a clear conscience before God and men all the time.
After a lapse of several years I came up with alms and 17
offerings for my nation,* and it was in presenting these that 18
I was found within the temple. I was ceremonially pure,
I was not mixed up in any mob or riot ; no, the trouble was
caused by some Jews from Asia, who ought to have been 19

* See Note on next page.

20
21

here before you with any charge they may have against me. Failing them, let these men yonder tell what fault they found with my appearance before the Sanhedrin!—unless it was with the single sentence I uttered, when I stood and said, ' It is for the resurrection of the dead that I am on trial to-day before you.' "

<hr/>

* It is hardly possible to make sense of the following Greek text, and none of the various readings or of the emendations that have been proposed is entirely satisfactory. All one can do is to reproduce the general drift of the passage.

<hr/>

Paul in his defence was fully a match for his adversary, and his speech is as lawyer-like as that of Tertullus. He opened with a compliment to Felix, whose long experience of Judaic Palestine qualified him to be an impartial judge. He then declared that only twelve days ago he had come to Jerusalem, and defied his accusers to prove that he had been guilty of disturbing the religious peace of the city. He next freely admitted that he worshipped his ancestral God (a strong point, as the Jew's religion had long been formally legalized), though after the manner which his enemies were pleased to call a sect or ' heresy.' The word *heresy* here and elsewhere in the New Testament does not imply erroneous doctrine. In Acts it is applied both to Pharisees and Sadducees (v. 17, xv. 5), as well as to Nazarenes. In the epistle to the Galatians it is coupled with divisions (Gal. v. 20) : a man that is a heretic (Titus iii. 10) is to be avoided, because he is a ' factious person.' [1] Paul's words, in fact, may be paraphrased thus : ' They say I am a party man : so I am ; but so are all who acknowledge that our Scriptures speak of **a resurrection of just and unjust.'**

Paul goes on to deal with the fatal charge that he had profaned the Temple. He had not been a week in Jerusalem (ver. 12, cf. xxi. 26, 27), and it was years since he had visited the city. He was engaged as a good Jew in purifying himself after a vow he had previously taken. He had never caused any disturbance by preaching in Jerusalem ; and the Jews

<hr/>

[1] In later theological language a heretic is one who errs in doctrine ; a schismatic severs himself from communion with the Church, even though his doctrine is unimpeachable.

from Asia who had charged him with introducing Trophimus were not present to give their evidence. One mistake he honestly admitted : that he had divided the Sanhedrin on the question of the Resurrection. His answer even in this brief form is complete ; as a lawyer Paul was more than a match for Tertullus. Tarsus, it must be remembered, was a great law school.

As Felix had a pretty accurate knowledge of the Way, he re- 22 manded Paul, telling the Jews, "When Lysias the commander comes down, I will decide your case." He gave 23 orders to the officers to have Paul kept in custody but to allow him some freedom and not to prevent any of his own people from rendering him any service.
Some days later Felix arrived with his wife Drusilla, who was 24 a Jewess. He sent for Paul and heard what he had to say about faith in Christ Jesus ; but when he argued about 25 morality, self-mastery, and the future judgment, Felix grew uneasy. "You may go for the present," he said ; "when I can find a moment, I will send for you " (though 26 at the same time he hoped Paul would give him a bribe). So he did send for him pretty frequently and conversed with him. But when two years had elapsed, Felix was suc- 27 ceeded by Porcius Festus, and as Felix wanted to ingratiate himself with the Jews he left Paul in custody.

Paul had virtually convinced Felix of his innocence, and the procurator behaved well to him. If he was as wicked as Tacitus declared him to have been, the conduct of Felix at the trial is a testimony to Roman justice. Paul must have had influential friends, judging by Luke's surmise that there was a prospect of getting a large sum of money to secure his liberation. Felix had had three wives according to Suetonius, all of whom were queens. Drusilla had been given in marriage to Azizus King of Emesa, who accepted circumcision in order to obtain her. But owing to the artifices of one Simon, a Cypriote magician, she deserted her husband to marry Felix, partly because her beauty had aroused the jealousy of her sister Bernice. There is a curious reading adopted by Westcott and Hort, 'Drusilla his *own* wife,' though the best MSS. omit the word.   There may be some sarcasm underlying it, if we believe Suetonius's *trium reginarum maritum et adulterum*. She bore Felix a son who perished in the great eruption of Mount Vesuvius in A.D. 79.   Perhaps Drusilla may have been interested in Paul, and caused Felix to listen to him, as is implied in the western text as restored by Blass.   In the Harklean Syriac it is suggested that Drusilla induced Felix to have Paul brought to him.

Of what happened to Paul for two years we know nothing, save that he was detained by Felix at Caesarea.   Josephus informs us that this period was one of constant disturbance, and that the Jews and Syrians in Caesarea were so bitter against one another that their disorders were only quelled with bloodshed.   Felix was sent to Rome to answer for his misgovernment, and only escaped by the influence of his brother Pallas.   His successor **Festus** did what he could to restore peace by the vigour of his methods (Josephus, *War*, ii. 14. 1), but died two years after his appointment.   The little we know of his administration helps us to understand his difficulties in dealing with the case of Paul.

XXV.

1 Three days after Festus entered his province, he went up from
2   Caesarea to Jerusalem.   The high priests and the Jewish
3   leaders laid information before him against Paul, and
     begged him, as a special favour, to send for him to Jeru-
     salem, meaning to lay an ambush for him and murder him
4   on the road.   Festus replied that Paul would be kept in
     custody at Caesarea, but that he himself meant to leave for
5   Caesarea before long—"when," he added, "your com-
     petent authorities can come down with me and charge the
6   man with whatever crime he has committed."   After
     staying not more than eight or ten days with them, he
     went down to Caesarea.   Next day he took his seat on the
7   tribunal and ordered Paul to be brought before him.   When

he arrived, the Jews who had come down from Jerusalem surrounded him and brought a number of serious charges against him, none of which they were able to prove. Paul's defence was, " I have committed no offence against 8 the Law of the Jews, against the temple, or against Caesar." As Festus wanted to ingratiate himself with the 9 Jews, he asked Paul, " Will you go up to Jerusalem and be tried there by me upon these charges ? " Paul said, 10 " I am standing before Caesar's tribunal ; that is where I ought to be tried. I have done no wrong whatever to the Jews—you know that perfectly well. If I am a criminal, 11 if I have done anything that deserves death, I do not object to die ; but if there is nothing in any of their charges against me, then no one can give me up to them. I appeal to Caesar ! " Then, after conferring with the council, 12 Festus answered, " You have appealed to Caesar ? Very well, you must go to Caesar ! "

On arriving at **Caesarea Festus** started for **Jerusalem** to consult with the chiefs of the priesthood and the leading men among the Jews, and was met by a request to send Paul to the Holy City to take his trial. It was **a favour** which it might have been politic to grant, and a new-comer like Festus might well have acquiesced. But the country was infested by the *sicarii*, who were murdering all whose loyalty to Judaism was suspected ; Festus, to his credit, refused to grant the demand of the Jews, and invited them to come with him to Caesarea and there make their charges against Paul. When they had done so, and Paul had uttered an emphatic denial, Felix (xxiv. 27), wishing to oblige the Jews (like Festus, xxv. 9), asked Paul to accompany him to Jerusalem and be judged, not by the Jews, but by the procurator there. Thereupon Paul made his famous appeal. As a citizen of Rome he had the right of appeal to the tribunes of the people, whose power now rested in the Emperor Nero. This *provocatio ad populum*, which was one of the most ancient rights of a citizen, dating from 449 B.C., could not possibly be disregarded. Festus took the advice of **the council,** which acted as assessors

to every Roman governor, and pronounced his sentence,
'You appeal to Caesar, you shall go to Caesar.'

13 Some days had passed, when king Agrippa and Bernice came
14 to Caesarea to pay their respects to Festus. As they were
spending several days there, Festus laid Paul's case before
the king. "There is a man," he said, "who was left in
15 prison by Felix. When I was at Jerusalem, the high
priests and elders of the Jews informed me about him and
16 demanded his condemnation. I told them Romans were
not in the habit of giving up any man until the accused
met the accusers face to face and had a chance of defending
17 himself against the impeachment. Well, the day after
they came here along with me, I took my seat on the
tribunal without any loss of time. I ordered the man to
18 be brought in, but when his accusers stood up they did not
19 charge him with any of the crimes that I had expected.
The questions at issue referred to their own religion and to
20 a certain Jesus who had died. Paul said he was alive. As
I felt at a loss about the method of inquiry into such
topics, I asked if he would go to Jerusalem and be tried
21 there on these charges. But Paul entered an appeal for
his case to be reserved for the decision of the emperor; so
I ordered him to be detained till I could remit him to
22 Caesar." "I should like to hear the man myself," said
Agrippa to Festus. "You shall hear him to-morrow,"
23 said Festus. So next day Agrippa and Bernice proceeded
with great pomp to the hall of audience, accompanied by
the military commanders and the prominent civilians of
24 the town. Festus then ordered Paul to be brought in.
"King Agrippa and all here present," said Festus, "you
see before you a man of whom the entire body of the Jews
at Jerusalem and also here have complained to me. They
25 loudly insist he ought not to live any longer. I could not
find he had done anything that deserved death, so I decided
26 to send him, on his own appeal, to the emperor. Only, I
have nothing definite to write to the sovereign about him.
So I have brought him up before you all, and especially

before you, O king Agrippa, in order that I may have
something to write as the result of your cross-examination.
For it seems absurd to me to forward a prisoner without 27
notifying the particulars of his charge." Then Agrippa xxvi.
said to Paul, "You have our permission to speak upon 1
your own behalf." At this Paul stretched out his hand
·and began his defence.

St. Luke's portrayal of **Agrippa** II leaves a pleasing impression of a Roman gentleman of Jewish birth. A great-grandson of Herod the Great and Mariamne, the last of the Asmonaeans, he was the last representative of the priest-kings of Judah ; and, as his family had long lived in Rome on familiar terms with the aristocracy of the capital, his sympathies were with the ruling race. His constant companionship with his sister **Bernice** caused much scandal (Juvenal, *Satire* vii. 56), but both of them, like many of the Herodian family, were capable of acting a creditable part. Bernice risked her life among the disorderly soldiers to intercede for the Jews whom the infamous procurator Gessius Florus was massacring in Jerusalem, and Agrippa did his best to avert the Jewish war (see his speech recorded by Josephus in *War*, ii. 16. 4). Agrippa was a friend and patron of Josephus, to whom he was remotely related. At this time he was a great magnate in Palestine, being **king** of Chalcis and holding large estates in Galilee. He also possessed, and constantly exercised, the right of appointing and deposing the high-priest.

Festus in this statement lays down a sound principle of Roman law, and represents his own conduct towards Paul in the most favourable light possible.

The word 'superstition' in the A.V., like the adjective in xvii. 22, gives an entirely wrong impression. Festus is evidently desirous of shewing every courtesy to Agrippa, and could not possibly have meant that Judaism, the king's **religion**, was a 'superstition.'

I should like is literally 'I was wishing.' The case of Paul was apparently already notorious, and the curiosity of the king may be compared with that of Herod Antipas, who had

221

desired to see Jesus when Pilate sent him to his tribunal (Luke xxiii. 7).

Here Luke introduces Paul's speech with a dramatic picture of regal pomp. Agrippa and Bernice are represented as sitting in judgment surrounded by the Roman tribunes and the magnates of Caesarea. When all are assembled Paul is introduced. **With great pomp** is an impressive touch. The Apostle is now about to make the greatest of his speeches recorded in the Acts, and the scene is appropriately set for so momentous an occasion. It is noteworthy that when Agrippa II made his great appeal to the Jews to avert war, Bernice also sat by him. The orator Quintilian says that he once pleaded a cause when Bernice sat among the judges. At this trial of Paul, Agrippa takes the leading part, and allows the Apostle to speak for himself.

xxvi.

2 " I consider myself fortunate, king Agrippa, in being able to defend myself to-day before you against all that the Jews
3 charge me with ; for you are well acquainted with all Jewish customs and questions. Pray listen to me then
4 with patience. How I lived from my youth up among my own nation and at Jerusalem, all that early career of
5 mine, is known to all the Jews. They know me of old. They know, if they chose to admit it, that as a Pharisee I lived by the principles of the strictest party in our religion.
6 To-day I am standing my trial for hoping in the promise
7 made by God to our fathers, a promise which our twelve tribes hope to gain by serving God earnestly both night and day. And I am actually impeached by Jews for this
9 hope, O king! I once believed it my duty indeed actively
10 to oppose the name of Jesus the Nazarene. I did so in Jerusalem. I shut up many of the saints in prison, armed with authority from the high priests ; when they were put
11 to death, I voted against them ; there was not a synagogue where I did not often punish them and force them to blaspheme ; and in my frantic fury I persecuted them even

to foreign towns. I was travelling to Damascus on this 12
business, with authority and a commission from the high
priests, when at mid day on the road, O king, I saw a light 13
from heaven, more dazzling than the sun, flash round me
and my fellow-travellers. We all fell to the ground, and 14
I heard a voice saying to me in Hebrew, ' Saul, Saul, why
do you persecute me ? You hurt yourself by kicking at
the goad.' ' Who are you ? ' I asked. And the Lord said, 15
' I am Jesus, and you are persecuting me. Now get up 16
and *stand on your feet,* for I have appeared to you in order
to appoint you to my service as a witness to what you have
seen and to the visions you shall have of me. *I will* 17
rescue you from the People and also *from the Gentiles—*
to whom I send you, that their *eyes may be opened* and that 18
they may turn *from darkness to light,* from the power of
Satan to God, to get remission of their sins and an inheritance among those who are consecrated by faith in me.' 19
Upon this, O king Agrippa, I did not disobey the heavenly
vision; I announced to those at Damascus and at Jerusalem 20
in the first instance, then all over the land of Judaea, and
also to the Gentiles, that they were to repent and turn to
God by acting up to their repentance. This is why the 21
Jews seized me in the temple and tried to assassinate me. 22
To this day I have had the help of God in standing, as I
now do, to testify alike to low and high, never uttering a
single syllable beyond what the prophets and Moses predicted was to take place. Why should you consider it 8
incredible that God raises the dead,* that the Christ is
capable of suffering, and that he should be the first to rise 23
from the dead and bring the message of light to the People
and to the Gentiles ? ''

* Restoring ver. 8 to its original position at the beginning of ver. 23.

Although this speech may appear to the general reader little
more than a repetition of that delivered by Paul at Jerusalem
on the steps leading from the Temple to the Antonia (xxii.
1–21), it was evidently not Luke's purpose to leave this impression. On the contrary, considering the setting in which

it is placed, and the distinguished company to whom it was delivered, it was intended to be the most important, as it is the last, of all the speeches of the Apostle. It is, in fact, a veritable *Apologia pro vita sua*, a fitting conclusion to the account of his missionary labours and trials in Acts, and it resulted in his acquittal by Agrippa II, the chief personage in the Jewish nation. Despite its resemblance to the address in chap. xxii., it has certain distinct features of its own : the language is stately and dignified as befitted the occasion ; the topics are well chosen to appeal to a Jewish judge, and the arrangement is excellent. (1) An introduction (vers. 2–3) leads to (2) a definition (vers. 4–7) of Paul's position, and (3) of his career (vers. 9–11) as a persecutor ; (4) vers. 12–18 give the story of the vision ; (5) vers. 19–20 describe his preaching ; then comes in ver. 21 (6) his arrest, and (7) the substance of his message (vers. 22–24).

(1) As in the speeches in chap. xxiv. before Felix, this begins with what was known as a *captatio benevolentiae*, a courteous address to the judge. Agrippa I, the father of this Agrippa, if noted for his profligacy in Rome, was equally conspicuous for his piety in Jerusalem ; and his son had obviously been trained in the laws and ceremonies of Judaism.

(2) Everyone who had known Paul must have been aware, though unwilling to admit the fact, that he had not only learned but practised the **strictest principles** of Pharisaism, belonging as he did to the most scrupulous **party** (Greek αἵρεσις = in classical language a philosophic school) of Jewish observance. As a Pharisee he shared in the hope of the **Twelve tribes,** i.e. of all Israel, a **hope** which has brought upon him the hostility of the priests of Jerusalem. If ver. 8 is rightly considered to be out of place here, Paul is not here alluding to the resurrection ; but speaking in general terms, implying that all good Israelites are looking forward to a great deliverance.

(3) But although he shared in the hope of Israel, Paul was violently opposed at first to the good tidings brought by Jesus of Nazareth, and was one of the bitterest persecutors of his followers. He gives some details of the persecution over

Stephen, which we should hardly infer from chap. viii. The protomartyr was not the only victim : on the contrary there was an organized attempt to put down the preaching of the new faith, in which several were brought to trial and condemned to death, Paul being certainly at this time a member of the Sanhedrin. One characteristic feature of the persecution was that the followers of Jesus were compelled to **blaspheme** or to curse him. This test, as we learn from Pliny's letter to Trajan, was in the second century applied by the heathen to those accused of being Christians.

(4) The varieties in the three descriptions of the vision have already been noted. The interesting additions here are the words, **You hurt yourself by kicking against the goad,** and the fact that Jesus spoke **in Hebrew** (i.e. Aramaic), as he is recorded to have done in the Gospels. The substance of what Jesus said to Paul is (in chap. ix.) told to Ananias, who healed his blindness.

(5) It is remarkable that in the letters of St. Paul there is little said of **repentance** being the subject of his preaching. Indeed, the language here is rather that of the Gospels when they speak of John the Baptist ; ' works meet for repentance ' in the A.V. is an echo of Matt. iii. 18.

(6) **This is why the Jews seized me,** etc., is a curiously brief summary of what is recorded elsewhere in Acts. Nor was such preaching the reason for Paul's arrest in the Temple. It is quite possible that Luke, knowing Agrippa had been informed of what had happened, condensed it in a brief verse.

(7) Paul now sums up. He has been marvellously delivered from peril by God, and still takes a firm stand in witnessing to his convictions. But these are not opposed to the religion of his people. Not only Moses, but every prophet since has taught what amounts to this, (a) that the Messiah is **capable of suffering** (our translation is more accurate than the A.V. ' that Christ should suffer,' the meaning here being that the Messiah is not merely a divine deliverer of Israel but one who can suffer with and for his people), and (b) that this Messiah (Paul does not mention the name of Jesus) must be **the first to rise from the dead and bring light,** not only **to the People** of

God, but to the nations of the world. The Messiah is, in fact, the firstfruits of them that slept (1 Cor. xv. 20).

Now follow remarks by Festus and Agrippa which add much to the vivid character of the scene.

24 When he brought this forward in his defence, Festus called out, " Paul, you are quite mad ! Your great learning is driving
25 you insane." " Your excellency," said Paul to Festus,
26 " I am not mad, I am speaking the sober truth. Why, the king is well aware of this ! To the king I can speak without the slightest hesitation. I do not believe any of it has escaped his notice, for this was not done in a corner.
27 King Agrippa, you believe the prophets ? I know you
28 do." " At this rate," Agrippa remarked, " it won't be long before you believe you have made a Christian of me ! "
29 " Long or short," said Paul, " I would to God that not only you but all my hearers to-day could be what I am—
30 barring these chains ! " Then the king rose, with the governor and Bernice and those who had been seated
31 beside them. They retired to discuss the affair, and agreed that " this man has done nothing to deserve death or
32 imprisonment." " He might have been released," said Agrippa to Festus, " if he had not appealed to Caesar."

Festus, like those who mocked Paul at Athens when he spoke of the resurrection, was astonished at this part of the Apostle's defence, and loudly exclaimed that Paul was **mad**. This was not intended to be an offensive remark ; perhaps the A.V. gives a truer impression, ' thou art beside thyself.' The Greek word μαίνομαι is of the same root as μάντις, a prophet or seer, and μαντευομένη (xvi. 16) is applied to the girl who told fortunes. If it is rendered *mad*, we must bear in mind that a madman was usually regarded in antiquity as one possessed by a power not his own, and when he raved it was supposed that a spirit spoke through him. Probably Paul ended his speech with a burst of oratory which we might call inspired, and Festus, with a true Roman distrust of mere oratory, declared that Paul was raving, and that these scriptures he was constantly referring to were unhinging his mind. In reply the Apostle declared that he was speaking true and sober words (*veritatis et sobrietatis*, Vulg.).

Agrippa now interposed, but what he actually meant must remain doubtful. The A.V. rendering has become proverbial: ' Almost thou persuadest me to be a Christian.' Editors of the MSS. realized the difficulty of these words. For ' thou persuadest me,' some read ' thou persuadest thyself,' and for ' to be ' (γένεσθαι) an alternative is ' to make me ' (ποιῆσαι). The words ἐν ὀλίγῳ have been rendered ' almost,' ' with little trouble,' ' in a short time.' At anyrate the saying befits a cynical but courteous personage. Paul's reply is a model of Christian zeal for the conversion of all present, and of consideration, with a touching phrase **barring these bonds** (' except these bonds '). The word **Christian** occurs only in two other places in the N.T. (in Acts xi. 26, and in 1 Pet. iv. 16, where the believer suffers as a Christian).

Agrippa pronounces the final verdict of ' Not Guilty,' and his words would be a suitable ending to Paul's biography in Acts. The last two chapters are really supplementary. Yet though they do not add to our knowledge of the case, they are of inestimable value to students of ancient navigation, to the curious as a revelation of the character of St. Paul, and to the devout as an indication of the great qualities which a sublime trust in God can evoke.

Chapter xxvii. falls into three main sections :

      I. The journey to Crete (vers. 1–8).
     II. The storm (vers. 9–26).
    III. The shipwreck (vers. 27–41).

As a technical knowledge of the navigation of the Mediterranean as well as nautical experience is demanded of anyone who presumes to interpret this account, and as the task has been admirably performed by those well qualified to deal with it, this voyage will necessarily be treated with brevity, though it is among the finest pieces of descriptive writing in the New Testament.

xxvii.

1 When it was decided we were to sail for Italy, Paul and some
other prisoners were handed over to an officer of the
2 Imperial regiment called Julius. Embarking in an
Andramyttian ship which was bound for the Asiatic sea-
ports, we set sail, accompanied by a Macedonian from
3 Thessalonica called Aristarchus. Next day we put in at
Sidon, where Julius very kindly allowed Paul to visit his
4 friends and be looked after. Putting to sea from there,
we had to sail under the lee of Cyprus, as the wind was
5 against us ; then, sailing over the Cilician and Pamphylian
6 waters, we came to Myra in Lycia. There the officer
found an Alexandrian ship bound for Italy, and put us on
7 board of her. For a number of days we made a slow
passage and had great difficulty in arriving off Cnidus;
then, as the wind checked our progress, we sailed under
8 the lee of Crete off Cape Salmonê, and coasting along it
with great difficulty we reached a place called Fair Havens,
not far from the town of Lasea.

Here the writer resumes the first person plural. Paul
embarks with **other prisoners** (ver. 42), among them perhaps
Aristarchus of **Thessalonica**. This **Aristarchus** was one of the
delegates who had accompanied Paul to Jerusalem with the
contribution to the poor (xx. 4), and had been with him at
the time of the Ephesian riot where he had been arrested by
the mob. His name occurs with that of Marcus in Col. iv. 10
as Paul's fellow-captive, and also in Philem. 24 (' Marcus,
Aristarchus, Demas, Lucas '). He must have been a prominent friend of the Apostle, and the mention of his name in
connexion with Luke's may well be used as an argument for
the Lucan authorship of the story of the voyage. Paul was
in charge of Julius, a centurion of the ' Augustan cohort.'
The word here rendered **Imperial** is in Greek ' Sebastan,' that
being the equivalent of Augustan. Josephus speaks of a
' turma ' or troop of horses called Sebastene, from Sebaste in
Samaria, which was so named by Herod the Great in compliment to his patron Augustus. What this cohort was is

unknown. Perhaps one may hazard a guess that Julius, who was evidently an officer of rank, belonged to the praetorians in Rome, and had been on a special mission to Caesarea. He certainly shewed Paul great consideration. The weather was stormy, and at Myra (Vulgate, *Lystra*), in the south-west corner of Asia Minor, they disembarked, and sought another ship **bound for Italy.** This change of vessels appears to have been usual, since Paul and his companions took another ship at Patara on their way to Syria (xxi. 2). They were now on board a large ship bound for the open sea, and reached **Cape Salmonê,** the easternmost part of Crete ; despite adverse winds, they coasted as far as a port called **Fair Havens.**

By this time it was far on in the season and sailing had become 9 dangerous (for the autumn Fast was past), so Paul warned them thus: " Men," said he, " I see this voyage is going 10 to be attended with hardship and serious loss not only to the cargo and the ship but also to our own lives." How- 11 ever the officer let himself be persuaded by the captain and the owner rather than by anything Paul could say, and, 12 as the harbour was badly placed for wintering in, the majority proposed to set sail and try if they could reach Phoenix and winter there (Phoenix is a Cretan harbour facing S.W. and N.W.). When a moderate southerly 13 breeze sprang up, they thought they had secured their object, and after weighing anchor they sailed along the coast of Crete, close inshore. Presently down rushed a 14 hurricane of a wind called Euroclydon ; the ship was 15 caught and unable to face the wind, so we gave up and let her drive along. Running under the lee of a small island 16 called Clauda, we managed with great difficulty to get the boat hauled in ; once it was hoisted aboard, they used 17 ropes * to undergird the ship, and in fear of being stranded on the Syrtis they lowered the sail and lay to. As we were 18 being terribly battered by the storm, they had to jettison the cargo next day, while two days later they threw the 19 ship's gear overboard with their own hands ; for many 20

---

* See Note on next page.

days neither sun nor stars could be seen, the storm raged heavily, and at last we had to give up all hope of being

21 saved. When they had gone without food for a long time, Paul stood up among them and said, "Men, you should have listened to me and spared yourselves this hardship and loss by refusing to set sail from Crete. I now bid you

22 cheer up. There will be no loss of life, only of the ship.

23 For last night an angel of the God I belong to and serve,

24 stood before me, saying, 'Have no fear, Paul; you must stand before Caesar. And God has granted you the lives

25 of all your fellow-voyagers.' Cheer up, men! I believe God, I believe it will turn out just as I have been told.

26 However, we are to be stranded on an island."

* Naber's conjecture βoειαις for the βoηθειαις of the MSS. yields this excellent sense. [βόειος means ox-hide. The master of a merchant-ship once, however, told the author that ropes would not keep a ship together, but a large sail-cloth might do so.]

It was now the end of September or the beginning of October, and the sea was considered no longer safe for navigation. The great Jewish **fast** of the *Yom-kippor* or Day of Atonement was over, and a council was held as to what should be done. Paul, who was a traveller of great experience, was invited to attend, and advised that they should stop where they were. Despite his warnings, **the owner** of the ship and the master who navigated it thought it possible to go a little farther and **reach Phoenix,** as a far more convenient stopping-place. The wind was favourable, till suddenly a violent storm drove them from the shores of the island. **Running** before the gale, there was a temporary respite owing to the wind being broken by the **small** islet of **Clauda,** of which they availed themselves by hauling up the *one* boat, undergirding the ship, and lowering the unwieldy mainsail. As **the storm** still continued, they threw over all they could to lighten the ship, and finally, after three days, cleared her of all her superfluous **gear.** It was then that Paul rose to the occasion and assured the despairing and famished crew that he had had a vision that all lives would be saved.

27 When the fourteenth night arrived, we were drifting about in

the sea of Adria, when the sailors about midnight suspected land was near.   On taking soundings they found 28 twenty fathoms, and a little further on, when they sounded again, they found fifteen.   Then, afraid of being stranded 29 on the rocks, they let go four anchors from the stern and longed for daylight.   The sailors tried to escape from the 30 ship.   They had even lowered the boat into the sea, pretending they were going to lay out anchors from the bow, when Paul said to the officer and the soldiers, ''You 31 cannot be saved unless these men stay by the ship.''   Then 32 the soldiers cut away the ropes of the boat and let her fall off.   Just before daybreak Paul begged them all to take 33 some food.   '' For fourteen days,'' he said, '' you have been on the watch all the time, without a proper meal. Take some food then, I beg of you ; it will keep you alive. 34 You are going to be saved !   Not a hair of your heads will perish.''   With these words he took a loaf and after 35 thanking God, in presence of them all, broke it and began to eat.   Then they all cheered up and took food for them- 36 selves (there were about * seventy-six souls of us on board, 37 all told) ; and when they had eaten their fill, they lightened 38 the ship by throwing the wheat into the sea.   When day 39 broke, they could not recognize what land it was ; however, they noticed a creek with a sandy beach, and resolved to see if they could run the ship ashore there.   So the 40 anchors were cut away and left in the sea, while the crew unlashed the ropes that tied the rudders, hoisted the foresail to the breeze, and headed for the beach.   Striking a reef, 41 they drove the ship aground ; the prow jammed fast, but the stern began to break up under the beating of the waves. Now the soldiers resolved to kill the prisoners, in case any 42 of them swam off and escaped ; but as the officer wanted 43 to save Paul, he put a stop to their plan, ordering those who could swim to jump overboard first and get to land, while the rest were to manage with planks or pieces of 44 wreckage.   In this way it turned out that the whole company got safe to land.

* Reading ὡς (B and Sahidic version) for διακόσιαι.

As the storm had lasted for a fortnight and they were without the guidance of sun or star, the navigators had no idea of where they were, and only knew they were in the Adriatic, not the modern gulf, but the sea between Greece and Italy.   As **soundings** were taken, and it was evident that they were near land, another peril threatened the passengers. There was, surprising as it may seem to us, only one boat for a large ship carrying at least seventy persons and possibly more, and the cowardly **sailors** resolved to abandon the vessel and those on board to their fate.   Paul, who knew well what it was to be wrecked (2 Cor. xi. 25), warned the centurion, and **the soldiers cut away the ropes of the boat,** thus compelling the sailors to remain on board.   It was now evident that the ship was hopelessly lost, and Paul once more took the lead, calling all to unite with him in a solemn, one may almost term it a eucharistic, meal.   The wheat with which the hold had been stored was now thrown into the sea.   The MSS. differ as to the number on board, the best reading (ver. 37) is **about seventy-six,** but a total of two hundred and seventy-six (as in A.V.) is not incredible.   Josephus says that when his ship was wrecked in the Adriatic, there were no less than six hundred on board (*Life,* 3).

xxviii.

1 **It was only after our escape that we found out the island was**
2   called Malta.   The natives showed us uncommon kindness, for they lit a fire and welcomed us all to it, as the rain had
3   come on and it was chilly.   Now Paul had gathered a bundle of sticks and laid them on the fire, when a viper
4   crawled out with the heat and fastened on his hand.   When the natives saw the creature hanging from his hand, they said to each other, " This man must be a murderer !   He has escaped the sea, but Justice will not let him live."
5   However, he shook off the creature into the fire and was
6   not a whit the worse.   The natives waited for him to swell up or drop down dead in a moment, but after waiting a long while and observing that no harm had befallen

him, they changed their minds and declared he was a god.

There was an estate in the neighbourhood which belonged 7 to a man called Publius, the governor of the island ; he welcomed us and entertained us hospitably for three days. His father, it so happened, was laid up with fever and 8 dysentery, but Paul went in to see him and after prayer laid his hands on him and cured him. When this had 9 happened, the rest of the sick folk in the island also came and got cured ; they made us rich presents and furnished 10 us, when we set sail, with all we needed.

We set sail, after three months, in an Alexandrian ship, with 11 the Dioscuri on her figure-head, which had wintered at the island. We put in at Syracuse, and stayed for three days. 12 Then tacking round we reached Rhegium ; next day a 13 south wind sprang up which brought us in a day to Puteoli, where we came across some of the brotherhood, who 14 invited us to stay a week with them.

In this way we reached Rome. As the local brothers had 15 heard about us, they came out to meet us as far as Appii Forum and Tres Tabernae, and when Paul saw them he thanked God and took courage.

The happenings at **Malta,** and the prosperous journey from thence to Rome, though interesting, throw but little light on the object of our quest, which is the contribution of Acts to the history and theology of the primitive church. But the concluding verses of this chapter are of great importance for our purpose, as they open up the question of the Apostle's connexion with the early Roman church. He was evidently well known to the Christian community, and his arrival eagerly expected. Since his meeting with Aquila and Priscilla he had been in communication with the church, and if the salutations in Rom. xvi. are addressed to residents in the city, he had many friends and even relatives there. The question, however, is an open one. Personally, the writer is disposed to believe that the last chapter of the letter was intended for the Romans rather than for the Ephesians. At anyrate the Roman

233

epistle seems to presuppose considerable acquaintance with the problems agitating their church. This will adequately account for the fact that the Roman Christians journeyed as far as **Appii Forum** and Three Taverns to meet him, those places being respectively forty and thirty miles distant from the capital. It is also worth noticing that there were believers ready to welcome the Apostle at **Puteoli,** where he disembarked and remained, by the courtesy of Julius, for seven days. This fact will account for the deputations from Rome being apprised of his arrival and starting forth to meet him. It was not the purpose of Luke to carry his readers farther than Paul's arrival and two years' sojourn in the imperial city, where, if not set at liberty, he was allowed the freedom of an honourable captivity. All that can be gleaned from the later epistles of St. Paul, the Pastoral Epistles, and Christian tradition, may be disregarded by those who are solely occupied in the interpretation of Acts.

16 When **we** did reach Rome, Paul got permission * to live by
17 himself, with a soldier to guard him. Three days later, he
called the leading Jews together, and when they met he
said to them, " Brothers, although I have done nothing
against the People or our ancestral customs, I was handed
18 over to the Romans as a prisoner from Jerusalem. They
meant to release me after examination, as I was innocent
19 of any crime that deserved death. But the Jews objected,
and so I was obliged to appeal to Caesar—not that I had
20 any charge to bring against my own nation. This is my
reason for asking to see you and have a word with you. I
am wearing this chain because I share Israel's hope."
21 They replied, " We have had no letters about you from
Judaea, and no brother has come here with any bad report
22 or story about you. We think it only right to let you tell
your own story; but as regards this sect, we are well
23 aware that there are objections to it on all hands." So
they fixed a day and came to him at his quarters in large
numbers. From morning to evening he explained the

* See Note on next page.

Reign of God to them from personal testimony, and tried
to convince them about Jesus from the law of Moses and
the prophets. Some were convinced by what he said, but 24
the others would not believe. As they could not agree 25
among themselves, they were turning to go away, when
Paul added this one word: " It was an apt word that the
holy Spirit spoke by the prophet Isaiah to your fathers,
when he said,   26

> *Go and tell this people,*
>   *' You will hear and hear but never understand,*
>   *you will see and see but never perceive.'*
> *For the heart of this people is obtuse,*   27
>   *their ears are heavy of hearing,*
>   *their eyes they have closed,*
> *lest they see with their eyes and hear with their ears,*
> *lest they understand with their heart and turn again, and*
>   *I cure them.*

Be sure of this, then, that this *salvation of God* has been sent 28
to the Gentiles ; they will listen to it." For two full years 30
he remained in his private lodging, welcoming anyone who
came to visit him ; he preached the Reign of God and taught 31
about the Lord Jesus Christ quite openly and unmolested.

* Omitting [ὁ ἑκατόνταρχος παρέδωκεν τοὺς δεσμίους τῷ στρατοπεδάρχῳ]
and [δέ].

Of more interest is Paul's relation to the Jewish leaders of
the synagogues in Rome, whom it was his evident object to
conciliate. That these should have been professedly ignorant
of the new Movement in Jewry may be surprising, but it is
not incapable of explanation. Certainly in later days the
Jewish rabbis maintained a silence with regard to Christianity,
or, if they allude to it, do so in terms which are studiously
ambiguous. It was the deliberate policy of the Jews to ignore
the rival religion. That the Jews of Rome had received **no**
letters concerning Paul may be explained by the supposition
that he had been sent thither very soon after his appeal to
Caesar ; the inclement winter would render communications
exceptionally slow. It also is possible that the Jewish com-

munity was not anxious to be mixed up in a case which might prejudice the urban authorities against their continuance in the capital. These, however, are no more than conjectures. It is more important to guess why Luke gives such prominence to the incident.

The explanation may be found by reference to what happened at Pisidian Antioch at the beginning of Paul's ministry and later at Corinth. At both places he had carried his message to the Jews, and when it was rejected he turned to the Gentiles. He carried out this principle consistently in Rome, and his words re-echo those of the Lord Jesus when he was asked why he spoke in parables (Matt. xiii. 14). The meaning of the incident may be that this was the beginning of a distinctively Gentile church in Rome, whereas hitherto the Jewish element had predominated.

The end of Acts resembles that of 2 Maccabees, which closes with the great victory of Judas Maccabeus over Nicanor, leaving the hero at the moment of his triumph, so soon to be followed by his defeat and death. Of the fate of the great Apostle his biographer was ignorant, or he does not see fit to tell us. But the conclusion of his story, if not satisfactory to us, is at least highly artistic. Paul had triumphed all along the line. He had been brought before the praetors of Philippi, and before the cultured Gallio at Corinth ; he had been supported by Asiarchs at Ephesus, he had defended himself before Felix, and had been acquitted by his countryman King Agrippa. Now at Rome he is left preaching freely to those who visited him in his own house, **unmolested,** or, as the Vulgate expresses it, *sine prohibitione.*